THE BEST NONFRANCHISE BUSINESS OPPORTUNITIES

Andrew J. Sherman, Esq.
Donna Tozzi Cavanagh

THE BEST
NONFRANCHISE
BUSINESS
OPPORTUNITIES

An Owl Book
Produced by The Philip Lief Group, Inc.

HENRY HOLT AND COMPANY · NEW YORK

Henry Holt and Company, Inc.
Publishers since 1866
115 West 18th Street
New York, N.Y. 10011

Henry Holt ® is a registered trademark
of Henry Holt and Company, Inc.

Library of Congress Cataloging-in-Publication Data
Sherman, Andrew J.
The best nonfranchise business opportunities / Andrew J. Sherman
and Donna Tozzi Cavanagh : produced by the
Philip Lief Group, Inc.—1st ed.
    p.   cm.
"An Owl book."
1. Small business—United States.   2. Service industries—United States.
I. Cavanagh, Donna Tozzi.   II. Philip Lief Group.
III. Title.
HD2346.U5S53   1993   92-34838
658'.041—dc20   CIP

ISBN 0-8050-2208-2

First Edition—1993

Designed by Victoria Hartman
Printed in the United States of America
All first editions are printed on acid-free paper.∞

10 9 8 7 6 5 4 3 2 1

Produced by The Philip Lief Group, Inc.
6 West 20th Street
New York, NY 10011

To my father, Sheldon Sherman,
and my mother, Deanna M. Robin,
who both always taught me
to pursue opportunity.
—*Andrew Sherman*

To Edward and Coleen
for all their support.
—*Donna Cavanagh*

Contents

Preface

The purpose of this book is to provide entrepreneurs with an overview of nonfranchise business opportunities that exist in the market today. Nonfranchise opportunities are the main focus here because only a limited supply of information on these companies is currently available to consumers and entrepreneurs. Magazines and industry publications frequently compile names and addresses of these companies, but their history and methods of operation often remain a mystery.

The 75 companies in this book were chosen because they provided open and detailed information on their business operation. These companies use a variety of methods to establish relationships with independent entrepreneurs including dealerships, distributorships, consulting, multilevel marketing programs, licenses, and direct sales programs. These profiled opportunities also offer a wide range of investment packages, support systems, and training requirements, and they bring to light businesses that do not require a full-time commitment.

Several well-known companies such as Amway, Mary Kay Cosmetics, and Avon declined to comply with our requests. With the general public aware of their presence, the marketing potential of a listing here could not persuade these companies to divulge a detailed description of their operations.

A three-part research process was used to determine which companies would be profiled. First, a questionnaire was sent to provide biographical data about a company. Company officers were asked to describe the type of business opportunity they offered entrepreneurs. Officers were also asked to supply legal documentation that prospective distributors, dealers, and so on would be expected to sign as a condition for their participation in the program. This questionnaire also included inquiries about their legal history, entrepreneurial investment needs, and the type and duration of training and support they each offer independent contractors.

The second step of the research process included personal interviews with the contact persons listed on the questionnaire. The interviews aided in the understanding of all aspects of the company, including their daily operation, their products, and their marketing strategies. The interviews also provided insight into the people behind the companies: the founders, inventors, chief executive officers, marketing executives, and personal assistants. It was discovered that these companies varied greatly in size. Some employed hundreds at their home-office facilities, and others were still based in a spare room in the house, with just two people handling all the daily demands.

Strict attention was paid to the investment requirements of each opportunity, and all expenses were strictly noted. This was impossible when it came to estimating rent, leasing costs, land purchases, employee salaries, and capital. Some companies were able to estimate these expenses, and others could not because these factors differ greatly from state to state, and sometimes from country to country.

The last part of the research process consisted of fact-checking our company profiles. Once again, our contact people at companies listened, corrected, and approved the information in the profiles.

It is hoped that this book acts as a helpful guide to all entrepreneurs considering business ownership. There are other business opportunities out there besides franchises, and these opportunities differ greatly from one another in time and money commitment.

Good luck!

PART·1

What's In It for Me?
An Overview of
Business Opportunities

This book introduces you to some new and exciting ways to enter a variety of different types of nonfranchised businesses in many diverse and growing industries. Included are auto detailing, computer maintenance, weight-loss and nutrition management, carpet and upholstery cleaning, advertising specialties and novelties, sports equipment and accessories, children's toys and books, recreational facilities, and advertising/publishing. The investment required starts at a low of $49.95 for a sales kit, to $3,000 for an initial set of vending machines, to more than $15,000 for the license of a proprietary software package or the purchase of heavy equipment. As shown in part I of this book, there's a business opportunity available in virtually every industry that might interest you and for almost all levels of available capital. Business opportunities are available for those who wish to work full time, part time, or even just earn a little extra money on the side. Part II of this book provides profiles of 75 of these opportunities, all of which were carefully evaluated. The following is an example of the types of business opportunities that are offered.

Profile

In 1982 Melissa Andrews believed in her commitment to be an "at-home" mom, but her hectic life with two toddler children left her with limited time for socializing with other adults. A friend invited Andrews to a Discovery Toys home party. The concept behind the California-based Discovery Toys interested Andrews immediately, and she signed up to become a distributor.

A direct sales marketer, Discovery Toys sells a mostly exclusive line of educational, entertaining, and durable toys, games, and books for children of all ages. Established in 1978, the company began as a part-time venture of educator Lane Nemeth, and today Discovery Toys grosses more than $83 million annually and has more than 25,000 distributors throughout the world.

"I just thought that this is what I was looking for," explains the 46-year-old Carmichael, California, resident. "A part of me wasn't fulfilled, but I knew the solution wasn't finding a full-time job."

Andrews is now on the top level of the Discovery Toys marketing chain. She oversees more than 600 independent distributors in her multimarketing network. For each sale they make, Andrews receives a percentage override.

The rise to the top of the distributor network took a great deal of commitment and hard work. Andrews admits that there are struggles and frustrations, but entrepreneurs will succeed if they put impatience and unrealistic goals aside.

"I tell the people I recruit that they have to want to work at this, and this is rewarding work. We provide great products for kids at the same time we promote family play," says Andrews, a former social worker. "Those who believe in this system will do fine, and they can build a profitable part-time or full-time business."

Andrews observes that this opportunity still attracts a number of "at-home" moms who have left the work force to raise their children. "They are intelligent women who don't want to give up the community or school activities, or miss going on that field trip, but they want something to build on. This business allows them the best of two worlds."

Discovery Toys consultants do not need to be full-time entrepreneurs to climb the distributor ladder. Andrews has never viewed this opportunity as a full-time commitment, and she is responsible for grossing more than $2,250,000 in more than ten years with Discovery.

As a manager-level distributor, Andrews divides her time between conducting sales shows and supporting the people who are in her own network. A person who enjoys sales, Andrews still finds time to conduct three to four home party shows per month and gross between $20,000 and $25,000 in personal sales per year.

"I am responsible for sponsoring training workshops, and I hold monthly training and leadership meetings for those within my group, but I would miss the sales if I stopped conducting shows."

According to Andrews, Discovery Toys are not hard to sell. Parents or grandparents usually attend the home parties, and they are willing to spend more money on quality toys for children than they are on merchandise for themselves.

"The smaller parties are nice because people can try out the toys and take a good look at what we offer," Andrews notes. "Larger parties are even better because there is an energy in the room, and parents and customers feed on the excitement and buy a great deal of merchandise."

Although there are many exciting business opportunities to consider, there are also many pitfalls to avoid. This book will help you evaluate your own strengths and weaknesses, choose among competing opportunities, and understand the legal and regulatory issues that affect the offer and sale of these nonfranchised businesses. Chapters will help you in the process of business planning, raising capital to get your business off the ground, and management tips and issues for continuing the growth and prosperity of your business.

Many reputable and viable companies offer programs to sell their products and services on a legitimate and cost-effective basis. Unfortunately, there are also unscrupulous and illegal companies that prey on every entrepreneur's desire to achieve the "American dream" and provide a better life for his or her family. The time to find out whether you have fallen into the hands of such a scam is not after you've left your job and triple-mortgaged your home or even after you have written a check for several hundred dollars. This book offers you check lists, company profiles and stories, legal guidelines, and red flags to help guide you toward finding the right offering that meets your personal goals and objectives.

This book discusses myriad business opportunities that are not franchises yet nonetheless allow you to get into a business for yourself without the need to start from scratch. We urge you to evaluate your strengths, weaknesses, and objectives, and use the results to choose the business opportunity that is right for you.

CHAPTER 2

Step One:
Understanding Yourself and Your Targeted Market

Before choosing a business opportunity, you must understand yourself and decide what you want to accomplish with your business. An honest self-evaluation can be difficult for anyone, but it is especially tough if you are on the brink of what you hope is a promising opportunity to earn much-needed income. Everyone would like to have the right business aptitude, managerial skills, education, and relevant work experience to be successful, but in order to prepare yourself for the challenges ahead, it is vital to be as objective as possible in assessing yourself and the business opportunities you want to consider.

In this chapter we look at some of the key issues and questions you must ask about your interests and strengths as well as the competition and room for growth in your targeted marketplace. The key to this chapter is to be honest and realistic in your evaluation of your interests, strengths, and weaknesses. Many entrepreneurs have a tendency to evaluate their strengths more favorably than would an independent third party. Others overestimate the need for a new product or service in a given market because they are blinded by their own enthusiasm. You are only fooling and hurting yourself and your family if you convince yourself that you have a particular strength or a talent in a specific industry. Similarly, you only create stumbling blocks in the way of your long-term success if you consider going into business to sell a new product or service when objective research shows you there is no market, or that the market is already oversaturated.

Of course, an entrepreneurial spirit and a positive mental attitude are still critical components in starting a new business. To succeed in business, we all need to have a little bit of the Little-Engine-That-Could mentality. But you must know that a small train cannot possibly get up a hill without any coal or an engineer, nor would it want to go up a hill if there were no passengers or freight to carry. Be objective as you answer the questions in the pages that follow.

Understand Yourself

Take a notebook and write down your answers to the following questions. Then, really examine your answers. If you can't form an objective opinion about your qualifications for buying and running a business, ask a friend to look at your answers. Honest responses to these questions may determine if nonfranchising is right for you.

Personal Attributes

- Describe your five strongest and weakest points.
- How will these assets and liabilities affect your ability to start and run a business?
- Do you have any specific weaknesses that could be an impediment to running a business successfully?
- For example, do you have a short temper or find it very difficult to speak before a group?

Motivation

- Are you emotionally and financially prepared to take risks? Can you deal with rejection?

- How will you feel if the first twenty potential customers slam the door in your face?
- How will you feed your family if the first fifty customers choose not to buy your product or service?
- What is your motivation for going into business?
- Are you willing to make the necessary sacrifices to start and own a business?
- Are you willing to work long hours, miss out on time with family and friends, give up leisure activities and hobbies?
- Will you make the time to commit yourself to community service projects and public-relations activities, eat leftovers five nights in a row, or trade in your European sports car for a used jalopy if necessary?

Financial Concerns

- What are our financial needs?
- Where are you now and where would you like to be?
- What are your realistic expectations about what you will earn from this business opportunity? On what basis have you arrived at these projections?
- What funds are immediately available to acquire the business and get it running?
- What additional funds will be required?
- Where will you get the money?
(For more details on this topic, see chapter 5.)

Leadership Ability

- Can you manage and motivate others?
- Have you displayed leadership qualities?
- How many employees will this business opportunity require?
- Do you feel comfortable in delegating key tasks and positions of responsibility to others?
- Will you be able to resist the impulse to second-guess them and interfere with their ability to work effectively?
- How strong are your organizational and decision-making skills?
- Do you consider yourself to be well organized in your man-

agement of day-to-day affairs, or are you constantly forgetting about things?

- Are you typically early or late for meetings and appointments? Are you prepared for them?
- Are you good at making plans, sticking to them, and then adjusting them when necessary?

Self-perception

- How would you describe yourself?
- Words typically associated with successful entrepreneurs include hardworking, ambitious, energetic, perseverant, enthusiastic, and well liked. Do you fit the bill?
- Or do you consider yourself a bit lazy, introverted, or lacking emotional and physical stamina?
- How will your own character traits and health affect your ability to overcome adversity, meet challenges, lead others, and face disappointments?

Support Systems

- Whom do you rely on for support and encouragement?
- Do your friends and family agree with your assessment of the particular business opportunity?
- Do you have time and resources to consult with an accountant or business attorney?
- Do you have a business mentor or role model?
- Can you consult with him or her about the business opportunity?

Creativity

- Are you creative?
- At work or at home, are you the one who comes up with new ideas?
- Are you always looking to improve or strengthen the way things are done, or do you take things for granted?

- Do you have an if-it-ain't-broke, don't-fix-it mentality, or are you uncomfortable with the status quo and always trying to make things better?

Understand Your Marketplace

Once you decide that owning your own business is right for you, the next critical task is to make sure that you've selected the *right type* of business. This involves matching your skills, strengths, and weaknesses to the business you would like to enter. For example, if you've determined that "people skills" are not your greatest asset, then you may want to select a business that requires only a few employees or one that targets a smaller number of individual customers instead of hundreds of retail consumers. Once you've selected the type of business, it is critical to make sure that the marketplace is ready and demands the particular product or service you plan to offer. The following questions will help you analyze your target marketplace.

Product/Service Demand

- Why do you feel that there is a demand for your intended product or service in your targeted marketplace?
- Is this based primarily on wishful thinking, or can you back it up with actual market research?
- On what data did you base your research?
- Did it come from reliable sources, such as industry groups, banks, chambers of commerce, and government agencies?

Competition

- Who are the direct competitors in your targeted marketplace?
- What about indirect competitors?
- What are their track records? How will you distinguish your product or service from those of your competitors?
- What makes yours better or different?
- Why would a typical consumer choose your company over a competitor's?

- Will you be able to offer the product or service at a competitive price?

The Market

- What is your targeted market?
- How big is it?
- On what basis have you defined this market?
- What changes in competition, demographics, or technology have influenced demand in your market?
- What future trends will influence demand in your market?
- What type of site or location does this product or service require?
- Are these types of sites available in your targeted market at a competitive price?
- Who are your targeted customers?
- How will you reach them? What factors influence their decision to purchase the product or service that you offer?

Product/Service Concerns

- How strong is the product or service that you intend to offer?
- Is it considered high quality?
- Or are you offering a lower-quality product or service in exchange for certain price benefits?
- Is the key value of your product or service based on a proprietary formula or trademark?
- How easily can it be duplicated by a competitor?
- Is your product or service "state of the art," or could it soon become obsolete?
- Is the product subject to a sharp change in consumer demand, as fad or gimmick products are?
- Could the product be considered seasonal or a luxury item?
- Is the offer and sale of this product or service subject to any special regulatory licensing, such as alcohol, tobacco, or firearms?

Use your answers to these questions to determine if a nonfranchised business opportunity is the best career choice for the person you are. Further, does the type of opportunity you have in mind still make the most sense? Take your time thinking about these issues—this decision may be one of the most important in your life.

CHAPTER 3

What's Out There: *Types of Business Opportunities*

The first step in making an informed decision about the type of opportunity to pursue is to understand the primary types of nonfranchised business opportunities that will be discussed throughout this book. These offerings fall generally into three primary categories: *general business opportunities; dealerships*; and *multilevel marketing, distributorships, and direct sales programs.* In later chapters you will learn how to select and evaluate various offerings, understand their legal and regulatory aspects, and even prepare a customized business plan in the event that third-party capital is required to start your new business. I will draw on my own experience as an entrepreneur and current experience as an attorney practicing primarily in the areas of franchising, distribution, and small business matters to provide valuable insight into the selection process and save you time and money by helping you avoid the wrong venture.

Business Opportunities

Business opportunities come in all different shapes and sizes. Some companies offer rather extensive support and assistance, akin to a franchise, and others offer a one-time purchase of a proprietary piece of equipment. It often seems as if no two offerings are exactly alike. Even lawyers and regulators can't agree on the exact definition of a business opportunity. Typically there is a lot of legal confusion as to the differences between a business opportunity offering and a franchise offering.

For example, let's look at the difference between a successful business opportunity in the field of auto care, Polishing Systems, a Pennsylvania-based nonfranchise business opportunity of car-cleaning equipment and supplies, established in 1980 with more than 4,000 distributors, and a well-recognized franchisor, SpeeDee Oil and Tune-Up, based in New Orleans, Louisiana. Polishing Systems offers a manual that details the use of the equipment and some general tips on marketing the business to attract consumers. It does not offer any type of ongoing support or assistance. Polishing Systems does not require the establishment and construction of a freestanding site for the operation of the business and does not allow the entrepreneur to use its trademarks. On the other hand, SpeeDee offers: (1) extensive training and support; (2) the rights to use an internationally recognized set of trademarks; (3) quality-control guidelines, systems, and procedures to assist franchisees in virtually every aspect of the business; and (4) national and regional cooperative advertising programs in exchange for an initial franchise fee, a royalty fee, and contributions to an advertising fund.

The key point to understand here is that one is not necessarily any better or worse than the other; rather, they are two different packages designed for two different types of entrepreneurs. The entrepreneur attracted to Polishing Systems may be looking for less support and assistance, fewer levels of control, and lower total capital costs. The prospective SpeeDee franchisee is looking for greater levels of initial and ongoing training, support and assistance, the affiliation with an internationally recognized series of trademarks, and is someone who is ready to take responsibility for a more extensive retail facility that would be open to the general public on a daily basis.

Some offerors of business opportunities either purposely or negligently avoid compliance with the franchise laws, to avoid the expense or because they have something to hide. If the offering that you are considering seems to fit closer to the definition of a franchise, as set forth below, and yet the offeror's representatives insist that they are not subject to applicable franchising laws, then you should consult with legal counsel or a regulatory authority. Call on their help to evaluate the offering and determine whether it is in fact a business opportunity or a franchise.

From a legal perspective, these are the most common differences between a business opportunity and a franchise:

Business Opportunity	Franchise
Payment is usually less than $500 and is for the purchase of particular goods or services.	Payment is more than $500 and is usually for the right of the franchisee to enter into an ongoing relationship with the franchisor.
Offeree (that is, the entrepreneur) generally has no rights to use trademarks of the offeror.	Franchisee licenses trademark as its total trade identity.
Offeree gets general training, if any, relating specifically to offer and sale of the products and not to the overall management and marketing of the business.	Training and support is extensive and mandatory on an initial and ongoing basis.
Offeree is generally *not* required to follow a prescribed marketing plan, operations manual, or method of conducting business.	Franchisee *must* follow a prescribed marketing plan and comprehensive operations manual; failure to meet and follow these quality-control standards and specifications is grounds for termination.

Business opportunities generally offer more freedom than a franchise, in exchange for a lesser degree of ongoing support and services. The fact that business opportunity offerors have relatively little control and supervision over the offeree may be especially attractive to someone seeking part-time, night and weekend work for supplemental income, rather than a full-time undertaking.

The legal structure of the business opportunity offering varies from company to company. Some are in the form of *dealerships and distributorships*, where the offeree buys and sells the business opportunity offeror's products or services, usually within the boundaries of an exclusive, conditionally exclusive, or nonexclusive territory, but operating under a separate business identity. An example of this type of business opportunity offering is Sport It, Inc., based in Naples, Florida, which awards sporting-goods dealerships for $2,500 but does not allow its dealers to use the Sport It trademark.

Others are in the form of a *license*, where the licensor provides to the licensee access to a proprietary piece of equipment, technical data, process, or technology (under which products can be made or services offered), or line of already finished products or services for direct resale to the consumer. For example, a business opportunity offeror may license the know-how for a proprietary method of cleaning bathroom tile to an offeree, but then not seek to control how or when the licensee offers the services to the general public.

A third distinct legal category of business opportunity structure, not featured in the profiles included in this book, is a *rack jobber*. Here the offeree essentially buys a route from the offeror, entitling him or her to restock the offeror's products on store shelves along the specified route. An example of a well-known rack jobber is Federal Music and Video Club, which, among other things, offers to its licensees an opportunity to distribute records, tapes, compact discs, and videotapes along specified routes.

Multilevel Marketing Offerings
A multilevel marketing company is typically defined as an entity that sells, distributes, or supplies goods, or services, through distributors at different levels, and in which participants may recruit other participants. Commissions or bonuses are paid as a result of the sale of the goods or services, or the recruitment of additional participants. The better and well-established multilevel marketing companies include Multi-Pure Drinking Water Systems and Shaklee Corporation, both of which have, over a period of time, proved to be valid and lucrative ways of distributing products and services.

Individual entrepreneurs in such companies often supplement their income and in certain cases even leave their salaried jobs to develop their sales network full time.

The following profile is an example of a multilevel marketing company.

Profile

Myra Breakey has dedicated most of her life to helping others. An outpatient alcoholism and addictions counselor, Breakey finds her life rewarding. However, retirement is around the bend for the 63-year-old counselor, and she decided four years ago that she had too much energy to retire quietly. Instead, she began building a profitable business as a part-time distributor for Multi-Pure Drinking Water Systems.

"I have always enjoyed helping others, and I needed to build a business that would allow me to continue to do that," explains Breakey, who has risen to be a Master Builder distributor in the company and oversees more than 500 distributors in her own subnetwork. "I am a health-conscious person. I researched product after product, and I determined Multi-Pure was the best that there was, and it was something I could be proud of."

The Multi-Pure system purifies water using a solid carbon filter. This filter removes most toxic substances from water and reduces drastically the amount of chlorine, lead, asbestos, and other dangerous elements. The company includes more than 85,000 independent distributors, and it has received recognition for its efforts from the U.S. government as well as private environmental organizations.

Breakey first heard about Multi-Pure from her son Jeff, who is also a top distributor for the company. Breakey's professional commitments have prevented her from working full time for Multi-Pure, but she still has managed to recruit distributors, conduct home demonstrations, and work up to the Multi-Pure multilevel marketing chain.

The more than 570 distributors Breakey oversees are located in all parts of the country. Breakey lends them support through sales meetings, workshops, and telephone and mail consultation.

"I used to advertise nationally for recruits," explains Breakey, who operates her home-based business under the name of Water Wellness. "But I couldn't provide as much personal support as I wanted. Being able to help my distributors out means a great deal to me. Now I advertise the product more, and I work with many organizations such as the Welcome Wagon."

Breakey credits Multi-Pure's support system with her success as a part-time entrepreneur. She is confident that this business opportunity will turn into a full-time career when she retires.

"I know I want to be able to travel to my distributors in other parts of the country and help them out with demonstrations and shows, but it still won't seem like a full-time job, because I'll take off when I want to take off and go where I want to go," she says. "I owe a great deal to the people at Multi-Pure for my business success. They have always been there to support me and assist me when I or my distributors needed help."

Retirement will not be difficult for Breakey because she is looking forward to helping people on a new level. "I know that I will still be working to improve the quality of their lives with this product, and I guess that's why I give so much time to it."

Consumers often confuse legitimate *multilevel marketing programs* (which are generally valid methods for distributing products and services to the public) with *pyramid schemes* (which are generally unlawful schemes subject to criminal prosecution in many states). Federal and state regulations have shut down the organizations of Glen Turner Enterprises, FUNDAMERICA, and others on the basis that their structures were more similar to an illegal pyramid than to a valid multilevel marketing program. Three ways to distinguish a legitimate multilevel marketing program from unlawful pyramid schemes are initial payment, inventory loading, and headhunting.

Initial Payment

Typically the initial payment required of distributors of products and services of a multilevel marketing program is minimal; often they are required to buy only a sales kit that is sold at cost. Because pyramid plans are supported by new recruits' payments, participants are often required to pay substantial sums as "entry fees," solely for the right to participate in the program.

Inventory Loading

Pyramid schemes typically require you to purchase large amounts of nonrefundable inventory as a condition for program participation. Legitimate multilevel marketing companies do not usually require this front-ended "inventory loading" and, in fact, will usually repurchase any remaining inventory if and when a distributor decides to leave the business. Many state laws require the company to repurchase any resalable goods for at least 90 percent of the original cost.

Headhunting

Pyramid plans generally encourage their participants to focus on the recruitment of new prospects ("headhunting") as a primary source of income instead of actually selling the products. Participants in multilevel marketing programs, on the other hand, are encouraged to earn income primarily through the sale of legitimate and bona fide products to consumers.

Multilevel marketing is a method of distributing goods or services without the need for a retail location. Thus the middleperson is cut out. Sales are not made through retail stores but rather through the efforts of independent distributors or sales agents who sell directly to consumers. These distributors have a great deal of flexibility in training their own salespeople and will earn a share of the revenue from the products sold by these salespeople (that is, the downline sales organization) as well as their own sales. Because the initial cost is often minimal, multilevel marketing is becoming more popular and attractive to individuals interested in supplementing their income or in some cases starting a full-time business.

Distributorships, Dealerships, and Sales Representatives

Many product-oriented companies choose to bring their wares to the marketplace through independent third-party *distributors* and *dealerships*. Although these two terms have essentially the same meaning, there is sometimes a distinction between the customers they service. Many times the distributor serves as a wholesaler or intermediary; the dealership is almost always a retailer. These types of arrangement are commonly used by manufacturers of electronic and stereo equipment, computer hardware and software, sporting goods, medical equipment, and automobile parts and accessories. Sometimes distributorships and dealerships are marketed as "business opportunities" to start-up entrepreneurs; in other cases they are available only through nontraditional channels, such as trade journals or industry contacts, which are likely to be made at a trade show. For example, a manufacturer of a new food processor attending the National Housewares Manufacturer's Association will seek out existing retailers to act as its dealers by adding its product to the current line. In that case, the new product line may account for a very small percentage of the existing retailer's total revenues. However, dealerships marketed as "business opportunities" will typically appeal to nonretailers and account for most or all of the newly established dealer's overall revenues.

Distributors and dealers are often taken for sales representatives, however, there are many critical differences. Typically, distributors *buy* the product from the manufacturer at wholesale prices. Title to the product passes to the distributors when the manufacturer receives payment. Distributors usually pay no initial fee for the grant of the distributorship, and they may carry competitive products. Distributors are expected to maintain some retail location or showroom where the manufacturer's products are displayed. Distributors must maintain their own inventory storage and warehousing capabilities. Distributors look to the manufacturer for technical support, advertising contributions, supportive repair, maintenance and service policies, new product training, volume discounts, favorable payment and return policies, and brand-name recognition. The manufacturer looks to the distributors for in-store and local promotion, adequate inventory controls, financial stability, preferred display and stocking, prompt payment, and qualified sales personnel.

The following two profiles are examples of dealers and distributors.

Profiles

Bruno Giannini is always planning something. As owner of Straight Shooter Productions in King of Prussia, Pennsylvania, the 31-year-old business owner makes his living planning special events for clients. To make these events successful, Giannini has at his disposal an assortment of promotional tools, including a pair of mechanically operated robots that spar and box like professional fighters.

As a dealer for the World Robotic Boxing Association, Giannini contracts with corporations, bars, schools, churches, and charity organizations to have his robots at ringside. Customers pay between $3 to $5 to enter the boxing match and operate the robots until one knocks the other robot's head off.

Giannini has been a dealer for more than five years. He bought a pair of robots when the World Robotic Association was just starting out in 1986.

"I love this kind of stuff," Giannini says with a laugh. He has been in the special events industry since his college days at Monmouth College in northern New Jersey. "I just thought it would help a lot of people have a good time, and it does."

Giannini says that at first he directed his robots at bar crowds, but in recent years he has received a great many requests from corporations who want them at special promotions or company parties.

"They are attention-getters, there's no doubt, and the people have a great time with them. They really get into these bouts," Giannini observes. "The audience for this has grown since we started carrying them. Once bars and taverns were 85 to 90 percent of our customer base, but now that number has fallen, and corporations and charity organizations are the major part of our clientele for the robots."

When Giannini first purchased the robots, he handled all aspects of the business operation. The increase in demand has forced him to concentrate on the management end of the business.

For Giannini, this dealership and his business are what he always wanted to do.

"It does take a great deal of hard work, but I have all these toys, and people want to pay me to let them borrow them," jokes Giannini. "This is not a bad life, and I know it's a cliché, but only in America can this happen. I'm lucky because I get to do what I enjoy doing the most—playing."

Steven and Stephanie Weber still receive sarcastic remarks from relatives about their chosen line of work. As distributors for Artistic Impressions, Inc., a direct sales company that markets oil paintings and other art media to customers through home shows and demonstrations, the Webers maintain an office in their home and an average workweek of 17 to 20 hours.

"They still kid us and say, 'When are you going to get a real job?' " jokes 35-year-old Steven Weber. "But I think we have the last laugh."

The Webers' have been distributors for Artistic Impressions for a total of five years. Stephanie first started with the company after the birth of the couple's first child, and now the couple supervise and train more than 47 distributors who together gross more than $700,000, by conducting shows in Hudson, Wisconsin, and the greater St. Paul and Minneapolis area.

"She wanted to be home with the baby and maybe work part time," recalls Steven. "She is trained in fashion design and apparel, and there were no opportunities that didn't require demanding hours or ridiculously low pay."

Stephanie stumbled onto the company when she attended an Artistic Impressions show at her sister-in-law's home.

"She really liked the idea, and I was the typical skeptic. I just didn't see how it was possible."

Steven's attitude changed when the couple began receiving financial rewards and commissions despite two moves into new communities.

"Stephanie got involved in community organizations such as Newcomers, and some fashion pageants and other events that allowed her to network and schedule shows," Steven says. "There were frustrating times for her, but she worked at it, and it really paid off."

Three years ago Steven also began selling the art on a part-time basis. Today both husband and wife view Artistic Impressions as their full-time careers. They each conduct shows on their own as well as together, and they both participate in the training and recruitment of new distributors.

"We are now management level, and that brings more rewards as well as responsibilities," Steven observes. "We're there to support our distributors and encourage their progress as well as our own. This takes time through meetings and seminars and workshops."

Sales Representatives

Unlike distributors and dealers, the sales representative or sales agent is an independent marketing resource for the manufacturer. If you serve as a sales representative for a company, then it is not likely that you will be required to take title to the merchandise, maintain inventories or retail locations, or engage in any special price promotions unless instigated by the manufacturer. Essentially, you are an independent contractor authorized to offer and sell products on behalf of the manufacturer in a given territory in exchange for a commission according to a predetermined schedule.

Cooperatives

The focus of this book is on business opportunities offered primarily as distributorships, licenses, sales representatives, and multi-level marketing offerings. However, you should know that certain types of business opportunities are offered as cooperatives. Cooperatives are generally limited to specific types of industries, and they are different from traditional types of business opportunities. Although we won't cover them extensively in this book, it is useful to understand how they work.

Over the years, cooperatives have been formed as associations of member companies in the same or similar industries to achieve operating, advertising, and purchasing efficiencies and economies of scale. Joining a cooperative as a member is an exciting and cost-effective way to start a new business or improve the performance of an existing small business. Typically members own and control the cooperative. Each cooperative has its own policies regarding membership recruitment, selection, and acceptance. An early-stage cooperative may actively solicit new members, while an older cooperative may accept a new member only to replace one who is leaving. Cooperatives have been especially effective in certain inventory-intense industries, such as hardware, automobile parts and accessories, pharmacies, and grocery stores. Perhaps the best-known cooperative associations are Ace Hardware stores and Best Western hotels. Typically each independent business may use a common trade identity in its advertising and promotion; however, the cooperative itself owns the actual trademarks. For more information on cooperatives, contact Stan Dreyer at the National Cooperative Bank (NCB) at 1-202-745-4691 or the National Cooperative Business Association at 1-202-638-6222.

Conclusion

Many companies do not label themselves clearly as being a franchise, business opportunity, or multilevel marketing plan. You will need to use the tools, evaluation guidelines, and check lists provided in this book to evaluate the opportunity offered, to understand how the offering is regulated and your rights as an offeree, and to determine how much capital will be required to open and continue to operate the business. This information will be invaluable, whether you are considering a business opportunity as a full-time and capital-intensive investment or whether you are looking at business opportunities as a source of extra income. Make sure that you fully understand the nature of the opportunity being offered and your rights as an offeree. You may need to hire a knowledgeable accountant and attorney to help you.

CHAPTER 4

Evaluating
Business Opportunities
and Distributorships

Having decided that you are ready for business and that your targeted market is ready for you, it's time to learn how to select from among competing offerings.

In chapter 2 our focus was on the evaulation of *your* strengths, weaknesses, and targeted marketplace. Now it is time to turn to the *offeror* of the business opportunity in order to ensure that: (1) there is a match between your needs and expectations and the package being offered; (2) the offeror has designed a program that features quality products and services and provides support and long-term growth potential; and (3) the offeror is credible, enjoys a good reputation, and respects its legal obligations and your legal rights both during the offer and sale process and over the course of the relationship.

Naturally, the appropriate questions to ask and the analysis to conduct in evaluating potential offerings will vary from company to company, from industry to industry, and among the various types of business opportunities. This chapter focuses on the types of questions that must be asked about *all* types of business opportunities. Special sections provide tips on how to analyze distributorship agreements and evaluate multilevel marketing opportunities. The chapter ends with some general "red flags" to look out for when evaluating business opportunity offerings.

The first step in evaluating an offering package is to determine the *type* of business opportunity being offered. Doing so will not only help you in identifying specific types of questions to be asked about the offeror, but will also help you determine which laws apply to the offer and sale of this opportunity.

As discussed in chapter 3, business opportunities come in a variety of shapes and sizes. Ask offerors whether they consider themselves to be offering dealerships, licenses, multilevel marketing, joint ventures, vending machines, rack jobber routes, cooperative memberships, or franchises. Remember that labels are not important if the offering materials or agreements seem to indicate a relationship that is different from the label offerors attach. Substance over form is the rule of thumb in analyzing these offerings. Use the definitions in chapter 3 and the legal guidelines in this chapter to help you in this determination. If you are still confused or feel you are being misled, use the resource directory in chapter 8 to contact the appropriate federal or state authorities. If you are unsure what to ask and how to ask it, have your professional advisors, such as your accountant or lawyer, do some further investigation.

Make sure that you are comfortable not only with how the offering is being characterized but also with the particular method that you will use to reach your customers. How will you sell the products and services? Do you need to establish a retail location? Or will sales be conducted primarily through direct selling? Multilevel marketing? Mail order? Telemarketing? Coin-operated devices? Special vehicles? Rack jobbers?

Evaluating the Offeror

The following are the key questions to ask when evaluating the offering documents and agreements of *all* types of business opportunities.

Company Health

- What is the organizational structure of the company?
- Does it own all of the intellectual property that is at the heart of its offering, or is it a licensee of a related entity?
- What happens to you if the license is lost or terminated?
- How long has the company existed?
- What is its financial strength?
- Is documentation available?
- What is its market share?
- Does it offer quality products and services?
- How many *current* distributors does it have?
- How does that compare with three years ago? Five years ago?
- How many are projected to be sold in the next two years? Five years?
- To what extent are current operating locations owned by the company?

Start-up

- Is training provided?
- Are written manuals provided?
- How long is the training program?
- How extensive are the manuals?
- How often are the manuals and/or training programs updated?
- What is the background of the management team of the offeror?
- How does the offeror's experience relate to this industry?
- Is the company overly dependent on a particular individual?
- What are the support and service obligations of the company to assist you before you open up for business?
- What about *after* you open?

Litigation History

- What is the litigation history of the company?
- Have disgruntled distributors filed lawsuits on the basis of fraud or misrepresentation?

- Have there been any regulatory inquiries into the affairs of the company? What were the nature of the allegations?

Registration Issues

- Has the company registered under any of the state business opportunity or multilevel marketing statutes? Why or why not?
- Do you agree with the company's explanation as to why registration is not necessary? Does your lawyer?
- Has the company received any legal opinion or regulatory determination that it is *not* subject to federal or state disclosure laws?
- Does a copy of such a determination exist?
- If the company did register, were any bonding or escrow requirements imposed?
- Did the state require any special disclosures or warnings to be included in the company's offering materials?
- Does the company have one or more federally registered trademarks? How about state registrations?
- Certain states exempt an offeror from state registration if the company has a registered trademark. Has the company relied on the "registered trademark" exemption under applicable state business opportunity statutes?
- If the company has, then does it meet the minimum net worth requirements now being imposed by certain states?
- Are you licensed to use these trademarks in connection with the operation of the business? Under what conditions or restrictions?

Earning Claims

- Does the company directly or indirectly provide earnings claims or statements to its prospective distributors?
- Have these earnings claims been prepared in accordance with federal and state legal guidelines?
- Are the earnings claims reasonable? Substantiated? Geographically relevant to your targeted territory? Truly representative of most of the company's other distributors?

Fees

- As a distributor, what initial and ongoing fees must you pay to the offeror?
- Under what conditions, if any, are these fees refundable?
- Are there any minimum ongoing payments?
- What are the offeror's estimates of the initial and ongoing costs and expenses in connection with the establishment and operation of the business opportunity? Are these figures realistic in your local market?

Equipment and Supplies

- To what extent does the company impose equipment specifications and quality-control standards on the products and services that must be used to operate the business?
- Can you purchase equipment and supplies from a source other than the company? Under what conditions?
- Are the offeror's prices for products and services competitive? Can you buy elsewhere?

Territory and Market

- Must you meet any performance standards as a condition to territorial exclusivity or to the renewal of an agreement?
- What type, if any, of territorial exclusivity is provided?
- How is the size of the territory determined?
- Is this market too large or too small?
- What site selection, architectural, engineering, and zoning assistance is available?
- Has the company conducted a study in order to determine how many distributors a given market will support?
- How does this compare with the size of the exclusive territory offered?

Promotion

- Are public figures used in connection with the promotion of the business?

- Must you pay a separate fee for their appearance?
- Would the business be adversely impacted if the public figure were no longer affiliated with the offering?

Relationship Termination

- Under what conditions can the company terminate your relationship?
- How and when does the distributor get notice that he or she has breached the agreement, and how much time, if any, is allowed to cure the breach?
- What are your obligations upon termination? Are any post-term covenants required?
- What is the company's sales and termination history?
- What restrictions are there on your ability to sell or transfer your business? Is the offeror's approval required? Must it be responsible?
- What reporting and record-keeping requirements, if any, are imposed by the offeror?
- What are your specific obligations under the agreement, if any, to continue to market and promote the products and services?

Outside Information

- Have you conducted any "independent" investigations of the offeror?
- Have you spoken to competitors, trade groups, and current distributors about the company's reputation?
- Have you ordered a credit report from any of the credit-rating organizations, such as Dun & Bradstreet?
- Is the company publicly traded?
- Have you obtained copies of its annual report or data from stock-rating services, such as Standard & Poor's or Moody's?
- Is the offeror in good standing in its state of incorporation or qualified to do business in your home state? (Remember that much of this information is easily obtainable from local libraries, newspapers and magazines, consumer advocacy groups, trade groups, and government agencies.)

Product Information

- How long have the offeror's products and services been on the market?
- Are these products and services of high quality and up-to-date?
- Are they scheduled to be replaced any time in the near future?
- If so, what will happen to your obsolete inventory on hand?
- Has the offeror promised that it will repurchase unsold or obsolete merchandise?
- Are these products or services in any way seasonal or faddish?
- How often does the product line change?
- What are your costs and training time commitments when products or services change?
- Is the product manufactured by the offeror or a third party? What happens if the third party goes out of business?
- Are there warranties that back up these products or services? At what cost to you?
- Who is responsible for the replacement or repair of broken or faulty products? Who pays for refunds or repairs?
- Whom do you contact if there is a problem in shipment or delivery?
- What discount programs are offered for bulk orders or prompt payment?

Personal Considerations

- Who else has evaluated the offeror's marketing literature and agreements?
- Has a lawyer, accountant, or business advisor reviewed all of the pertinent documents?
- Have you discussed this opportunity with friends and family? What was their reaction?
- Have you spoken to others who have acquired this opportunity? Are they happy with their earnings? Do they speak highly of the offeror?
- What do they think about the viability of your targeted marketplace?

- Has the offeror evaluated *you* carefully?
- Does the company have objective criteria for evaluating *its* potential distributors, and do you meet these criteria? (*Note:* You do *not* want to acquire a business opportunity from an offeror who will sell to anyone whose check will clear. This demonstrates a lack of integrity and a lack of understanding of what it takes for offerees to succeed.)

Distributorship Agreements

When reviewing the offeror's proposed distribution agreement, be sure that you and your lawyer are clear about the answers to the following questions.

- What is the scope of the appointment?
- Which products are you authorized to distribute and under what conditions?
- What is the scope, if any, of the exclusive territory to be granted?
- To what extent will product, vendor, customer, or geographic restrictions be applicable?
- What activities will you be expected to perform in terms of manufacturing, sales, marketing, display, billing, market research, maintenance of books and records, storage, training, installation, support, and servicing?
- What obligations will you have to preserve and protect the intellectual property of the manufacturer?
- What right, if any, will you have to modify or enhance the offeror's warranties, terms of sale, credit policies, or refund procedures?
- What advertising literature, technical and marketing support, training seminars, or special promotions will the offeror provide?
- What sales or performance quotas will be imposed on you as a condition to continue to distribute the offeror's products or services?
- What are the rights and remedies of the offeror if you fail to meet these performance standards?

Multilevel Marketing Opportunities

Many types of business opportunities are discussed in this book, and all must be evaluated carefully. You must be especially careful and diligent, however, when investigating and evaluating multilevel marketing programs. While many legitimate companies with established track records use multilevel marketing as a system of distribution, scam artists and perpetrators of fraud abound in this area.

Use the following questions in evaluating a multilevel marketing opportunity. Analyze your answers using the legal guidelines pertaining to multilevel marketing in chapters 3 and 4:

Start-up

- How are participants recruited?
- Are high-pressure sales tactics and pie-in-the-sky promises made as inducements to join the sales network?
- Are you required to attend high-energy motivational sales and recruitment meetings in large groups?
- What is the dropout rate among representatives? (*Note:* The dropout rate in a multilevel marketing offering is very high, reaching sometimes 80 to 90 percent annually in some companies.)
- Are you required to pay any up-front fees as a condition to participating in the program?
- Is there any type of entry fee or initiation fee beyond the mandatory purchase of a basic sales kit?

Basic Structure

- How is the multilevel marketing network structured?
- How and when are commissions paid?
- What are the guidelines for recruiting other sales representatives who will then become part of your "downline"?
- What are the rules for "breakaway distributors" who establish their own downlines?
- What percentage do you get of the breakaway sales?
- Are you subject to any minimum purchase requirements or performance standards? (*Note:* These requirements often lead

to "inventory loading" and a lot of unwanted merchandise in your basement or garage.)

Product Questions

- Is the product a one-time purchase, such as water filters, security systems, or air cleaners, or does the company offer products that consumers will purchase again and again, such as vitamins, cosmetics, toiletries, housewares, pantyhose, jewelry, or toys?
- What is the primary emphasis in the sales and marketing training program and literature?
- Are you encouraged to sell more and more products or services, or is the emphasis really on building your network? (*Note:* If the main emphasis is on "headhunting" rather than the sale of a bona fide and financially viable product, both you and the offeror may run into federal and state regulatory problems.)
- Do you believe in the quality of the product that you are selling?

Support

- Are you comfortable with the multilevel marketing (MLM) method of sales, or are you concerned about the possible negative reaction of friends and relatives?
- What tools does the company provide to assist you in product sales and in the recruitment of additional representatives?
- Does the company provide brochures? Flip charts? Audiocassettes? Videotapes?
- What initial training and ongoing support does the company provide? Are you responsible for managing, training, and motivating your downline network on an ongoing basis? (*Note:* Many states require the active management of the distributors in your network to avoid characterization as an illegal pyramid.)
- Will you receive any type of an exclusive or protected territory?
- How many other distributors already exist in your immediate market?
- Is there sufficient demand for the products within the market to support all of these distributors?

Earnings Claims

- Did the company and/or a marketing representative make earnings claims to you during the recruitment process?
- Were the claims substantiated, reasonable, and geographically relevant?
- In what form were the earnings claims presented?
- Get promises in writing and make sure that the literature was generated and approved by the company's headquarters. Many multilevel marketing companies have a problem with the use and distribution of unauthorized marketing materials. (*Note:* Do not view becoming a distributor in an MLM network as a get-rich-quick scheme. The MLM company and recruiting distributor should make it clear that it will take a long time, perhaps a year or more, to build a stable business. Do not give up your full-time job too hastily. In fact, the MLM opportunity and your earnings are likely always to be a part-time project.)

Company Health

- What is the company's reputation and track record?
- How long has the company been in business?
- What is the experience of its management team?
- Has the company ever been investigated by the Federal Trade Commission (FTC) or the Securities and Exchange Commission (SEC)? At the state level by the Attorney General's Office or the Consumer Protection Division?
- If yes, what were the outcomes of these investigations? Is the company, or its principals, subject to any administrative orders, injunctions, or other legal restrictions?

Company Safeguards

- What steps does the company take to prohibit distributors from making unauthorized representations about earnings potential or the attributes of the products?
- Does the company seem to be committed to legal compliance?

- Will you be expected to sign an independent distributor agreement? What are its terms and conditions?
- Under what conditions can the agreement be terminated?

Unsold Merchandise

- What is the repurchase policy for unsold inventory?
- Are you able to return any merchandise which you were unable to sell? At what discount rate? (*Note:* The Direct Selling Association recommends a 90 percent buy-back policy, less any overrides or bonuses that have already been paid. Seven states, Georgia, Louisiana, Maryland, Massachusetts, New Mexico, South Dakota, and Wyoming, *require* a 90 percent buy-back policy.)

Red Flags in Offering Documents

When you review the offering documents and agreement, there are several red flags that should be of special concern. Naturally, the specific red flags will vary from company to company, but they commonly include the following.

- Unregistered trademarks and lack of truly proprietary products or services.
- Extensive litigation or regulatory inquiries concerning the offeror.
- Weak financial statements or refusal to disclose financial condition.
- Contractual provisions that require the distributor to purchase all or virtually all inventory or supplies from the offeror or an affiliate.
- An excessive number of "hidden fees" that are charged by the offeror.
- Extensive and burdensome covenants against competition during and after the term of the distributorship or license agreement.
- Overly stringent conditions to the renewal or transfer of the business opportunity.
- Little to no assurance of geographic exclusivity being granted to the distributor (which could result in market saturation).

- An unclear or ambiguous statement of the exact duties and support services that the offeror will provide to the distributor.
- An inexperienced management team or an overly strong dependence on a particular person.
- A very short training program (which may imply a shallow foundation for the system) or a very long training program (which may imply a high degree of difficulty in teaching the underlying concepts).

Conclusion

In assessing your analysis of the offeror's package, one of the key questions you should ask yourself is: "What can this company do for me that I can't do for myself?" In other words, there should be a series of good reasons *why* you are willing to pay some initial and possibly ongoing fees to the offeror for the right to be in this business. If the offeror has a weak background, lacks financial strength, offers inferior products or services, provides little or no territorial protection, or enjoys a poor reputation in its industry or among its current distributors, then you are better off going into business for yourself without it. If, on the other hand, you are truly convinced that the tangible list of benefits and services directly outweighs the costs and risks, then it's time to get on with the tasks of understanding your legal rights, preparing a business plan, raising necessary capital, and opening up for business. This is the focus of chapters 5, 6, and 7.

CHAPTER 5

Business Plans
and Raising Capital

E ach business opportunity will have its own unique set of initial and ongoing capital requirements that the entrepreneur must meet. Some opportunities can be obtained and operated with a very small capital base, such as a multilevel marketing or direct sales opportunity, where the initial capital requirements may only be several hundred dollars for a sales kit and some business cards. Other opportunities, such as retail-oriented product distributorships and dealerships, may require initial purchases of inventory, construction, and fit-out for a retail location, extensive equipment, or a large amount of initial or ongoing advertising. This chapter focuses on two areas: *business planning,* which *all* entrepreneurs should engage in regardless of whether they will require capital from outside sources or not, and *strategies for raising capital,* which are designed to give you some ideas and approaches for raising money when you need third-party financing to acquire and operate the business opportunity.

Step One: Preparing a Business Plan
The first step in raising capital for funding the operation of your business opportunity is to prepare a business plan. The business plan will serve as your road map to success in business and will demonstrate to prospective lenders and investors that you have done

your homework in evaluating the opportunity and analyzing the local market.

A typical business plan that should be used in the acquisition of a business opportunity, license, or distributorship follows.

I. *Executive Summary*

This section is an overview of the type of business you plan to open, the amount of capital you require, and your plan for operating and managing the business.

II. *Business Summary* (brief paragraph)
   A. Describe unique features of the business opportunity and the principal products or services you will offer.
   B. How and why will your business successfully compete?
   C. When will your business open?
   D. What hours and days of the week will you be in operation?

III. *Management Team and Ownership*
   A. Provide an organization chart and responsibilities.
   B. Name key management personnel. (Describe who will actually manage the operation on a day-to-day basis and what functions each person will perform.)
   C. Describe the related experiences, skills, and educational accomplishments of each person who will be responsible for managing a part of the business.
   D. How do you intend to attract and compensate your employees?
   E. Describe in detail any training the managers will require and the costs of such training.
   F. Will there be other partners or stockholders?
   G. List professional support. (Describe the strengths and background of your attorneys, accountants, consultants, advertising agency, bank, and service organizations.)

IV. *Financial Plan*
   A. Provide the lender or investor with a projected balance sheet, and income and cash-flow statements for the first

three years. (Provide projections for the first year on a monthly basis.)

B. Give a projected break-even analysis.

C. Cite assumptions and explanatory footnotes consistent with the narrative and based on some type of historic data (that is, traffic flow count, demographics, and so on).

V. *Location*

A. Describe the area in which you intend to operate business.

B. Cite the present and expected population for the next five years.

C. Cite market demographics. (Why is this an appropriate area for your proposed product or service?)

D. Who are the competitors in the area?

E. What are the general population trends (that is, population per square mile, age, ethnic origin, number and size of families, number of single homes, apartments, average income level, education level, number employed and unemployed, retail spending habits, etc.)?

F. Is your territory well defined? Is it large enough? What are your expansion possibilities?

VI. *Products or Services*

A. Describe product lines or services.

B. Compare them to competitor's products.

C. Cite the present buying habits regarding the product or service.

D. Does this product or service have an enduring consumer appeal (that is, not a fad or so highly stylized that it will be outdated before you have a chance to recoup your capital expenditures and earn a profit)?

VII. *Market Research and Analysis*

A. Customers

1. Who and where are your major customers?

2. What are the key factors that influence their purchasing decisions (that is, price, quality, service)?

3. What plans do you have to take these factors into consideration when marketing your own product or service?

B. Competition
1. Identify the key competitors in your market.
2. Discuss the strengths and weaknesses of each of your key competitors and its products or services.

C. The Industry
1. What industry are you in?
2. Cite the current status and size of the industry.
3. List its chief characteristics.
4. Project major trends in the industry.
5. Is the industry in a growth position?
6. Where is the industry going in the future?

VIII. *Analysis of the Offeror*
A. What is the experience level behind the company that offers the business opportunity?
B. What is its track record? How long has the offeror been in business, both as a company and as a business opportunity offeror?
C. Does the offeror have a good reputation for quality, service, and fairness? Have you spoken to other distributors? Are they happy? Profitable?
D. How many new distributorships does the company intend to award during the next twelve months, three years, five years? Is the company growing too fast or too slow? Why or why not?
E. Has the company been involved in any legal action against its distributors or vice versa? Are there any suits pending?
F. What is the company's current financial condition?
G. Who are the company's directors and officers and what is their related business experience?

IX. *Analysis of the Distributorship Agreement*
A. What is the term of the agreement?
B. What are the conditions for renewal? Are there any fees payable at the renewal date?
C. What are the provisions for location selection?

    D. What, if any, exclusivity rights are granted to distributors?

    E. What are the initial and ongoing fees and cash requirements?

    F. Under what conditions may the agreement be canceled or terminated? Do you have a right to cure (that is, correct the reason for which you are being terminated)? Is it reasonable?

X. *Exhibits to the Business Plan*
    A. Provide biographies of the management team.
    B. Provide news and promotional information about the offeror, the industry, or you.
    C. Provide pictures of sample products, sample location, and so on.

Tips on Preparing the Business Plan

You should be aware of four major guidelines in preparing to draft a business plan for the financing and operation of your business opportunity.

The final draft of the business plan must be concise and well written and must focus on the principal areas of concern to a lender or investor. Avoid overly technical descriptions of your intended operations. Investors will commit funds based on the quality and clarity of the document, not its thickness. Although business plans ought to be presented professionally, a very expensive binder or presentation will often demonstrate that your priorities and resources are misplaced.

The business plan should be written primarily by the person seeking the capital, not by a friend, relative, or advisor. Ideally, the business plan should be developed by the entrepreneur and *then* reviewed by qualified experts, including the company's accountants, attorneys, and board of directors. The business plan should never be prepared solely by outside advisors without your valuable input. A lender or investor will be quick to recognize a "cookbook" plan or one that reflects the views and efforts of your professional advisors rather than your own. You will be responsible for running the company on a day-to-day basis.

Be realistic and objective in preparing your business plan. Naturally, the business plan should demonstrate your enthusiasm about the founders of the company as well as generate excitement in the reader. This should not, however, be an excuse for a business plan that lacks credibility and accuracy. Investors and lenders will want to know all of your proposal's strengths *and* its weaknesses. In fact, a realistic discussion of your projected problems, along with a reasonable plan for dealing with these various risks and challenges, will have a much more positive impact on the prospective investor or lender.

Remember that business plans are *not* written only when a company needs to raise capital. Although most business plans are written in connection with the search for capital, a well-written business plan will benefit you in a number of ways. The plan is a management tool that can serve as a road map for your company's growth. It reflects a realistic self-appraisal of your company's progress to date as well as your projected goals and objectives.

Step Two: Deciding on the Type of Capital

Before turning to a discussion of the various sources of capital, it is critical to determine how much money you will need initially to open and then to continue to operate your business. This process is always a difficult challenge, and many entrepreneurs fail in their early years because they underestimate the amount of money they need to *stay* in business after they've opened. The business may not generate the level of income and profit you had originally anticipated, which will put pressure on your ability to pay bills and meet your obligations at both a business and a personal level. Therefore, it is critical to plan to obtain and have available extra working capital and cash revenues in the event that your business gets off to a slow start.

Getting a Handle on Start-up and Operating Costs

The nature of the start-up costs of getting your business open will also dictate your options in determining the appropriate source of capital. For example, if your business opportunity requires the expenditure of primarily "soft costs," such as advertising, promotion, letterhead, and business cards, then it will be very difficult to get a bank loan unless you can pledge other collateral to secure the loan. In these situations equity capital, such as money from a friend or family member in exchange for a percentage of the profits, may be a more viable route. On the other hand, if your business opportunity requires the purchase of equipment or inventory, then banks, commercial finance companies, equipment lessors, state and local government small business loan programs, and thrifts or savings and loan institutions may all be viable sources of capital. In fact, some equipment-oriented business opportunity offerors will make special arrangements with finance companies to provide loans or lease financing to their qualified offerors.

Your start-up budget should take into account the following categories of expenses.

Initial License or Distributorship Fee	$_____
Initial Product Inventory	$_____
Special Equipment and Parts	$_____
Training Costs	$_____
Travel	$_____
Legal and Accounting Fees	$_____
Deposits to Landlord and Equipment-Leasing Companies	$_____
Grand Opening and Advertising Promotion	$_____
Phone and Utilities Deposits	$_____
Business Cards, Stationery, and Office Supplies	$_____
Preopening Salaries or Consulting Fees	$_____
Insurance	$_____
Construction Costs and Improvements (Furniture or Fixtures)	$_____
Licenses and Tax Deposits	$_____
Working Capital	$_____
Total Start-up costs	$_____

To determine the figures that will go in each of the blank spaces, talk to your accountant, research your industry, meet with your offeror and other distributors, read industry periodicals and trade magazines, study your competitors, and contact trade associations.

The process of determining start-up costs must not be a guessing game, nor should it be done on the assumption that you can really get started on a shoestring budget. Plan to have a working capital cushion just in case your initial estimates were wrong.

Many of the costs just outlined need to be factored into your analysis of the ongoing costs of your business. Prospective lenders and investors will want to know *not only how much it will cost to start, but also how much it will cost to stay open.* The preparation of a monthly projected cash-flow statement should include an estimate of the income that will be earned and the ongoing monthly costs of operating your business. These recurring costs will include rent, royalty fees or any other type of continuing fee to the offeror (where applicable), inventory replenishment, insurance, interest (if and when money is borrowed), payroll and your salary, advertising and promotion, maintenance and repair of equipment, supplies, postage and printing, professional fees, taxes, utilities, and telephone. In preparing these projected monthly cash-flow statements, be sure to take into account any applicable industry trends, shifts in competition or consumer demand, seasonality (where applicable) of your products and services, economic conditions in your territory, and the prospects for growth within your market.

Step Three: Determining the Source of Capital

The last step in determining how capital will be raised is to determine whether the funds will be in the form of debt or equity and where they will come from. Each method has its share of costs and benefits. With debt comes the obligation to meet the monthly payments to the lender, pledge collateral to secure the debt, and struggle with many restrictions on the operation and management of the business that are likely to be found in the loan documents. With equity comes a dilution of your ownership interests in the company, the need to share profits with your shareholders and partners, the fiduciary obligations owed to additional investors who will not be taking an active role in the business, the increased risk of securities law if the business plans of the company are not met, and the possible loss of control of the company.

Debt-Financing Alternatives

The debt-financing alternatives to a start-up entrepreneur are basically either to borrow from a lending institution or issue debt securities, such as debentures or promissory notes to family, friends, or passive private lenders. The nature and amount of debt that you will be able to handle will depend on a wide variety of factors, such as: the direct cost of borrowing the capital; your ability to meet debt service payments; the amount of collateral available to secure the loan; projected cash flow and earnings; current and anticipated tax obligations; key industry ratios and norms; and whether all or part of the debt will be convertible into equity.

Sources of Debt Capital

Many sources of debt capital are available to today's start-up entrepreneurs. Although the focus here is on loans from traditional lending institutions (such as banks, thrifts, credit unions, and equipment lessors), you should also consider and investigate the lending programs offered by federal, state, and local governments. Many of these agencies have special programs for small businesses, community development projects, and businesses owned by women and members of minority groups. These agencies still have criteria and loans that are far from automatic; however, they may be more flexible with respect to collateral requirements, interest rates, operating covenants, and other key terms of the transaction.

The Small Business Administration (SBA) has significantly reduced its direct loan program in recent years; however, it is still an active provider of loan guarantees for small businesses. A call to your local SBA office will yield a list of certified lenders in your area who will consider applications for start-up entrepreneurs for loans under the SBA loan guaranty program. In addition to the SBA, many states have active small business direct loan and loan guaranty programs. A call to your state's department of commerce or economic development agency should be a good starting point for learning about these programs. In addition to federal and state programs, many city and county governments offer small business financing programs. At an even more local level, community development corporations may be an excellent source of start-up capital for your small business.

Getting a Bank Loan

Before commencing the process of applying for a bank loan, it is crucial to understand the lender's perspective. Banks are in the business of selling money. Capital is the only product in their inventory. Remember, however, that banks are not well known as risk-takers, especially in these turbulent economic times. The shareholders and board of directors of any bank expect that their loan officers will take all necessary steps to minimize the risk to the institution in each transaction and obtain the maximum protection in the event of default. Therefore, the types of loans available to start-up entrepreneurs, the terms and conditions of loan agreements, and the steps taken by the bank to protect its interest all have a direct relationship to the level of risk that the lending officer and the loan committee perceive.

Most lenders will require the start-up entrepreneur to prepare and present a loan proposal package. Although the exact elements of such a package vary depending on the projected size of your business, the industry, the amount of capital required, and how it will be allocated, most lenders want the following fundamental questions answered:

- Who is the borrower?
- How much capital is needed and when?
- How will the capital be allocated? For what specific purposes?
- How will the borrower service its debt obligations (for example, application and processing fees, interest, principal, or balloon payments)?
- What protection can the borrower provide the bank if he or she becomes unable to meet the obligations?

Notice that the answers to these questions are all designed to assist bankers in their assessment of the risk factors in the proposed transaction. However, these answers are also designed to provide commercial loan officers with the information necessary to persuade the loan committee to approve the transaction. Start-up entrepreneurs must understand that loan officers, once convinced of your creditworthiness, will then serve as advocates on your behalf in presenting the loan proposal to a loan committee. The loan documentation, terms, rates, and covenants that the loan committee will specify as a condition to making the loan are directly related to the ways in which you demonstrate your ability to manage and operate the business successfully and, as a result, are in a position to repay the loan.

Understanding and Negotiating the Loan Documents

Assuming that you have prepared an effective loan proposal and convinced the bank of your creditworthiness, the next and most important step is to carefully review and negotiate the loan documents that you will be expected to sign and comply with throughout the term of the loan.

Five types of documentation are involved in a typical term loan: the loan agreement, security agreement, financing statement, promissory note, and guaranty.

Loan Agreement

The loan agreement sets forth all of the terms and conditions of the transaction between the lender and the borrower. The key provisions are:

- amount
- term
- repayment schedules and procedures
- special fees
- insurance requirements
- conditions precedent
- restrictive covenants (small business borrowers should be especially careful of negative covenants, which are a series of acts that cannot be performed without the lender's prior written consent)
- the borrower's representations and warranties (with respect to status, capacity, ability to repay, title to properties, litigation, and so on)

- events of default, and the lender's remedies in the event of the borrower's default.

The provisions of this agreement should be reviewed carefully by an experienced attorney and a knowledgeable accountant. The long-term legal and financial impact of the restrictive covenants should be analyzed. You should always try to negotiate to establish a time-table under which certain covenants will be removed or modified as your company's ability to repay is clearly demonstrated. Do not rely on verbal assurances by the loan officer that a waiver of a default on a payment or covenant will be available.

Security Agreement

The security agreement will identify the collateral to be pledged in order to secure the loan. The security agreement usually references terms of the loan agreement as well as the promissory note (see below), especially with respect to the restrictions on the use of the collateral and the procedures upon default of the debt obligation. The remedies available to the lender under the security agreement in the event of default range anywhere from selling the collateral at a public auction to taking possession of the collateral and using it for an income-producing activity.

Financing Statement

The financial statement is the document that is actually filed with state and local officials in order to record the interests of the lender in the collateral. It is designed to give notice to the borrower's other potential creditors that a senior security interest (a holder of a security interest that has priority over you and your security interest) has been granted in the collateral specified in the financing state-ment. Specific rules regarding this document and the priority of competing creditors can be found in your state's version of the Uniform Commercial Code (UCC).

Promissory Note

The promissory note is the actual instrument that serves as evi-dence of the borrower's obligation to the lender. Many of its terms are also included in a loan agreement, such as the interest rate, the length of the term, the repayment schedule, the ability of the borrower to prepay without penalty, and the ability of the lender to accelerate the note in the event of default.

Guaranty

Virtually all start-up entrepreneurs are asked to execute a personal guaranty as further security in order to protect the lender in the event of a default. The terms of this guaranty should be carefully reviewed and negotiated, especially with respect to length, scope, the rights of the lender in the event of default, and the type of guaranty provided.

Sources of Equity Capital

An alternative to borrowing money that you need to open and operate your business is to take on a partner or other shareholders who will get an ownership interest in the business in exchange for their capital. The sources of capital when an equity financing is selected include individual private investors, institutional venture capital funds, and private placements.

Private Investors

Many small companies get their initial start-up capital from one or more private investors. Commonly known as "angels," these people range anywhere from your wealthy Uncle Bob, to your tennis partner, to an old college roommate who inherited his father's business. Typically these people do not expect the structure of the deal to be anything fancy and do not expect actually to manage or control the business. Entrepreneurs offering to sell stock to friends and relatives, however, must be sensitive to the applicable corporate and securities law issues, even at this level, that such an investment may trigger.

Institutional Venture Capital

The term venture capital has been defined in many ways. In general, it refers to the early-stage financing of young, relatively high-risk, emerging growth companies. The high risk is typically attributable to the company's newness or the entire industry's. Most venture capitalists look for investment opportunities that offer significant potential capital appreciation and return on investment, a strong management team, a company that is well positioned to exploit an opportunity within its industry, and a likelihood of an initial public offering within three to five years. The venture capitalist almost always wants to exercise some control and influence over a company's growth and development, both directly through a consulting arrangement or membership on the board of directors as well as indirectly through a wide variety of restrictive covenants in the investment documents.

If you decide to show your business plan to venture capitalists, you *must* take the time to learn the investment criteria and industry preferences of each venture capital company and then arrange for a personal introduction to the particular fund manager. Proceed in this manner only when your company has developed to the point where venture capital would be appropriate—when the company has actually been producing revenues and profits for at least one or two years.

Private Placement

A private placement is an offering of your company's securities to a limited number of investors under one or more specific exemptions from the registration requirements imposed by federal securities law. Many early-stage companies that do not necessarily possess the characteristics required by an institutional venture capitalist (or that simply want to avoid the typical controls required by a venture capitalist) should pursue this method of equity financing.

Most smaller offerings will be pursuant to Rule 504 of Regulation D under the federal securities laws, which is available for private offerings of up to $1,000,000. In addition, it is necessary to comply with the individual state laws that govern the offer and sale of securities. While federal law does not set forth any detailed requirements in conjunction with a Rule 504 offering, some state laws set forth certain disclosures that must be made in the private placement memorandum.

In preparing the disclosure document that will be used in connection with a Rule 504 offering, it is also important to recognize that the underlying purpose of the securities laws is to ensure that investors are able to make an informed decision based on full and fair disclosure of all material facts relevant to the investment. As a result, the document should fully describe any risks connected with the offeror or the offeror's securities for the protection of both the issuer and the purchaser. The SEC's Rule 10b-5, which penalizes an issuer for fraudulent misrepresentations (or omissions) in connection with the offer or sale of securities, is being applied more often these days.

Private placements are especially useful when a number of people have expressed an interest in investing in the company, but where no single individual has enough capital to meet all of your needs under the business plan. It is critical that you consult qualified and experienced lawyers and accountants prior to pursuing a private placement offering.

CHAPTER 6

Check List for Managing Your Business

O nce you've gone through all of the preliminary steps of:

- reviewing the company's offering documents,
- reviewing and negotiating the distributorship or license agreement,
- raising the necessary funds for starting the business,
- seeking advice from attorneys, accountants, and friends,
- obtaining the necessary business permits and licenses,
- opening bank accounts,
- obtaining business cards,
- obtaining a business telephone,
- obtaining Yellow Pages advertisements and initial advertising materials,
- buying office supplies,
- and hiring the initial staff needed to offer your products and services,

there still remains the formidable task of *managing your business on an ongoing basis.*

The key to the successful management and operation of a small business is for the owner to stay closely involved with three critical issues: (1) *personnel* (for example, ask "How do I continuously manage and motivate people to offer my products and services on a cost-effective basis and in a quality fashion?"); (2) *customers and markets* (for example, ask "How do I keep my customers happy and loyal, while keeping in touch with changes in demand and the entry of new competitors?"); and (3) *capital and cash flow* (for example, ask "How do I make sure that I have enough money to pay my expenses and still have some left for a profit?"). Although an extensive discussion of the specifics of small business management is beyond the scope of this book, this chapter provides a check list of key questions that you must ask at various stages of your company's growth. Naturally, not all of the questions will apply to your business right away, especially at the outset, when you are in all likelihood operating as a sole proprietorship. However, as your venture begins to grow and new employees are hired, you will find that more and more of the issues set forth must be examined periodically, both internally and with your team of external advisors.

Periodic Business Checkups

The best way to stay on top of these three key areas of small business management is to continue to evaluate *where you are* and *where you want to be* from a business and personal perspective. Too many owners of small businesses get and stay too closely involved in the day-to-day operation of their business to see the "big picture." They have fallen into the classic trap of being so close to the forest that they can't see the trees. The following is a list of business and legal issues that you should examine periodically, perhaps annually, in order to make sure that you stay on the right track.

Company Status

- Under what form of ownership is the company operated?
- When was this decision made? Does it still make sense? Why or why not?
- Have all annual filings and related actions such as state corporate annual reports or required director and shareholder meetings been satisfied?

FUTURE PLANS

- What are the company's capital requirements in the next twelve months?
- How will this money be raised?
- What alternatives are being considered?
- What issues are triggered by these strategies?
- Have applicable federal and state securities laws been considered in connection with these proposed offerings?
- Will key employees be offered equity in the enterprise as an incentive for performance and loyalty?
- Is such equity available?
- Have the adoption of such plans been properly authorized? Up to what point?
- Have all necessary stock option plans and employment agreements been prepared and approved by corporation shareholders and directors?
- Will any of the company founders be retiring or moving on to other projects?
- How will this affect the current structure?

CURRENT STRUCTURES

- If the company is a corporation, was an election under Subchapter S ever made? Why or why not?
- If the entity is a Subchapter S corporation, does it still qualify?
- Is such a choice unduly restrictive as the company grows (for example, ability to attract foreign investment, taxation of undistributed earnings, and so on)?
- If the entity is not a Subchapter S corporation, could it still qualify?
- Is this a more sensible entity under the new tax laws?

COMPANY LEGITIMACY

- Have bylaws been prepared and carefully followed in the corporation operation and management?
- Have annual meetings of shareholders and directors been properly held and conducted?
- Have the minutes of these meetings been properly and promptly entered into the corporate record book?
- Have transactions "outside the regular course of business" been approved or ratified by directors (or where required by shareholder agreements or bylaws) and resolutions been recorded and entered into the corporate records?
- Have quorum, notice, proxy, and voting requirements been met in each case under applicable state laws?

Business Planning Matters

- How and when was the business plan prepared?
- Has it been reviewed and revised on a periodic basis, or is it merely collecting dust on your bookshelf?
- Has it been changed/supplemented to reflect any changes in your plans or objectives?
- To whom has the plan been shown and for what purposes?
- Have you taken steps to preserve the confidential nature of the document?

Compliance with Government Regulations

- Have you filed all required federal and state tax forms (that is, employer's quarterly and annual returns, federal and state unemployment tax contributions, and so on)?
- Are federal and state record-keeping requirements being met for tax purposes?
- Have all payroll and unemployment tax accounts been established?
- Have all necessary state and local business permits and licenses been obtained and renewed?

- Have you checked on the need to obtain resale licenses (for sales tax collection)? Business licenses? Zoning permits? Fire permits? Health inspections? Bulk mail permits?
- Have you been qualified to "do business" in each state where such a filing is required?
- Have all required local business permits and licenses been obtained?
- Are the company's operational policies in compliance with the Occupational Safety and Hazard Agency (OSHA), the Equal Employment Opportunity Commission (EEOC), the National Labor Relations Board (NLRB), and zoning requirements?
- Have you developed smoking, maternity leave, and child care policies and programs that are in compliance with federal, state, and local laws?
- When is the last time the company consulted these statutes to ensure that current practices are consistent with applicable laws?

Employment Matters

- Have you determined your current and future staffing needs?
- What steps have you taken to ensure that you will always have sufficient human resources to run your business?
- Have you considered temporary or part-time employees?
- Have you developed employee policies and handbooks?
- Do you have hiring, performance review, and firing procedures?
- Have you adopted equal employment policies?
- Have all employees completed job applications? W-2 forms? I-9 forms?
- Will your company adopt a medical reimbursement plan? Group life insurance? Retirement plans? Disability plans? If not, should they be adopted?
- If yes, are all amendments to the structure and ongoing management of these plans being made to maintain qualification?

Contractual Matters

- On which material contracts is the company directly or indirectly bound?

- Are you bound personally as a guarantor on any of these contracts?
- Were these agreements drafted in compliance with applicable laws, such as your state's version of the Uniform Commercial Code?
- Is your company still able to meet its obligations under these agreements?
- Is any party to these agreements in default? Why?
- What steps have been taken to enforce the company's rights and/or mitigate damages?
- To what extent are contractual forms used when selling company products and services?
- When is the last time these forms were updated? What problems have these forms triggered?
- What steps have been taken to resolve these problems?
- Are employees who possess special skills and experience under an employment agreement with the company?
- When was the last time the agreement was reviewed and revised?

SALES REPRESENTATIVES

- What about sales representatives of the company?
- Are they under some form of a written agreement and commission schedule?
- Has the scope of their authority been clearly defined and communicated to the third parties with whom they deal?

INDEPENDENT CONTRACTORS

- To what extent does the company hire independent contractors?
- Have agreements been prepared with these parties?
- Have the intellectual property law issues, such as "work for hire" provisions, been included in these agreements?

COMPETITORS' FORMER EMPLOYEES

- Have you recently hired a former employee of a competitor?
- How was he or she recruited?
- Does this employee use skills or knowledge gained from the prior employer?
- To what extent has the prior employer been notified?
- What steps are being taken to avoid a lawsuit involving misappropriation of trade secrets and/or interference with contractual regulations?

Marketing Issues

- Have you clearly defined the market for your company's products and services?
- Who are your key competitors?
- What are their respective market shares, strengths, weaknesses, strategies, and objectives?
- What new players are entering your market?
- What barriers exist to new entry?
- What is the saturation point of this market?
- What steps will you take to protect your customers and market share?

Advertising and Public Relations

- What advertising and public relations strategies were initially used to promote your new business?
- Did you keep track of what worked well and what didn't?
- What steps will you take to modify your advertising and public relations strategies?
- Can you afford to implement these new strategies?
- Will these strategies reach your targeted market in a cost-effective manner? Have you tried direct mail, door flyers, coupons, civic activities, Little League team sponsorship, chamber of commerce participation, seminars, or writing articles in community or business periodicals?

Choosing a Legal Form for Your Business

Choosing a corporate form is a crucial decision for the first-time entrepreneur. The following chart outlines the major pros and cons of each structure.

Organizational Structure	Advantages	Disadvantages
Sole Proprietorship: Attorney's fees for your start-up will be less than for other business forms as less documentation is required. To set a sole proprietorship up, find a location and begin. There are fees for registering your business and obtaining necessary licenses.	• Easy to launch • Income tax advantages in very small firms • Maximum authority • Flexibility and freedom of action	• Unlimited liability • Limited access to capital; • Lack of business continuity; business ceases with death, illness • Growth limited to personal energies • Limited business and/or organizational skills
Partnerships: Association of two or more persons who engage in business as co-owners sharing the assets, liabilities, and profits. Can be formed by oral agreement or attorney's written contract.	• Partner offers feedback, moral support, and "two heads are better than one" • Access to larger pools of capital • Better credit rating than corporations of similar size	• Death, withdrawal, or bankruptcy of one partner endangers business • Difficult to get rid of bad partner • No clear definition on authority could lead to conflicts

Organizational Structure	Advantages	Disadvantages
Corporation: You can incorporate without an attorney, but it's not wise to do so. Corporate form is usually the most costly to organize as it is the most complex.	• Limited stock-holder liability • An ability to attract large amounts of capital • Easy to transfer ownership • Access to larger pools of talent and skill	• Limited liability could give owners false sense of security • Time and expense to incorporate • Heavier taxes • More legal formalities

CHAPTER 7

Troubleshooting:
An Overview of
Laws and Regulations

M any laws at the federal and state level are designed to protect your legal rights once you've made the decision to participate in a business opportunity. Some of these laws protect you during the offer and sale process by requiring the offeror to provide you with certain minimum levels of information about the company and the package offered. Other laws are designed to protect you even after you've opened up for business, such as the antitermination statutes that eighteen states have passed. And still another set of laws has been passed to protect you in specific types of situations, such as multilevel marketing and pyramid statutes, special laws pertaining to automobile dealers and service station operators, and laws requiring how and when earnings claim information may be presented.

This chapter discusses the various federal and state laws that are designed to protect you in the event that you are duped into participating in a fraudulent scheme by a high-pressure, fast-talking salesperson.

Regulation of Business Opportunities under the FTC Rule

Certain types of business opportunity offerings are regulated under federal law by the Federal Trade Commission (FTC). Its trade regulation Rule 436, which is formally titled "Disclosure Requirements and Prohibitions Concerning Franchising and Business Opportunity Ventures," was formally adopted on December 21, 1978, and became effective on October 21, 1979 (the FTC Rule).

Although trade regulation Rule 436 typically is referred to in the context of franchising, it *also* applies to companies that sell certain types of business opportunities *if* the seller offers a "package" that has all three of these characteristics:.

1. The distributor sells goods or services that are supplied by the offeror or a person affiliated with the offeror.
2. The offeror assists the distributor in any way with respect to securing accounts for the distributor, or securing locations or sites for vending machines or rack displays, or providing the services of a person able to do either.
3. The distributor is required to make payment of $500 or more to the offeror or a person affiliated with the offeror at any time before to within six months after the business opens.

The FTC Rule exempts fractional franchises, which are opportunities that result in less than 15 percent of your total revenue. The rule also excludes relationships between employer and employees and among general business partners; membership in retailer-owned cooperatives; certification and testing services; and single trademark licenses.

Among other things, the FTC Rule requires the sellers of certain types of business opportunities to deliver an offering circular (containing certain specified disclosure items) to all prospects within certain specified time requirements. The FTC has adopted and enforced its rule pursuant to its power and authority to regulate unfair and deceptive trade practices. The FTC Rule sets forth the *minimum* level of protection that shall be afforded to prospective candidates.

A person cannot sue in an individual capacity for a violation of Rule 436. However, the FTC itself may bring an enforcement action against a company that does not meet its requirements. Penalties for noncompliance have included asset impoundments, cease-and-desist orders, injunctions, consent orders, mandated recision or restitution for injured distributors, and civil fines of up to $10,000 per violation.

If the offering of the company that you are considering meets the three elements just set forth, then you must be provided with a disclosure document that includes information on the following 20 subjects:

1. Identifying information about the offeror;
2. Business experience of the offeror's directors and key executives;
3. The offeror's business experience;
4. Litigation history of the offeror and its directors and key executives;
5. Bankruptcy history of the offeror and its directors and key executives;
6. Description of the offering;
7. Description of any money that you as the distributor must pay to obtain or commence the business;
8. Continuing expenses that you will incur in business operation that are payable in whole or in part to the offeror;
9. List of persons, including the offeror and any affiliates, with whom you are required or advised to do business;
10. Real estate or personal property and services, and so on, that you are required to purchase, lease, or rent, and a list of any person with whom such transactions must be made;
11. Description of consideration paid (such as royalties, commissions, and the like) by third parties to the offeror or any of its affiliates as a result of your purchases from such third parties;
12. Description of any financing assistance the offeror will provide for your purchase of an offering;
13. Restrictions placed on your conduct of your business;
14. Whether the offeror requires your direct personal participation in the business;
15. Termination, cancellation, and renewal of the offering;

16. Statistical information about the number of opportunities that have been sold by the offeror and their rate of termination;
17. Offeror's right to select or approve a site for the offering;
18. Training programs provided by the offeror;
19. Celebrity involvement or affiliation with the offeror;
20. Financial information about the offeror.

The information in the disclosure document must be current as of the end of the offeror's most recent fiscal year. In addition, the document must be promptly revised whenever there has been a material change in the information it contains. The disclosure document must be given to a prospect at the earlier of either (1) the prospect's first personal meeting with the offeror, or (2) ten days prior to the execution of a contract or payment of money relating to the offering. In addition to the disclosure document, prospects must receive a copy of all agreements that they will be asked to sign at least five days prior to the execution of the agreements.

The FTC Rule also requires that a completed distributorship agreement and related agreements be provided to the prospect *five business days* before the agreements are executed. (A business day is any day other than Saturday, Sunday, or the following national holidays: New Year's Day, Washington's Birthday, Memorial Day, Independence Day, Labor Day, Columbus Day, Veteran's Day, Thanksgiving, and Christmas.)

These timing requirements apply nationwide and preempt any lesser requirements in state laws. The ten-day and five-day disclosure periods may run concurrently, and sales contacts with the prospective distributor may continue during those periods.

It is an unfair or deceptive act or practice within the meaning of the FTC Act for any offeror or offering broker to:

1. Fail to furnish prospective distributors, within the time frame established by the rule, with a disclosure document containing information on 20 different subjects relating to the offeror, the underlying business, and the terms of the offering agreement;
2. Make any representations about the actual or potential sales,

income, or profits of its existing or prospective distributors except in the manner set forth in the rule;

3. Fail to furnish prospective distributors, within the time frame established by the rule, with copies of the offeror's standard form of distribution agreement and copies of the final agreements to be signed by the parties; or

4. Fail to return to prospective distributors any funds or deposits (such as down payments) identified as refundable in the disclosure document.

State Regulation of Business Opportunities

Several states have enacted legislation that requires specific prior written disclosure regarding business opportunities. Many of these state laws were passed in response to fly-by-night scams in the 1960s and 1970s by criminals and perpetrators of frauds engaged in franchising and business opportunity offerings. These state laws vary widely but generally define a business opportunity as the sale of goods or services to enable a purchaser to start a business accompanied by specific kinds of representations by the offeror to the purchaser, such as that the investment is "risk-free" or that the offeror will buy back any unsold products.

Thus, the *first* element of a business opportunity is the sale or lease of goods or services that allows the purchaser to begin a new business or materially alter an existing one. The *second* element is based on one or more of several specified types of organizations. These representations may be categorized as follows:

- Assertions by the offeror that the purchaser will be provided locations for the use or operation of vending machines, racks, display cases, currency-operated amusement machines, or other similar devices;
- Promises that the offeror will buy any products that the purchaser produces with the seller's goods or services;
- Claims by the offeror that the distributor will be provided with a surefire or guaranteed sales or marketing plan; or
- Guarantees that the buyer will derive income from the opportunity exceeding the amount paid for it; that the investment will be refunded if the buyer is dissatisfied; or that the offeror

will repurchase the goods or services sold to the buyer if the buyer is not satisfied. These are typically known as "buyback options" or "investment guarantees."

Business opportunity statutes commonly define their scope in terms of the offeror's conduct rather than by categorizing the business transaction, and they explicitly describe prohibited practices. Business opportunity offerors are required, in twenty-four states, to file a registration statement with the appropriate state agency (usually the Securities Division or Consumer Protection Agency) and to file with the agency a disclosure statement (similar to that required of franchisors), which would then be provided to each prospective offeree. The following states have adopted business opportunity statutes:

Alabama	Louisiana	Oklahoma
California	Maine	Ohio
Connecticut	Maryland	South Carolina
Florida	Michigan	South Dakota
Georgia	Minnesota	Texas
Indiana	Nebraska	Utah
Iowa	New Hampshire	Virginia
Kentucky	North Carolina	Washington

Many statutes require offerors to obtain surety bonds to protect the offeree within the state or establish escrow or trust accounts in favor of the offeree. The amount of these bonds and trust accounts can range from a low of $10,000 to a high of $75,000. Some business opportunity statutes require specific contractual or disclosure terms in the areas of cancellation rights, the specific delivery dates for goods bought by the offeree from the offeror, terms and conditions of payment, and the details of any representations made by the offeror to repurchase the goods or inventory acquired by the offeree. Many of these state laws require a presale cooling-off period, and some even require a postsale think-it-over-one-more-time period under which the offeree can *cancel* within three days after the contract is signed.

By way of example, the state of Washington has what could be considered a typical business opportunity statute. It defines a "business opportunity" as the offer for sale or lease of products, supplies, or services sold for the purpose of starting a business *and* in which the offeror represents any of the following five items: (1) it will provide locations for vending machines, display cases or racks; *or* (2) it will repurchase products made by the distributor; *or* (3) it will refund all or a part of the investment; *or* (4) it will guarantee any level of income or profit; *or* (5) it will provide a sales or marketing program if the distributor pays $300 or more. The offeror must provide a disclosure document to residents of the state at least forty-eight hours prior to the signing of any agreements or any money changing hands. The disclosure document must be registered with the state, and if the offeror makes any representations pursuant to item (4), then it must post a performance bond of not less than $50,000. The agreement between the offeror and the distributor must be in writing and must include certain provisions dictated by the state. Failure by the offeror or its agents to comply with these laws could expose the company to a wide range of penalties, including civil fines, permanent injunctions, and even criminal imprisonment for the commitment of a Class B felony.

Regulation of Multilevel Marketing (MLM) Offerings

MLM companies are regulated by a variety of overlapping laws that vary from state to state. MLM programs are affected by a combination of pyramid statutes, business opportunity statutes, multilevel distribution laws, offering and securities laws, various state lottery laws, referral sales laws, the federal postal laws, and Section 5 of the Federal Trade Commission Act.

Recently many MLM plans have been targeted for prosecution and litigation pursuant to these laws. To date, enforcement of statutes and regulations has been rather selective and arbitrary, and many regulatory officials are skeptical regarding the legality of virtually all MLM programs. Therefore, from a legal standpoint, MLM is an uncertain and speculative activity, and there is no assurance that even the most legitimate MLM progam will be immune from legal attack.

Six states, however, have laws that specifically regulate companies that adopt multilevel marketing programs. They are Georgia, Louisiana, Maryland, Massachusetts, New Mexico, and Wyoming. Any MLM company operating in any of these states typically must file an annual registration statement giving notice of its operations in that state and must appoint the state's secretary of state as its agent for service of process. This means that if you are sued, the state will accept the litigation papers on your behalf. Because the statutes include "sales kit exemptions," MLM companies are often not covered by the business opportunity laws. Under such exemptions, "required payment" for the cost of demonstration equipment or materials sold at the company's cost are not considered to be "required payments."

In addition to imposing the annual registration requirement, several states have additional regulations governing the activities of MLM companies. These states may:

1. Require that MLM companies allow their independent representatives or distributors to cancel their agreements with the company. Upon such cancellation, the company must repurchase unsold products at a price not less than 90 percent of the distributor's original net cost;
2. Prohibit MLM companies from representing that distributors have or will earn stated dollar amounts;
3. Prohibit MLM companies from requiring distributors to purchase certain minimum initial inventories (except in reasonable quantities);
4. Prohibit compensation to be paid solely for recruiting other participants.

Pyramid Schemes
Numerous laws and regulations have been enacted in the United States to prohibit pyramid schemes. Pyramid schemes are prohibited under a myriad of state laws, some of which declare unlawful "pyramid sales schemes," "chain distributions," "referral selling," "endless chains," and the like. Pyramid distribution plans have also been declared unlawful as lotteries, unregistered securities, violations of mail fraud laws, or violations of the Federal Trade Commission Act.

Broadly speaking, a pyramid distribution plan is a means of distributing a company's products or services to consumers. Pyramid schemes generally consist of several distribution levels through which the products or services are resold until they reach the ultimate consumer. A pyramid differs from a valid multilevel marketing company in that in its elemental form, a pyramid is merely a variation on a chain letter and almost always involves large numbers of people at the lowest level who pay money to a few people at the highest level. New participants pay a sum of money merely for the chance to join the program and advance to the top level, where they will profit from the initial payments made by later participants.

One of the most common elements of pyramid schemes is an intensive campaign to attract new participants who serve to fund the progam by providing the payoff to earlier participants. Some schemes use high-pressure sales techniques such as "Go-Go Chants" and "Money Hums" to increase crowd enthusiasm. Often meetings are held in distant locations with everyone traveling to them by bus as captive audiences. These bus rides and meetings may include an emotional pep-rally type recruiting approach. In one case, prospective recruits who did not sign up at the initial meeting were taken on a charter plane trip to the company's home office. During the flight, known as a "Go Tour," they were subjected to intense pressure to sign contracts before the plane landed. On the plane, references were made to the success of others, large amounts of money were displayed, and, at times, piles of cash and contracts were dropped onto prospects' laps.

The format of the meetings is often completely scripted and prepared strictly in accordance with the company's guidelines and policies. These scripts invariably make reference to the financial success that awaits those who participate. In the aforementioned case on the airplane, recruits were told that they could easily become millionaires.

A certain number of participants fail in all pyramid schemes. A pyramid can work only if there are unlimited numbers of participants. When the pyramid fails to attract new participants, those individuals who joined later will not receive any money because there will be no new bottom level of participants to support the plan.

In order to avoid prosecution, the promoters of pyramid schemes often attempt to make their plans resemble multilevel marketing companies, which are legitimate methods of doing business that utilize a network of independent distributors or sales representatives to sell consumer products or services. Pyramid schemes often claim to sell products or services to consumers, but products or services are often of little or no value. No one truly tries to sell the goods; rather, the emphasis remains almost solely on signing up new participants who are needed to "feed the machine."

The following five sections summarize other laws that have been used to prosecute promoters of pyramid plans and also regulate multilevel marketing companies.

Referral Sales Statutes

Some states prohibit referral sales programs that are generally defined to include the payment of some compensation to a buyer in return for the furnishing to the seller of the names of prospective recruits. Thus, any scheme in which buyers are told that they can receive a return of the money paid if they provide a list of names to the seller is an unlawful referral sale.

Lottery Statutes

Many states prohibit pyramid programs as lotteries, because financial success in the program is not based on skill and judgment but on the element of chance: for example, an endless stream of new participants will join the program causing the original participant to receive a return higher than the initial entry fee paid to join.

Securities Laws

The sale of a security that is not registered is a violation of state and federal law. According to the Securities and Exchange Commission (SEC), the money paid by a prospect to participate in a scheme (with the expectation of profit based primarily on the activities of other parties) is considered an investment contract or security that must be registered with the SEC or fit within the bounds of one of its exemptions from registration.

Mail Fraud Laws

Pyramid programs have been prosecuted under mail fraud laws that prohibit endless chain schemes involving the exchange of money or other things of value through use of the U.S. mail.

Federal Trade Commission Act

Section 5 of the FTC Act prohibits unfair methods of competition in commerce and unfair or deceptive practices. This broad provision has been used to justify FTC action against pyramid programs. In one of its most famous cases, the FTC argued that Amway Corporation was an illegal pyramid program. The FTC ultimately determined that Amway is *not* a pyramid scheme because the only required "investment" is a sales kit sold to distributors at cost. Amway guaranteed it would repurchase unsold inventory, and the *sponsoring distributor received nothing from the mere act of sponsoring* but rather began to earn money only when the newly recruited distributor sold products to consumers.

Federal Laws Affecting Dealerships in Specific Industries

Two common types of nonfranchised business opportunities are auto sales dealerships and service station dealerships. These dealerships have their own sets of federal laws that affect the relationship between the manufacturer and the dealer. A brief summary of these statutes follows.

Automobile Dealer Act (ADA)

The Automobile Dealer Franchise Act is frequently referred to as the automobile dealer day-in-court law. It provides that a dealer shall be permitted to recover damages and costs from a manufacturer that fails to "act in good faith in complying with any of the terms or provisions of the dealership agreement." A suit may be brought in the district in which the manufacturer resides without regard to the amount in controversy as long as the suit begins within three years of the cause of action.

Certain states have also enacted legislation governing automobile dealers. For example, in 1984 Pennsylvania enacted the Board of Vehicles Act, which established a state board of vehicle manufacturers, dealers, and salespersons to regulate the motor vehicle industry. The statute prohibits manufacturers from terminating or not renewing a franchise without just cause, good faith, and sixty days' notice. Dealers may protest terminations and nonrenewals to the board, which will conduct hearings and issue rulings on the protests. Termination or nonrenewal does not become effective until the board has made a final determination. Unlawful acts by manufacturers include:

1. Coercing dealers into accepting unwanted vehicles;
2. Forcing participation in advertising campaigns;
3. Coercing dealers into refraining from managing or investing in another line of vehicles;
4. Unfairly discriminating among dealers in warranty reimbursement;
5. Encroaching within a dealer's market area;
6. Unreasonably withholding consent to a franchise transfer.

The board is authorized to suspend or revoke licenses or fine dealers and manufacturers for violation of the law. A civil action for compensatory and punitive damages, attorneys' fees, and costs is also provided.

Petroleum Marketing Practices Act (PMPA)

The PMPA is similar to the ADA in that its primary purpose is to protect distributors and retailers of motor fuel with respect to termination or nonrenewal by refiners and manufacturers. The statute covers both oral and written contracts insofar as they address motor fuel marketing or distribution obligations and responsibilities. Unlike the federal provisions governing automobile dealers, however, the PMPA supersedes state law and specifically addresses grounds for termination and nonrenewal.

Understanding the Earnings Claims Laws

Naturally, information concerning the anticipated profitability of a business opportunity is a key issue for prospective distributors and their sources of financing. Knowing this, many companies or their sales representatives are tempted to tell distributors that a franchised business will "make a million dollars a year" or "allow you to buy the Porsche you've always wanted." These claims, however, are strictly governed by federal and state laws that pertain to "earnings claims."

The FTC defines an "earnings claim" as: "any oral, written or visual representation made to a prospective distributor or prepared for general dissemination in the media which states or suggests a specific level or range of potential or actual sales, income, or gross or net profits." In other words, it is anything that implies or guarantees that you'll make a certain amount of money if you invest in this business opportunity.

When an earnings claim is made, it must be in a specified form and prepared in accordance with specified standards under federal and state law. Therefore, any projected income statements, cash flows, statements from other stores, or any related data or claims provided by the company should comply with applicable laws. Counsel to the offeree should carefully review these documents to ensure compliance with the law. Note that the earnings claims laws do not cover mere claims of "puffery," such as "Opportunity of a Lifetime" or "Make Big Money Today!" A statement or document that does not specify or suggest some specific level of sales, income, or profits is probably not covered by the law of earnings claims.

State-Level Antitermination Statutes
Affecting Distributorships and Dealerships

Eighteen states* have statutes that govern distributorships and dealerships, typically prohibiting an offeror from terminating the relationship except for good cause. The definition of "good cause" varies from state to state.

States also vary as to which types of relationships fall within the bounds of the antitermination statutes. Arkansas, on one hand, defines the relationship as the right to use an offeror's trademark or the right to sell goods or services plus the granting of an exclusive territory. Similarly, Connecticut requires only a "community of interest," without requiring any fee. Florida requires that the offeror grant the right to offer or sell goods or services, that the distributor/

---

*Arkansas, California, Connecticut, Delaware, Florida, Hawaii, Illinois, Indiana, Kentucky, Michigan, Minnesota, Mississippi, Missouri, Nebraska, New Jersey, Virginia, Washington, and Wisconsin.

dealer constitute a component of the offeror's distribution system, and that the distributor/dealer be substantially reliant on the offeror for his or her supply of goods.

As an example, the Wisconsin Fair Dealership Law (WFDL) provides that: "No grantor, directly or through any officer, agent or employee, may terminate, cancel, fail to renew or substantially change the competitive circumstances of a dealership agreement without good cause. The burden of proving good cause is on the grantor."

Common Law Issues

Fraud and Misrepresentation

Common law claims of fraud and misrepresentation are often raised in cases involving the offer and sale of business opportunities and multilevel marketing plans. The offeror or agents often make statements to prospects that are clearly designed to induce them to participate in these programs. Inaccurate statements about potential profits, capabilities of the products, the experience of the offeror's management team, or the size of the distributor's "protected" territory all may amount to fraud. In order to prove fraud at common law, the distributor generally must show that:

1. The offeror or its agent made a false representation about an existing material fact.
2. The offeror or its agent knew the statement was false.
3. The offeror or its agent intended the distributor to rely upon the misrepresentation.
4. The distributor justifiably relied upon the misrepresentation.
5. The distributor sustained injury as a result of its reliance.

Although the definition may differ from state to state, these basic principles are common throughout the nation.

Unfair Competition Law and Related Business Torts

In addition to federal and state antitrust and consumer protection laws, a broad and growing body of state and local unfair competition laws may be interpreted to protect the interests of a distributor or an offeree who feels that he or she has been treated unfairly. The nature and scope of the law of unfair competition will vary from state to state. Most jurisdictions recognize some form of the following business torts (damage or injury) that usually fall under the unfair competition umbrella: trade libel; product disparagement; interference with existing or prospective contractual relations; misappropriation and infringement of intellectual property; invasion of privacy; commercial bribery; price-fixing; and price discrimination. Although a detailed state-by-state analysis is beyond the scope of this book, distributors and participants in multilevel marketing programs should keep these laws in mind if there is a problem with the manufacturer or offeror.

IMPLIED COVENANTS OF GOOD FAITH AND FAIR DEALING

Many state courts have been increasingly willing to read certain implied covenants of good faith and fair dealing into the provisions of today's licensing, distribution, and franchising agreements. As a result, licensees and distributors who have been treated unfairly could obtain some protection and relief *even* if their contracts say otherwise. Although not all courts have implied these covenants into contracts, the implied duty is a very worthwhile argument to consider in a dispute with a licensor or manufacturer.

INTEFERENCE WITH CONTRACTUAL RELATIONS

Although the antitrust laws are designed to foster competition, state courts will not tolerate excessive competitive zeal in approaching competitors' customers and suppliers. Improper solicitations of a competitor's customers or suppliers that are designed to encourage a breach of an existing or even prospective contract could cause the competitor to file a civil cause of action. In determining whether the alleged act or practice was improper, most courts will consider the nature of the actor's conduct, the proximity of the actor's conduct to the alleged interference, the current status of the relationship that was interfered with, and the interests of the third-party supplier or consumer that dealt with the competitor. The bottom line is that there is a large gray area separating a legitimate effort to take business away from a competitor and an improper attempt to induce a breach of contract.

PASSING OFF

This common law business tort is closely related to trademark infringement and trade secret misappropriation. It attempts to penalize a company that copies the packaging, design, name, shape, appearance, taste, color scheme, or general physical characteristics of the products or services offered by a competitor where the intent is to confuse the consumer as to source of origin. Therefore, although competitors are all equally entitled to ensure that their products and services offer attractive features and are presented in an attractive manner, no competitor is entitled to confuse the public by posing as another company.

EQUITABLE SERVITUDES AND COVENANTS

A seller's attempt to restrict the use of a product following the sale is an equitable servitude, which is generally unenforceable as an illegal restraint of trade. Similarly, most state courts will not tolerate an unreasonable covenant against competition following the termination of an employment or franchise relationship. If a company has a legitimate business justification for the use of such covenants or servitudes, then it will also bear the burden of proving the reasonableness of the provision when challenged.

CHAPTER 8

Directory of Resources

M any sources of help and information can assist you in evaluating business opportunities, distributorships, multi-level marketing offerings, and cooperatives. This chapter provides you with a directory of federal and state agencies, trade associations, trade show promoters, and publications that can be invaluable resources to you, not only during the evaluation stage but also in the event of a problem with your opportunity after you've opened your business.

The directory begins with a list of state agencies that specifically administer state business opportunity laws. This is often the best place to start when making an inquiry into the background or status of a particular offeror. The next section lists certain federal agencies that directly or indirectly affect the activities of a business opportunity offeror. For example, the Federal Trade Commission (FTC) is a good resource to check if you are concerned about a company's regulatory track record. Similarly, you can contact the U.S. Patent and Trademark Office (USPTO) to confirm the existence of a patent or trademark that an offeror purports to have registered.

The last three sections of the directory deal with certain trade associations and private companies from which you can gather information about business opportunity offerings. For example, to confirm an offeror's membership in the Direct Selling Association (DSA) (and its obligations to follow the Code of Ethics included at the end of this chapter), call the DSA for its membership directory.

Government Agencies Administering
the State Business Opportunity Laws

A variety of states regulate, and in certain cases register and bond, many types of business opportunity offerors before an offer or sale can be made. The following list specifies the state agencies that administer these laws. These state agencies can be useful in confirming that your particular offeror has met obligations under all applicable laws. These agencies are also a good place to start if there is a problem with the offeror, before *or* after the agreement is signed. Not all states are listed because not all states have their own business opportunity statutes. If your state is not listed and you have questions or concerns about a particular company, contact the state's attorney general's office or the consumer protection agency.

State	Address/Contact

California	Office of Secretary of State
	Limited Partnership or Statutory
	   Certification
	P.O. Box 704
	Sacramento, CA 95803
	Attn: Statutory Certification,
	   Bonds and Filings Unit
	1-916-324-6778

Connecticut	Department of Banking Securities Division 44 Capitol Avenue Hartford, CT 06106 Attn: Tia Damato 1-203-566-4560 ext. 8332
Florida	Department of Agriculture Consumer Services Mayo Building, Room 508 Tallahassee, FL 32301 Attn: Dick Brown 1-904-488-2226

Georgia	Office of Consumer Affairs 2 Martin Luther King Drive, S.E. Plaza Level, East Tower Atlanta, GA 30334 Attn: Dobbs Jordan 1-404-656-3790
Indiana	Consumer Protection Division Attorney General's Office 219 State House Indianapolis, IN 46204 Attn: David A. Miller or Deniece Rogers 1-317-232-6330/6331
Iowa	Securities Division Lucas State Office Building Des Moines, IA 50319 Attn: Dennis Britson 1-515-281-4441
Kentucky	Attorney General's Office Consumer Protection Division 209 St. Clair Frankfort, KY 40601-1875 Attn: Darlyn Asbil 1-502-564-2200
Louisiana	Department of Urban & Community Affairs Consumer Protection Office P.O. Box 94455, Capitol Station Baton Rouge, LA 70804 Attn: Ida Washington 1-504-925-4401 (gen. info), 1-504-925-4405

Maine	Department of Business Regulations State House—Station 35 Augusta, ME 04333 Attn: Karen L. Bossie 1-207-298-3671
Maryland	Office of the Attorney General Securities Division 7 North Calvert Street Baltimore, MD 21202 Attn: Delia Burke 1-410-576-6360
Michigan	Michigan Department of Attorney General Consumer Protection Division 670 Law Building Lansing, MI 48913
Minnesota	Department of Commerce Commissioner of Commerce 500 Metro Square Building St. Paul, MN 55101 Attn: Ann Hagestad 1-612-296-6328
Nebraska	Department of Banking and Finance P.O. Box 95006 Lincoln, NE 68509-5006 Attn: Thomas Sindelar, Neal Nelson 1-402-471-2171
New Hampshire	Attorney General Consumer Protection and Antitrust Bureau State House Annex Concord, NH 03301 Attn: Terry Robertson 1-603-271-3641

North Carolina	Secretary of State's Office Securities Division Legislative Annex Building 300 Salisbury Street Raleigh, NC 27602 Attn: Daniel Bell 1-919-733-3924
Ohio	Attorney General Consumer Fraud & Crime Section State Office Tower, 15th Floor 30 East Broad Street Columbus, OH 43215 Attn: Rick Sheffield, Chief; Rita Brown, Investigator 1-614-466-8831, 1-800-282-0515
Oklahoma	Oklahoma Securities Commission 2915 Lincoln Boulevard Oklahoma City, OK 73105 Attn: Sonya Singer, Faye Morton 1-405-521-2451
South Carolina	Secretary of State P.O. Box 11350 Columbia, SC 29211 Attn: Eric Pantsari 1-803-758-2244
South Dakota	Department of Commerce and Regulation Division of Securities State Capitol 910 East Sioux Avenue Pierre, SD 57501 Attn: Debra Bollinger, Dir. of Securities; Jeff Adel, Franchise Administrator; Dorothy Adams, Licensing Asst.; Melita Bisbee, Admin. Asst. 1-605-773-4013

Texas

Office of the Secretary of State
Business Opportunities Section
P.O. Box 13563
Austin, TX 78711-3563
Attn: Colleen Lloyd
1-512-463-5559

Utah

Consumer Protection Division
160 East 300 South
P.O. Box 45802
Salt Lake City, UT 84145-0801
Attn: Kathleen Bertelsen
1-801-530-6601

Washington

Department of Licensing
Securities Division
P.O. Box 648
Olympia, WA 98504
Attn: Claude Kennedy
1-206-753-6928

Federal Agencies

At the federal level, the Federal Trade Commission is the best place to bring a complaint or concern about a particular business opportunity offeror or when you suspect that a company is engaged in foul play. Keep in mind that the FTC has limited resources and will not be able to investigate every complaint. In some cases, the FTC may recommend that you discuss the matter with your state's consumer protection bureau or with an attorney to pursue a private right of action. Even those business opportunity offerors that are subject to the FTC's trade regulation Rule 436 need *not* register with the agency. Therefore, do not call the FTC to obtain a copy of an offeror's disclosure statement. The FTC may be able to tell you, however, whether there has been a prior or current investigation of the offering you are considering. The U.S. Patent and Trademark Office and the Library of Congress are excellent resources to determine whether the offeror has properly protected its trademarks, patents, or copyrights. The U.S. Small Business Administration (SBA) and its various field offices are excellent sources of materials and assistance on small business management, resources, and finance.

Federal Trade Commission
Consumer Protection
  Division
6th & Penn. Avenue,
  N.W.
Washington, D.C. 20580
1-202-326-2222

Register of Copyrights
Library of Congress
Washington, D.C. 20559
1-202-287-9100

U.S. Patent and Trademark
  Office
Box 5
Washington, D.C. 20231
1-703-557-3158

U.S. Small Business
  Administration
409 Third Street, S.W.
Washington, D.C. 20416
1-202-205-6631

Trade Associations

Many of the following trade associations consist of various companies that offer business opportunities, multilevel marketing offerings, direct mail, cooperatives, and franchises. These associations often publish directories of their members, which can be a valuable resource in choosing between competing offerings. Bear in mind that these associations typically require their members to follow a code of ethics, such as those published by the Direct Selling Association and reprinted at the end of this chapter. There are also trade associations for specific industry groups, such as housewares, sporting goods, and automobile services. Most of these associations have headquarters in New York, Washington, D.C., Chicago, or Los Angeles. These industry group associations can be a valuable resource for industry data, trends, and statistics that are critical for investigation of the opportunity as well as the preparation of your business plan. Also listed are the national offices of the Better Business Bureau and the National Consumer Law Center, which are important resources for evaluating problematic offerings or when the offeror fails to meet ongoing promises or contractual obligations.

Better Business Bureau
1012 14th Street, N.W.
Washington, D.C. 20005
1-202-393-8000

Direct Marketing Association
6 East 43rd Street
New York, NY 10017
1-212-689-4977

Direct Selling Association
1776 K Street, N.W.
Suite 600
Washington, D.C. 20006
1-202-293-5760

International Franchise Association
1350 New York Avenue, N.W.
Suite 900
Washington, D.C. 20005
1-202-628-8000

Licensing Executive Society
71 East Avenue
Norwalk, CT 06851-4903
1-203-852-7168

Multi-Level Marketing International Association
119 Stanford Court
Irvine, CA 92715
1-714-854-5488

National Consumer Law Center
11 Beacon Street
Boston, MA 02108
1-617-523-8010

National Cooperative Business Association
1401 New York Avenue, N.W.
Suite 1100
Washington, D.C. 20005
1-202-638-6222

Trade Show Management Companies
The following companies offer business opportunity and franchise trade shows in various cities across the country. Contact them directly for a schedule of upcoming trade shows.

Business World Expo
P.O. Box 162
Landenberg, PA 19350
1-215-268-8690

Q. M. Marketing, Inc.
Westlawn Professional Center
1515 West Chester Pike
Suite B-2
West Chester, PA 19382
1-215-431-2402

SC Promotions
901 S. Glendale Avenue
Suite 500
Glendale, CA 91205
1-818-500-0005

Spectrum Shows, Inc.
Blenheim Exhibitions Group, PLC
1133 Louisiana Avenue
Suite 211
Winter Park, FL 32789
1-407-740-0018

Publications

The following periodicals offer articles on business opportunities and entrepreneurship. Many of these magazines publish annual or semiannual listings and directories of business opportunity offerors.

Enterprise Magazine, Inc.
(publishes the *Business Opportunities Handbook*)
1020 North Broadway
Suite 111
Milwaukee, WI 53202

Entrepreneur Magazine
(publishes the *Annual Business Opportunity 500*)
2392 Morse Avenue
P.O. Box 19787
Irvine, CA 92713

Inc. Magazine
38 Commercial Wharf
Boston, MA 02110

Income Opportunities Magazine
380 Lexington Avenue
New York, NY 10168-0035

IncomePlus Magazine
Opportunity Associates
73 Spring Street
Suite 303
New York, NY 10012

Info Press, Inc.
(publishes directories and newsletters on franchises
and business opportunities)
728 Center Street
P.O. Box 550
Lewiston, NY 14092

New Business Opportunities Magazine
2392 Morse Avenue
Irvine, CA 92713-9440

Success Magazine
Lang Communications
230 Park Avenue
New York, NY 10169

DIRECT SELLING ASSOCIATION
CODE OF ETHICS

PREAMBLE

The Direct Selling Association, recognizing that companies engaged in direct selling assume certain responsibilities toward consumers arising out of the personal contact method of distribution of their products and services, hereby sets forth the basic and fair ethical principles and practices to which member companies of the association will continue to adhere in the conduct of their business,

INTRODUCTION

The Direct Selling Association is the national trade association of the leading firms that manufacture and distribute goods and services sold directly to consumers. The Association's mission is "to protect, serve and promote the effectiveness of member companies and the independent businesspeople marketing their products and to assure the highest level of business ethics and service to consumers." The cornerstone of the Assocation's commitment to ethical business practices and consumer service is its Code of Ethics. Every member company pledges to abide by the Code's standards and procedures as a condition to admission and continuing membership in the Association. Consumers can rely on the extra protection provided by the Code when they purchase products or services from a salesperson associated with a member company of the Direct Selling Association. For a current list of Association members, contact DSA, 1776 K Street, N.W., Washington, D.C. 20006, (202) 293-5760.

A. CODE OF CONDUCT

1. Deceptive or Unlawful Consumer Practices.

No member or company of the Association shall engage in any deceptive or unlawful consumer practice.

2. Products or Services.

The offer of products or services for sale by member companies of the Association shall be accurate and truthful as to price, grade, quality, make, value, performance, quantity, currency of model, and availability.

3. Terms of Sale.

A written order or receipt shall be delivered to the customer at the time of sale, which sets forth in language that is clear and free of ambiguity:

a. All the terms and conditions of sale, with specification of the total amount the customer will be required to pay, including all interest, service charges and fees, and other costs and expenses as required by federal and state law;

b. The name and address of the salesperson or the member firm represented.

4. Warranties and Guarantees.

The terms of any warranty or guarantee offered by the seller in connection with the sale shall be furnished to the buyer in a manner that fully conforms to federal and state warranty and guarantee laws and regulations. The manufacturer, distributor and/or seller shall fully and promptly perform in accordance with the terms of all warranties and guarantees offered to consumers.

5. Pyramid Schemes.

For the purpose of this Code, pyramid or endless chain schemes shall be considered consumer transactions actionable under this Code. The Code Administrator shall determine whether such pyramid or endless chain schemes constitute a violation of this Code in accordance with applicable federal, state and/or local law or regulation.

B. RESPONSIBILITIES AND DUTIES

In the event any consumer shall complain that the salesperson or representative offering for sale the products or services of a member company has engaged in any improper course of conduct pertaining to the sales presentation of its goods or services, the member company shall promptly investigate the complaint and shall take such steps as it may find appropriate and necessary under the circumstances to cause the redress of any wrongs which its investigation discloses to have been committed.

Member companies will be considered responsible for Code violations by their solicitors and representatives where the Administrator finds, after considering all the facts, that a violation of the Code has occurred and the member has either authorized such practice found to be violative, condoned it, or in any way supported it. A member shall be considered responsible for a Code violation by its solicitors or representatives. For the purpose of this Code, in the interest of fostering consumer protection, companies shall voluntarily not raise the independent contractor status of salespersons distributing their products or services under its trademark or trade name as a defense against Code violation allegations and such action shall not be construed to be a waiver of the companies' right to raise such defense under any circumstance.

The members subscribing to this code recognize that its success will require diligence in creating an awareness among their employees and/or the independent wholesalers and retailers marketing under the Code. No subscribing party shall in any way attempt to persuade, induce or coerce another party to breach this Code, and the subscribers hereto agree that the inducing of the breach of this Code is considered a violation of the Code.

PART·II

PART II

INTRODUCTION

The 75 companies profiled here represent a cross section of the various types of business ventures, including general business opportunities, dealerships, multilevel marketing, distributorships, direct sales programs, licenses, and vending operations. While an investment in most of the profiled companies results in a long-term relationship between the entrepreneur and the company, some of these ventures require only a one-time purchase of equipment and supplies.

It is important to note that terms used throughout the book to describe the relationship between entrepreneur and company, such as distributor and dealer, do have a specific and legal definition. But in practical, everyday operations, many of the companies use these terms interchangeably. Although not completely accurate, this practice is acceptable, but a novice entrepreneur may find it confusing. The lesson here is not to get bogged down in titles and nomenclature when investigating an opportunity. Rather than the title, it is the function of the entrepreneur in that business opportunity that should be understood.

In writing these profiles, in general, companies were selected that exhibited a successful expansion track record. A few selected companies do not fall into this category. Some, such as The World Garden Society, are new offerings that are marketing interesting and unique products or services. Other companies—for example, Fit By Five—are well established with noteworthy programs and credentials but follow a less-than-aggressive marketing strategy in attracting entrepreneurs.

The first part of the information in the profiles is listed in outline form. These data are extremely important, providing the vital statistics entrepreneurs should know when investigating a company. This information is organized in essentially three categories: required capital investment, company history, and industry focus. Additionally, the Company Advantages section overviews a company's place in a specific industry.

"Initial investment" refers to the money an entrepreneur is expected to give to the company as a sign of serious interest. It may come in the form of a deposit or a fee for receiving legal, promotional, or private company literature. The required fee is listed here. In many profiles, this initial investment matches the figure for "Total investment," or the entire amount of money an entrepreneur is required to give the company as a sign of the commitment. Some entries show a range of figures here. This range is seen mainly when companies offer a variety of investment and equipment packages to attract entrepreneurs of various financial capabilities.

The total investment figure refers only to the amount of money the company deems necessary to run the business opportunity, not to what an individual needs for necessities, such as food, clothing, and the costs associated with maintaining a certain standard of living. It is impossible for an outsider or company to estimate these costs, but every entrepreneur should weigh these expenses and include them when deciding if a business opportunity is affordable.

"Ongoing fees" refers to any charge a company passes on to entrepreneurs on a regular basis. These fees include licensing dues, dealership contract renewals, organization affiliation dues, and equipment rental. Entrepreneurs should include these items when listing expected expenses for a business opportunity.

Some entrepreneurs feel more secure investing in an opportunity with a well-recognized name. For that reason, under "Right to use trademark and logo," each entry indicates whether entrepreneurs purchase with their investment the right to use the company's trademark and logo as part of their own business name. This right is not an essential ingredient to success, and, in fact, some of the more successful opportunities profiled in this book do not have a registered trademark or logo. Some companies have registered trademarks but prohibit entrepreneurs from using them in their business name, while other companies require entrepreneurs to display the company's trademark and logo prominently. There is also a group of companies that allows entrepreneurs to represent themselves as dealers or distributors and use the company's trademark and logo in conjunction with their own name.

"Expansion History" details the growth rate of an individual company. Some companies established a sound track record with their product or services before they endeavored to sell business opportunities to entrepreneurs. Other opportunities were started and expanded simultaneously. Neither course of action is a telltale sign of company stability. A company's growth rate depends on the popularity of the idea, the market for the product, and the company's ability to support and monitor an expansion effort.

Also included in the expansion history is the number of entrepreneurs who have invested in the company and set up their own businesses or purchased equipment and supplies from the company. Most companies were able to supply this number, but some equipment manufacturers and suppliers do not keep track of this figure. Some companies also prefer not to disclose in a guidebook of this type the number of distributors, dealers, licensees, and so on, that exist; rather they divulge this statistic and provide references only to those interested in committing their time and money to the business opportunity. In these cases, it is noted that this figure is not available.

The purpose of listing the number of existing dealers, distributors, licensees, and the like is to give entrepreneurs an idea of how quickly the company has expanded. Again, please note that a company with 50,000 distributors does not automatically spell success, and a company with 4 distributors does not automatically spell failure. Some business opportunities require more capital investment from entrepreneurs and are more complex to operate and therefore expand slowly. Other opportunities require little capital, training, and equipment, and entrepreneurs can begin operating immediately.

"Industry Focus" tells the reader what products and services the company offers. This is a brief and general statement about the industry in which the company belongs. Some industries contain numerous companies that compete vigorously for market share, while other industries have only a few key players who can easily make room for more entrepreneurs. Entrepreneurs would be wise to study the growth patterns of the industry in which a certain company or business opportunity belongs.

"Company Advantages" gives entrepreneurs an idea of how the profiled company fits into the market picture. Does it have a great deal of competition? Does it produce and sell a unique product or service? Does the company offer potential entrepreneurs a solid support system, corporate image, and creative products to market? This section may also include some personal history, such as the founders' names, education, and reasons for starting the company. The narrative body of the profile is designed to give an overall picture of the company, its history, its expectations, and its responsibility to entrepreneurs who become dealers, distributors, licensees, consultants, and the like. In this section entrepreneurs learn what the company requires of them financially and personally. The role of the entrepreneur is explored. Is the entrepreneur mainly a salesperson, technician, or manager? Is this opportunity a one-person show, or does the entrepreneur need to hire employees to operate the business successfully? The text also reveals what kind of time commitment is expected of entrepreneurs. Is the business operated on a full- or part-time basis? Can the business opportunity be run as a home-based venture? Is an entrepreneur expected to run a direct mail or telemarketing campaign? The distributor may need to display products at home parties, craft shows, or flea markets and travel to reach customers. When the information was available, the typical dealer or distributor as to sex, average age, educational background, and any other pertinent characteristics is detailed.

The profile explains what is included in an entrepreneur's investment in terms of equipment, training, and company support. Readers may notice that some opportunities require formal training classes at the company's home office; others require dealers or distributors only to read a manual or view an instructional video at home. Training requirements and fees are also highlighted, especially if the cost of training is not included as part of the investment package.

Following the training requirements, the profile outlines the company's follow-up support program. Some companies, especially the larger distributorship firms, hold regular meetings, seminars, and workshops. Any bonus incentives or special promotions that exist for acheiving higher sales volumes are noted. This part of the profile also discusses the entrepreneurs' potential for advancement within a company's network. For example, multilevel marketing distributors earn higher commissions if they recruit and train other distributors. When the information is available, commission structures, the average gross earnings of entrepreneurs, and estimated working capital expenditures are also provided.

"Future Outlook" reviews the company's product or service and how it compares with the marketplace in general. A company's future cannot be predicted, but its history of expansion and support for its dealers, distributors, and the like gives clues about its potential performance. Also noted in this section is any new product, service, or business opportunity scheduled to be introduced. These new opportunities represent growth by the company, and although they were not yet in practice at the writing of this book, they nevertheless deserved mention.

The future outlook may also emphasize business courses entrepreneurs must pursue in order to achieve success. For instance, some opportunities require an entrepreneur to participate in cold-call sales to attract customers. Mention of this practice warns entrepreneurs who detest sales to look elsewhere for a business opportunity.

Finally, the "Contact Information" section gives readers the names and titles of personnel who can best provide information about specific business opportunities. This section also includes the businesses' addresses and telephone numbers.

It is hoped that these profiles will give readers and potential entrepreneurs enough facts to begin their investigation into a company. Any business undertaking, whether part time or full time, requires serious contemplation. Entrepreneurs should not be afraid to ask thorough questions. Not every opportunity requires thousands of dollars, but it does require time and commitment. Entrepreneurs must have a clear understanding of their place and rights in any business opportunity.

Last, investing in a business is not a quick road to success. No matter what the business opportunity, entrepreneurs must exhibit patience and determination. These are the hallmarks of the successful businessperson. Opportunities exist, but individuals must take care to find the right opportunity that matches their personal and financial constraints. Entrepreneurs should look for assistance in setting up their business venture from the legal profession and from government groups, such as the Small Business Administration. Entrepreneurs can also tap local organizations and chambers of commerce for assistance. Many retired business owners and executives volunteer their consultation service to new entrepreneurs. Investigation and preparation are the keys to developing a successful business.

General
Business Opportunities

ADVERTISING AND PROMOTION

I. ROBOTICS, INC.

(Rent a Robot)

Initial investment: $2,500 to $14,000
Total investment: $2,500 to 14,000
Ongoing fees: None
Right to use trademark and logo: No

Expansion History
Company operating since: 1981
Offering robot rental business opportunities since: 1981
Number of I. Robotic independent business owners: 161+

Industry Focus
Robots give an image of high technology, and many companies and industries want to relate this image to their present and potential customers.

Robots have come a long way in the last decade. They provide entertainment at the same time they are relaying information to the consumer.

Company Advantages
I. Robotics provides ample support and post-support training to entrepreneurs who purchase a robot from them. The company supplies robotic upgrades to fit customers' needs.

The I. Robotics robots are well recognized at trade shows, promotional events, store grand openings, and charity functions.

Entrepreneurs purchase the equipment from I. Robotics. There are no fees or royalties assigned to this purchase, and entrepreneurs can rent the robot to other businesses for professional displays.

In a competitive business world, companies and business owners need a sales promotion that will hold a customer's attention. I. Robotics, Inc., gives business owners that tool with its walking, talking, high-technology robots. Founded in 1981, I. Robotics markets its robots through a network of more than 161 independent entrepreneurs, who rent the high-tech promotional tool to corporations, charity organizations, and other businesses or associations.

The key to I. Robotics's success is the "personality" of the robots that entertain and educate potential customers about products through dance routines, speeches, and other physical antics.

The I. Robotics entrepreneur is an independent rental agent. Entrepreneurs market their robots to corporations, trade show hosts, flea market managers, charity organizations, and anyone else who needs to bring customers and patrons through the doors. Entrepreneurs set their own rental prices, but most charge between $150 and $250 per hour for a robot's appearance. The rental costs depend on the robot's routine and capabilities. Basic robots are equipped to perform standard walking and spinning movements as well as to play recorded audio messages. Entrepreneurs can upgrade their robot by purchasing optional equipment that can create special vocal effects, play videotapes, inflate balloons, dispense promotional literature, or greet customers by tipping a hat. Entrepreneurs can also purchase tuxedos and elf and Santa costumes to enhance the robot's appearance.

To purchase an I. Robotic robot, entrepreneurs invest between $2,500 and $14,000. The lower investment purchases a basic robot that walks, talks, and spins; the higher investment purchases the company's Star Commander Robot, which contains omnidirectional mobility, a colorful light display, a remote transmitter, stereo speakers, and other upgrades.

Entrepreneurs receive robot-operating instruction at the company's home office in Boston as well as at the entrepreneur's site. I. Robotics brings in experienced operators to teach new entrepreneurs how to attract people of all ages to the display, amuse people, and respond to people's questions and reactions. I. Robotics also provides entrepreneurs with a well-tested marketing plan that is designed to gain new customers and teach entrepreneurs how to run successful direct mail and advertising campaigns. The plan also instructs robot owners how to hire and train other robot operators. The initial investment package also includes support items, such as rechargeable batteries for the robot, a radio control transmitter, protective covers, a carrying bag, a pattern for costumes, operating manuals, and promotional photos.

As an added service, the company sponsors the National Robot Rental Exchange. This exchange lists I. Robotic entrepreneurs from all over the United States and Canada. It allows I. Robotics operators to locate their colleagues for out-of-town or national customers and contract their services. The entrepreneur who referred the other I. Robotic operator receives a 20 percent commission for the sales effort. I. Robotics also maintains a toll-free number for operators in need of assistance. The company warranties all electromechanical parts and labor on the robot models for one year. The warranty does not cover items such as the charging unit, replaceable batteries, and lamps.

Future Outlook

Robots are a sign of technology. Few people see robots in daily operation, so they are fascinated to meet one face-to-face. The business is purely marketing, and it requires an entrepreneur who has a strong desire to sell this service.

Overhead for this business is low. Entrepreneurs do not need an office, nor do they need a staff. As business grows, entrepreneurs may purchase more robots or upgrade the ones they own. The increase in business may push the entrepreneur into a more commercial environment and a professional marketing and operating staff.

Contact Information

Address: 66 Marion Street, Boston, Massachusetts 02128
Telephone: 1-800-447-6646 or 1-617-561-0400
Contact person: Edna Oshiro, general manager

AUTOMOBILE MAINTENANCE

TU-GROOVES

(Trademark of IIG Ltd.)

Initial investment: $5,050
Total investment: $8,050
Ongoing fees: None
Right to use trademark and logo: Yes

Expansion History
Company operating since: 1979
Offering Tu-Groove machine package since: 1985
Number of Tu-Groove owners: 62

Industry Focus
   Windshield safety grooves remove oil, dirt, snow, ice, and other hazardous elements from the windshield wiper.
   Safety grooves aid all transportation vehicles. Public transportation companies, airlines, and individual car owners rely on this grooved process to improve visibility in poor weather.

Company Advantages
   Tu-Grooves founder and president Ted Kallman imported this process from Europe in 1985, and he owns the only company in the United States that has exclusive marketing rights on the process.
   Tu-Grooves has added a new product, Wiper Wipers, which are polycarbonate plastic strips that contain adhesive backing for easy installation on windshields. This product is more temporary than Tu-Grooves, but consumers can do the installation themselves.

■ ■ ■

Heavy rain- and snowstorms can deposit dirt and oil on a windshield, drastically reducing the wipers' cleaning capabilities and the driver's visibility. Michigan-based Kallman Ltd. offers a process that consists of etching two grooves into the lower portion of a windshield in the direct path of the wiper blades. Wiper blades travel over the grooves, where dirt and other material is removed from their edges. The grooves are permanent and measure only three-tenths of a millimeter deep. They do not weaken windshields, and they can actually extend the normal life of wiper blades up to four times.

IIG Ltd. previously franchised this concept, but found that the franchise system was too costly and time-consuming to operate efficiently. IIG Ltd. redirected its expansion program in 1988, and now markets the tools and a complete training program to independent entrepreneurs as a general business opportunity.

The Tu-Grooves owner needs no experience in glass or windshield installation and repair. Tu-Grooves provides all materials and training. Entrepreneurs who own established glass or automobile service companies can add the Tu-Grooves process to their list of services.

Entrepreneurs can run their Tu-Grooves operation in a variety of ways. Some establish retail locations, while others choose to own a mobile company and go to the customer's site. The Tu-Grooves machine is hand-held and requires little room for storage. The machine does need an air compressor and water supply to run, but these accessory tools can easily fit into the back of a van. The flexibility in business operation attracts both part-time and full-time entrepreneurs.

The cost for installing the Tu-Grooves process ranges from $30 to $50 per vehicle, depending on the entrepreneur's location. The process takes about fifteen minutes to complete, and entrepreneurs can earn a 40 percent profit or more on each installation. Entrepreneurs market this service to individual consumers as well as truck companies, bus fleets, airlines, and any other person or business that operates a vehicle with a windshield.

An initial investment of $5,050 in the Tu-Grooves business opportunity is required. This investment purchases the Tu-Grooves machine and accessory items as well as one day of training at IIG Ltd.'s Lansing, Michigan, headquarters. This fee also includes the right to sell the company's newer product, Wiper Wipers. Made of polycarbonate plastic, these easily installed groove strips are attached to windshields by an adhesive material. Tu-Grooves sells polygroove strips to individual consumers who install the strips on their cars themselves.

Kallman recommends that entrepreneurs keep an additional $3,000 in reserve to cover the costs of insurance, printing and advertising expenses, and working capital. Other costs, such as leasing a retail location or customizing a van for mobile operation, depend on the Tu-Groove owner's market area.

Kallman offers Tu-Groove ongoing marketing and technical support. The company maintains a toll-free number for owners and provides a referral service for contracts and job assignments as well. The Tu-Grooves machine comes with a 90-day guarantee.

Future Outlook

IIG Ltd. provides a valuable and viable service. Tu-Grooves has won the support of the transportation industry. The simple product design improves driver visibility, which leads to fewer accidents and lower vehicle and windshield repair costs.

Contact Information
Address: 205 W. Saginaw, Lansing, Michigan 48933
Telephone: 1-800-678-1236 or 1-517-484-2415
Contact person: Ted Kallman, president

AUTOMOBILE UPHOLSTERY RESTORATION

FITZGERALD'S VINYL AND VELOUR REPAIR, INC.

Initial investment: $219.95 to $3,995
Total investment: $219.95 to $3,995
Ongoing fees: None
Right to use trademark and logo: None

Expansion History
Company operating since: 1978
Offering vinyl repair equipment and training since: 1981
Number of vinyl repair operators: 500+

Industry Focus
   Car vinyl and upholstery restoration can save consumers hundreds of dollars in replacement costs.
   Established car dealers or repair operations take on this service for customers. Vinyl and upholstery restoration is a simple process, and it produces a high profit margin.

Company Advantages
   Fitzgerald's Vinyl and Velour Repair is both a manufacturer and distributor of vinyl, velour, plastic, and leather repair equipment and supplies.
   The company has expanded without the aid of mass advertising. Most of its success comes from word-of-mouth referrals and trade journal listings.

   A torn vinyl roof or a torn velour seat cover can reduce the value of an automobile. Fitzgerald's Vinyl and Velour Repair restores vinyl and velour back to their original form. Established in 1978, Fitzgerald manufactures its own products at its 5,000-square-foot facility in Stockton, California. Along with the vinyl and velour restoration products, Fitzgerald also offers supplies for the repair and restoration of plastic, leather, and car bumpers.

The demand for the restoration products led the company to expand its distribution practice and open up two more company locations—in southern California and in South Carolina. At these three locations, entrepreneurs and established business owners learn the restoration process and purchase supplies for the vinyl repair business. Fitzgerald's has trained more than 500 entrepreneurs at its facilities, and the company has more than 1,000 clients for its equipment and supply products.

Entrepreneurs who purchase Fitzgerald equipment and supplies need no background in any type of automobile maintenance or repair. They do not have to be established business owners, and they do not have to take on this opportunity as a full-time career. Those who do not have established business locations may not need to lease commercial premises. Most entrepreneurs travel to their customer's location, carrying all equipment in a van or truck. The mobile nature of this business may eliminate the need for expensive commercial space.

The company advises marketing its services to car dealerships; restaurants that use vinyl chairs, stools, and booths; and many other businesses as well as individual consumers. Business owners not only repair damaged materials, they match colors for upholstery and wood grains for dashboards and repair damaged car bumpers as well. The target market for these services is large, and Fitzgerald advises entrepreneurs to explore a number of marketing strategies including direct mail, telemarketing, and person-to-person sales. An investment ranging from $219.95 to $3,995 purchases a variety of vinyl restoration packages. The highest-price investment purchases equipment and supplies to restore vinyl, velour, plastic, and leather. Included in this package is a master color-matching system; a bumper repair kit; a turbo-spray system with a 15-foot hose; a paint spray respirator; a 30-can, color-coat matching package; 10 large and 10 medium assorted heel pads; and weatherstrip adhesive. The package also contains a professional hand masker, a cut-off blade for it, a tape dispenser, masking tape, masking paper, and an electrostatic velour applicator. Fitzgerald's also includes in this deluxe package a training seminar videotape and three days of personal training.

The company also markets a basic starter package that costs $2,395, not including the three days of training; the 30-can, color-coat package; or the velour applicator. Both these packages are for the entrepreneur looking to establish a full-service vinyl and velour repair business.

The lower-price packages are for established business owners in need of supplies or further training. Entrepreneurs can also purchase separate kits for all restoration services, including color matching and plastic repair.

Those who choose a lower-priced kit can register for training separately. Entrepreneurs who want individual training at one of the company's three facilities pay an additional $300 for a half-day session. Those who prefer to attend a group training seminar for 40 to 50 people pay an additional $79 above their kit price.

Fitzgerald's maintains a toll-free line for entrepreneurs who experience technical problems or need to order new materials and supplies. The company also offers updated training seminars on its new products and publishes regular newsletters.

Future Outlook

Vinyl, velour, plastic, and leather are in almost every product in the marketplace today. It is not economically or ecologically sound to throw away many products just because they have torn or faded. Fitzgerald saves customers hundreds of dollars by bringing these materials back to their original form. The products are Environmental Protection Agency (EPA) approved, which also justifies restoration instead of disposal.

Contact Information

Address: 221 North American Street, Stockton, California 95202-2513

Telephone: 1-800-441-3326 or 1-209-463-1483

Contact person: Dean Fitzgerald, president

BUSINESS SERVICES

INKY DEW

Initial investment: $1,500 to $10,000
Total investment: $1,500 to $10,000
Ongoing fees: None
Right to use trademark and logo: Yes

Expansion History
Company operating since: 1988
Offering business opportunities since: 1989
Number of Inky Dew independent contractors: 60+

Industry Focus
Computer printer ribbons can be reinked 50 or more times before they have to be replaced. Reinking ribbon costs only half as much as ribbon replacement.

Company Advantages
The founders of Inky Dew researched the idea of recycled printer ribbons for one year before they launched the Inky Dew Company.

Inky Dew contractors can start on a part-time basis and build the business gradually into a retail or full-time sales office and service company.

The company has also branched out into new-ribbon sales for equipment such as cash registers and time clocks as well as computers.

Computer systems do make life easier, especially for small businesses, but the replacement of simple parts such as printer ribbons could become an annoying expense. Inky Dew of San Diego, California, tries to alleviate this cash outlay with its unique service that reinks used computer ribbons for less than half the price of ribbon replacement.

Established in 1988, Inky Dew is the product of Dr. Eugene Cummings and his wife, Eileen, who developed the process. The couple spent hundreds of dollars replacing computer ribbons during their graduate school days, and they became intrigued by the possible market for reinked ribbons. The Cummingses researched the longevity and demand for the recycled ribbons for one year and then launched their company. The result is a network that includes more than 60 Inky Dew independent contractors throughout the world.

Initially the company successfully focused only on reinked ribbons, but the Cummingses noticed a growing market that preferred to buy new ribbons—even at the higher price. Inky Dew expanded its target area and introduced new-ribbon sales and service for line printers, dot matrix printers, cash registers, and time clocks. Currently half of the company's total volume is still dedicated to ribbon recycling, while the remainder focuses on new ribbon sales.

"The ribbon's endurance is not compromised with the reinking process," says Eileen Cummings. "But many customers feel more secure with spending a few dollars more and buying a replacement ribbon. We appeal to both customers, and our contractors are prepared for each customer."

For a minimum investment of $1,500, an Inky Dew contractor purchases all equipment needed to start a ribbon recycling and replacement business. For this investment, contractors receive an exclusive territory based on population plus two inking machines and four adapters that fit 98 percent of the most popular printer makes and models. Inky Dew also supplies materials to reink the most popular spools and cartridge ribbons, plastic and sealer to mail reinked ribbon back to customers, a potential customer list, and promotional brochures and materials.

This entry-level package allows contractors to work from home on a part-time basis. Contractors contact potential customers through person-to-person sales, telemarketing, and direct mail campaigns. Contractors target both small and large businesses that use line printers, dot matrix printers, cash registers, and time clocks. Contractors can eventually direct their businesses into retail locations or professional office space as business volume develops. Inky Dew does not set pricing standards for its contractors, but the company encourages them to investigate to determine what is the local competitive rate for ribbon replacement. Inky Dew charges no ongoing royalty fees, but contractors do order supplies and ribbons from the home office.

Inky Dew also offers a higher-priced investment package. Contractors pay a $10,000 fee for supplies and equipment, including a ribbon-splicing machine. This package targets the entrepreneur who wants to start out with a full-time business immediately. Inky Dew urges entrepreneurs to start with the lower-priced package and build their businesses slowly.

As part of its support program, Inky Dew provides all contractors with videos and manuals that emphasize sales and marketing strategies. The videos and manuals also teach contractors the reinking process through examples and diagrams. Inky Dew's independent contractors do not need previous mechanical or computer experience. The reinking and ribbon replacements are not difficult tasks, and the company maintains that most ribbons take less than 20 minutes to reink or replace.

Inky Dew does not require in-person training, but the company sponsors a toll-free line for all contractors who have questions about the sale of ribbons or the reinking process.

Future Outlook

Inky Dew increased its customer draw by offering both new and reinked ribbons. For customers concerned about reducing office expenses, the reinking process is acceptable. The ribbon is not damaged, and most ribbons can be reinked 50 or more times before they need to be replaced. For customers who are wary of recycled ribbons, the company offers new-ribbon sales. Inky Dew plans to stay in this specialized niche of the office products market. This allows the company to study the market and adjust its product line to it.

Contact Information

Address: 935 E. Street, San Diego, California 92101-6511

Telephone: 1-800-262-INKY (U.S.) or 1-800-248-INKY (Canada) or 1-619-233-4344

Contact person: Eileen Cummings

PACK 'N MAIL

Initial Investment: $17,500
Total Investment: $55,000
Ongoing fees: None
Right to use trademark and logo: Yes

Expansion History
Company operating since: 1981
Offering independently owned stores since: 1985
Number of stores: 147

Industry Focus
Consumers have accepted private mail services and rely on them to deliver important parcels.

Private companies can provide post office boxes as well as pickup and delivery services. In order to be competitive with the U.S. Postal Service, private companies offer lower rates.

Company Advantages
As part of the $17,500 investment fee, Pack 'N Mail provides site-location services as well as lease negotiations for its operators. The company receives no royalties from operators who use the Pack 'N Mail name.

The company also negotiates with United Parcel Service (UPS) and other parcel services on behalf of all Pack 'N Mail store owners without charging an additional fee.

Pack 'N Mail may convert to a franchise. If this happens, all existing operators will not pay any additional charge or royalty fees. A grandfather clause in the franchise contract will protect all existing operators from these charges. However, the operators will receive the same support that future franchisees receive.

Pack 'N Mail of Lubbock, Texas, is an alternative to the over-worked postal system. In 1985 the company developed a network of independently owned parcel and package retail centers, which provide parcel pickup and delivery service, messenger service, Western Union, rental post office boxes, and UPS service as well.

Pack 'N Mail was one of the first entrants into the private mail industry more than 11 years ago. Today Pack 'N Mail consists of 147 stores throughout the United States and Canada, and the company estimates that 1,000 will exist by 1996. Pack 'N Mail is the second largest private mail company in the United States and competes with large franchise chains such as Mailboxes, Etc., and Mail Box U.S.A.

For an initial investment of $17,500, Pack 'N Mail will locate a suitable site for the retail store, negotiate a lease, allow the use of the Pack 'N Mail name and logo, and teach the company's method of operation. Pack 'N Mail will also assure the new store owner an exclusive territory, consisting of a three-mile radius around the store. In addition to the initial investment, a Pack 'N Mail owner should expect to need $37,500 for the purchase of inventory and equipment. The additional funds also cover the costs of leasehold improvements in the required 1,500-square-foot retail space. Owners of already established, private parcel mail centers can convert to a Pack 'N Mail store by paying a discounted investment fee of $10,000. Unlike many of its competitors, who have opted for expansion through franchising, the company charges no ongoing royalty fees.

"We attract investors and customers because we offer more than package pickup and delivery," says Pack 'N Mail president Mike Gallagher. "We experiment with new services and pass the successes on to our store owners. There may be a creative idea out there that can work for everyone."

The Pack 'N Mail owner offers customers all services that exist in the home office. Stores are open six days a week, from 9:00 A.M. to 6:30 P.M. Monday through Friday and 10:00 A.M. to 5:00 P.M. on Saturday.

Pack 'N Mail owners attend a 14-day training class. Classes focus on the mail services offered to customers, and there is also instruction in management, personnel recruitment, and marketing. Once stores are in operation, Pack 'N Mail will send field representatives to the site for three days to assist the owners in operating the business. The company maintains telephone support with store owners, and it provides in-field assistance. Pack 'N Mail publishes a newsletter every two months to keep owners informed on services and retail additions. Pack 'N Mail also negotiates contracts with major parcel and delivery companies on behalf of all store owners. These contracts are designed to lower the costs of parcel shipping for Pack 'N Mail owners.

Future Outlook
The company depends on its independent owners for a solid reputation and referral. Pack 'N Mail makes money on the sale of new locations. With no royalty fees, continued growth is essential to the company's survival.

Pack 'N Mail is considering converting to a franchise. Company executives have delayed this decision because they know it will slow down their expansion efforts and put them in direct competition with larger companies. As a nonfranchise opportunity, Pack 'N Mail has attracted more entrepreneurs, but it has lost revenue that would come automatically with royalty fees. If it turns to franchising, the company maintains it will charge lower royalties than any of its competitors, and all existing operators will be excluded from any future franchise fees or royalty fees by a grandfather clause.

Contact Information
Address: 5701 Slide Road, Suite C, Lubbock, Texas 79414
Telephone: 1-806-797-3400
Contact Person: Mike Gallagher

SALSBURY INDUSTRIES

Initial investment: $12,000 to $26,000
Total investment: $12,000 to $26,000
Ongoing fees: None
Right to use trademark and logo: None

Expansion History
Company operating since: 1936
Offering postal box equipment since: 1936
Number of private mail store owners: 5,000+

Industry Focus

Private mail centers have gained popularity in the last decade. Stores attract customers by offering one-stop shopping for their mail, fax, and copy needs.

Private mail centers work with many parcel companies as well as the U.S. Postal Service to provide speedy package and mail pickup and delivery services.

Company Advantages

Founded in 1936, Salsbury Industries is a manufacturer of post office equipment. The company is the leading equipment source for the U.S. Postal System. Salsbury has also pioneered the development of the private mail center industry by offering consumers equipment and marketing plans for a retail mail establishment.

For almost 60 years, Salsbury Industries has been an undisputed leader in post office equipment manufacturing. The emergence of the private postal center industry in the 1980s increased the demand for Salsbury's products, and the company worked with entrepreneurs to build the private mail industry into a multimillion-dollar entity.

Salsbury Industries is a manufacturer and consultant. The company supplies entrepreneurs with aluminum or brass postal boxes, collection stands, meter stations, and other equipment needed to run a one-stop postal center efficiently. Salsbury also provides a detailed manual that outlines the costs, marketing strategies, and daily operations associated with running a private mail retail store.

Entrepreneurs who purchase Salsbury equipment do not purchase a turnkey or ready-to-operate business opportunity. The company supplies the equipment and will assist entrepreneurs in the design and layout of the store. It is up to the entrepreneur to find and lease a suitable site, negotiate agreements with private parcel companies, determine what services to offer customers, and market the store appropriately. Salsbury's manual assists entrepreneurs in the step-by-step process, but the company does not maintain an ongoing contract with them.

Entrepreneurs who purchase Salsbury equipment should first discover who their customers are. Most private mail centers use the term suite instead of box numbers for company addresses. This feature attracts small business owners and home-based entrepreneurs who want to display a more professional address. The private mail centers also cater to individuals whose local post office branches have no available boxes for rent.

Other customers patronize mail centers for their auxiliary services, which may include photocopies, package wrapping and shipping, passport photos, key making, and faxing. Not all private mail centers need to offer the same services, and Salsbury emphasizes that services can be added as business volume grows.

Salsbury recommends that mail center entrepreneurs lease a minimum of 700 square feet. The center should be in a high-traffic shopping center that has ample parking for customers. The company also suggests that the minimum population in the store's area total 10,000 residents.

An investment ranging from $12,000 to $26,000 purchases all equipment and inventory needed to operate a private mail center effectively. Salsbury estimates that $5,600 to $10,000 of the investment covers the cost of the aluminum or brass postal boxes. The price difference depends on the number of boxes and the materials used. The remaining portion of the investment purchases items such as a fax machine, small copier, passport photo camera, key machine, word processor, scale, and stamp machine. Leasehold improvements, office signs, stationery, rent and utility deposit, and security are also included in the initial investment. Salsbury recommends that entrepreneurs also keep in reserve $2,500 to $4,500 for working capital and miscellaneous expenses.

The Salsbury manual provides entrepreneurs with business and marketing procedures. Salsbury offers telephone support to its customers, and the company will assist in developing store design, business name suggestions, and promotional or grand-opening ideas.

Future Outlook

The private mail center industry is still relatively new. Store owners can capture a large percentage of an area's population by offering reliable services. The private mail centers do not deliver mail. Their main functions are to receive and sort mail for their customers. The more services a center offers, the larger the customer base. Location means everything in this business. Entrepreneurs should take great care to select a site that is on a major highway or street and offers safe, ample parking.

Owners of these retail outlets should be prepared to be open for business seven days a week. Customers also should have access to their boxes 24 hours a day. Store designs should separate the postal box area from the other services.

Contact Information
Address: 1010 E. 62nd Street, Los Angeles, California 90001
Telephone: 1-800-323-3003 or 1-213-232-6181
Contact person: Brian P. Fraher

SIGNET SYSTEMS, INC.

Initial Investment: $8,895
Total Investment: $8,895
Ongoing fees: None
Right to use trademark and logo: None

Expansion History
Company operating since: 1976
Offering hot stamp or foil imprinters since: 1976
Number of imprinters sold: 1,000 +

Industry Focus
Foil imprinting or hot stamping uses a dry-heat, transfer process to print words, symbols, or logos on almost any flat surface.

Foil imprinting does not compete with full-service printers. Owners of these businesses often subcontract to printers, who would not earn a high enough profit completing short-run assignments themselves.

Company Advantages

Signet Systems has helped to establish more than 1,000 entre-preneurs in its hot-stamping, printing business. This opportunity does not demand long hours, and entrepreneurs can work on a part-time basis.

The hot-stamping machine imprints on a variety of surfaces, in-cluding paper, leather, vinyl, plastics, and wood. The imprinter is available as a manual or air compressor model, and it stands no more than three feet in height. The compact size allows entrepre-neurs to operate the machine in a small area.

Signet Systems markets a complete turnkey operation, and the company supplies initial training, ongoing advice, and a five-year guarantee on the imprinting machine. Signet Systems emphasizes that its imprinter is a commercial machine, not a hobby machine.

Signet Systems, Inc., equips entrepreneurs with the tools needed to launch a personalized imprinting business in the comfort of their own homes.

"Our business is getting people into their own business right with the right tools," explains Ross Connell, president. "This hot-stamp-ing or imprinting machine is meant for the entrepreneur and not for the person looking to find a creative outlet. There are less durable machines for hobby enthusiasts. That is why we back our machine with a five-year guarantee. We believe in its durability and capa-bility."

The main target market for Signet imprinter owners is the full-service and "quick" print industry. Signet entrepreneurs can sub-contract short-run assignments from retail printers who would not earn an adequate profit margin on these jobs. For full-service retail printers, short-run jobs tie up automatic printing equipment and high-priced labor that can be used more efficiently for larger volume work.

Individual Signet owners decide what type of operation they wish to run. As with many home-based persons, the Signet Systems printer usually begins as a part-time operator, learning the operation of the equipment and building a customer base. Entrepreneurs print or hot-stamp a variety of products, including business cards, pre-sentation folders, matchbooks, napkins, and specialty items such as buttons and three-dimensional cards. Entrepreneurs can also contract large-volume orders with customers, such as wedding invitation and matchbook packages. With orders this size, Signet operators do not do the printing themselves; rather they contract one of the company's wholesale printers to complete the assignment and deliver it to the customer directly.

Signet owners who develop regular retail accounts often turn the part-time endeavor into a full-time career. Most experienced full-time operators can produce as many as 1,000 business cards in an hour on the hot-stamp machine. This level of productivity translates into an hourly rate of $35 to $100 per hour or more.

An investment of $8,895 purchases a complete turnkey operation, including the Signet Systems imprinter and a full inventory stock of paper, enamel, leather, metal, and silk business cards. Also included is an assortment of novelty items, such as buttons, coasters, matchbooks, napkins, playing cards, and presentation albums. Signet also includes 25 replacement rolls of foil as well as 50 card-packing boxes, business card holders, instruction and marketing manuals, display signs, a sample book, and advertising flyers.

Entrepreneurs receive on-site personal training from a Signet Systems' representative. Initial training time varies, but most entrepreneurs need no more than three hours with the Signet agent. The company also provides a five-year guarantee on its imprinter, and it offers entrepreneurs ongoing technical assistance by telephone. Entrepreneurs can purchase additional supplies from Signet, but the company does not require them to do so.

Future Outlook

Retail printing stores must offer customers more than just printing if they want to survive the competitive market. Many chains and individual stores now offer copy, fax, graphic design, and word processing services in addition to their printing services. These added items usurp valuable time and labor and leave printers overworked and behind schedule. Signet owners subcontract with printers and complete the smaller printing jobs for them. Printers have come to view Signet operators as welcome assistance instead of economic competition.

Signet provides ample training and support for owners of this business opportunity. The company stands behind its equipment, and offers entrepreneurs sound marketing and operational advice. Signet has expanded throughout North America.

Contact Information
Address: 50 High Street, Suite LL7, Buffalo, New York 14203
Telephone: 1-416-662-2220
Contact person: Ross Connell

CAR WASHES AND POWER WASH EQUIPMENT

AUTOMATION EQUIPMENT, INC.

Initial investment: $6,225 to $36,500
Total investment: $6,225 to $36,500 plus extra equipment costs that depend on the number of wash bays and the costs of leasing or purchasing land
Ongoing fees: None
Right to use trademark and logo: Yes

Expansion History
Company operating since: 1971
Offering car wash equipment since: 1971
Number of independent car wash owners: 325

Industry Focus
Automatic and self-service car washes offer consumers a professional cleaning system at a reasonable price.

Consumers are cost conscious when it comes to car maintenance. Uncertain economic times make car owners hold onto their vehicles longer. Proper washing and buffing treatments can protect a car against the natural elements that can erode its exterior.

Company Advantages

Automation supplies automatic and self-service coin-operated car wash systems. This type of business requires only one on-site employee. An entrepreneur can add more equipment and washing bay areas as business volume grows.

Entrepreneurs can enter the car washing industry with an investment of $6,225. Automation provides entrepreneurs on-site assistance in finding a suitable location as well as in installing and operating the equipment. The company also maintains ample post-opening support.

Many American consumers subscribe to the do-it-yourself theory, especially when it comes to the care of their cars. Automation Equipment, Inc., simplifies car maintenance with its line of Apollo Car Wash equipment and cleaners that let consumers wash and wax their own automobiles professionally.

Automation car wash owners are independent businesspersons. They choose the size and type of facility they wish to operate. Automation offers entrepreneurs two types of car wash systems: a "no-touch" automatic car wash and a self-service car wash.

The automatic car wash is operated by computer controls. Consumers key in their choice for one or more of the four cleaning services, which include a combination of soap, rinse, and wax. Customers pay the "computer cashier" and drive their cars into the washing bay. The automatic car wash cleans automobiles professionally without the assistance of an attendant in less than two minutes.

Entrepreneurs who choose the automatic system need to invest a minimum of $36,500 for the purchase of the equipment, which includes an auto cashier, an entrance switch, galvanized wheel wash and undercarriage spray pipes, a stop switch assembly, a free-standing overhead track assembly, and a stainless steel, five-panel illuminated instruction sign. The investment also covers the purchase of a pumping unit, a motor starter, a computerized control panel, a 150-gallon cold water holding tank, a presoak pumping unit, a soap mixer tank, a wax holding tank, a water heater, and an automatic antifreeze system. Automation estimates that car wash owners may need an additional $5,000 for equipment installation costs.

This cost can be reduced or eliminated if entrepreneurs install the equipment themselves.

Automatic car wash owners can establish this business as a lone enterprise or in conjunction with an already established car wash or service station business. Entrepreneurs need a minimum bay area measuring 12.5 feet in width, 24 feet in length, and 10 feet in height for the washing chamber, plus added space to house the equipment.

Along with the automatic car wash system, Automation also offers entrepreneurs a self-service car wash system. An entrepreneur need not already own the automatic car wash system in order to invest in the self-service type. This operation requires entrepreneurs to construct a one- to eight-bay structure. Consumers drive into a washing bay and manually wash their cars using the state-of-the-art Apollo hoses, equipment, and cleaners. Investors can purchase a basic equipment package that ranges in price from $6,225 for a one-bay operation to $36,500 for an eight-bay operation.

For the initial investment, car wash owners receive trigger shut-off hand guns with high-pressure hoses, a center-mount swivel hose boom, a coin meter, a vault-type coin box, and a wash and wax selector switch, plus a bay instruction sign. The equipment room contains a plunger pump with ceramic plungers, an electrical control panel mounted on the pumping unit, a soap concentrate supply system, a 15-gallon polyethylene wax supply tank, a water heater, and a glass-lined tank with approved automatic controls.

Both the automatic and the self-service car wash owner can choose to offer higher-grade cleaners, such as the Apollo Final touch road film remover, the Magic Rinse spot reducer, the Foam Brush system, and the Whitewall tire cleaner. These added features are not included in the original investment packages, and they range in price from $175 to $925 per bay. Automation discounts the costs for owners who purchase the extra cleaning systems for more than one bay.

Entrepreneurs can invest in one or both of these car washing systems. The size and scope of the business depends on the amount of land available to the entrepreneur.

Future Outlook

Automation car wash systems do not carry high labor costs. Operators need only one attendant on duty, and some entrepreneurs keep no employees on duty. The Automation car washing systems provide entrepreneurs with the flexibility of operating twenty-four hours a day.

Entrepreneurs set their own prices for car washes, but all operators are careful to underprice the full-service car washes. The less costly washing system attracts frugal consumers who want a professional wash without the high price tag.

Contact Information
Address: P.O. Box 3208, Tulsa, Oklahoma 74101
Telephone: 1-800-375-4462 or 1-918-582-0025
Contact person: Orville Strout

EXPRESS WASH, INC.

Initial investment: $765 to $1,385
Total investment: $2,365 to $2,985
Ongoing fees: None
Right to use trademark and logo: None

Expansion History
Company operating since: 1985
Offering car wash equipment since: 1985
Number of independent car wash owners: 500+

Industry Focus

Many car owners detest the chore of washing their cars. They prefer to have it done professionally, but they also want to avoid the lines at drive-through wash centers.

Mobile car wash services bring a full-service car wash to parking lots or a customer's doorstep. The costs and overhead expenses in this type of venture are low, but there is a potential for a high profit margin.

Company Advantages

Express Wash, Inc., provides entrepreneurs with all the equipment and marketing tools to operate a mobile car wash properly.

The company offers four investment packages. Entrepreneurs who do not have a great deal of capital can enter this industry for $765. As business grows, entrepreneurs can upgrade equipment and add more services for their customers.

At one time, consumers had to go to a car wash for service. Amherst, New York-businessman Peter Dale changed all that with his novel business idea: mobile car washing and detailing. Established in 1985, Express Wash, Inc., eliminates the tiresome, long lines that are associated with full-service car wash centers. The mobile car wash concept has struck a chord with time-strapped consumers, and the company has attracted more than 500 entrepreneurs from all over the world.

The success of the Express Wash system lies in the exclusive car-washing equipment that fits into the rear of a hatchback car, station wagon, or pickup truck. The equipment is powered by the vehicle's battery through the cigarette lighter. The washing, polishing, and detailing equipment offered by Express Wash may be compact, but they are state-of-the-art professional tools.

Express Wash owners are service specialists. They go where potential customers exist in number. Many Express Wash owners market their service to employees who work in corporate centers or large office parks. Entrepreneurs contract to wash cars in the parking lots while their owners are at work. This type of strategy usually results in many car-washing assignments at the same location on a regular basis. Express Wash owners also view apartments and condominiums, hospitals, private residences, airports, golf and country clubs, limousine and car rental companies, and hotel chains as potential locations for the mobile service.

The Express Wash owner working alone can usually complete a simple wash and chamois wipe on a car in 15 minutes. For this on-location service, customers pay between $10 and $15. Entrepreneurs can also offer a "quick wash" service. This abbreviated process takes only 10 minutes to complete and costs $5 to $7.

Entrepreneurs receive all the equipment needed to run a mobile car washing operation. Express Wash offers entrepreneurs a choice of four packages that come with a 30-day, no-risk money-back guarantee and a three-year warranty.

The lowest investment price for the basic package is $765. This package is ideal for the entrepreneur who already has an automobile-detailing business and wants to add an additional service. Included in this package are two dome-molded polyethylene tanks, an Express Wash pressure pump, a 30-foot premium hose, a brass spray gun, and a brass extension and spray tip. It's necessary to have a sedan or hatchback to transport this equipment. In addition, Express Wash provides a training manual and video as part of the investment.

The second package, or System I package, is geared for the entrepreneur who owns a large-enough vehicle (a hatchback or small station wagon) to accommodate the extra equipment. Along with the basic equipment, warranties, and training material included in the basic package, the $1,075-priced System I includes a hose reel wash, Wash 'n Wax auto soap, Tire Brite whitewall tire cleaner, vinyl cleaner, carpet and upholstery shampoo, glass cleaner, a chamois, a lambswool mitt, dispensers, and brushes.

System II, the third selection, is for the entrepreneur who wants to build a high-volume car-washing business. This package requires an investment of $1,385 and contains all equipment and accessory items of System I plus two more polyethylene tanks.

For entrepreneurs who want to concentrate their business efforts only on automobile detailing, a comprehensive detailing package is available. This system does not contain general car-washing equipment, but it does include the necessary materials and equipment needed to start a detailing business. For $865, entrepreneurs receive a heavy-duty orbital polishing machine, a drive pad and drive pad protector, and reusable polishing bonnets. This system also includes a rubber vinyl dressing, detail towels, Teflon diamond seal, Simoniz Teflon TFE, Super Glaze acrylic sealer, a polishing compound, and body prep solution that removes tar, wax, and silicone.

Express Wash estimates that entrepreneurs will need an additional $1,600 for the initial costs of advertising, insurance, and working capital no matter what package they purchase.

Mobile car wash owners do not need to attend any formal training. The training manuals and videos detail all aspects of the business operation, including equipment use and maintenance and the implementation of successful marketing strategies. Express Wash does maintain a toll-free line for entrepreneurs who have questions or need to reorder washing and detailing supplies.

Future Outlook

Express Wash provides a convenient service to consumers who have little spare time to attend to a chore such as washing a car. The on-site service justifies the $10 to $15 fee for most car owners, and those who want to pay less have the choice of a quick wash.

The Express Wash process does not drain a car's battery power. The system is not costly to use, and entrepreneurs need no professional office space to run this operation.

Contact Information
Address: 415 Lawrence Bell Drive, #2, Amherst, NY 14221
Telephone: 1-800-876-4164 or 1-716-692-4631
Contact person: Peter Dale

WASH AMERICA

Initial investment: $4,995 to $24,995
Total investment: $4,995 to $24,995
Ongoing fees: None
Right to use trademark and logo: Yes

Expansion History
Company operating since: 1986
Offering power wash systems since: 1986
Number of independent contractors: 100 +

Industry Focus

Power wash systems are a practical way to clean building exteriors, large transportation vehicles, and warehouse floors at an affordable price.

Power washing is less time-consuming and more effective than ordinary cleaning methods with a scrub brush and hose.

Company Advantages

Wash America has a six-year track record in this industry. Competition in the industry comes from franchise chains, but Wash America charges no ongoing royalty fees to entrepreneurs who purchase the company's cleaning systems.

Wash America offers entrepreneurs eight investment packages, according to their financial capabilities.

The company has also recently introduced an acoustical ceiling cleaning system as an additional service for Wash America entrepreneurs. Contractors go to their customers' sites and refurbish soiled and smoke-stained ceilings using Wash America cleaning products and equipment. This newer service enables Wash America entrepreneurs who live in areas where it is cold in the winter to develop an all-year-round business.

Wash America, Inc., provides entrepreneurs with mobile power wash equipment that erases dirt and grime from a building's surface. The company's cleaning systems are also successful in acid-washing brick, masonry, and swimming pool surfaces as well as degreasing restaurant kitchen equipment, engines, service stations, and warehouse floors. Established in 1986, the Orlando, Florida-based Wash America relies on its more than 100 independent consultants to market its power wash services throughout the United States.

During the initial stages of business ownership, many Wash America consultants act as both salespersons and technicians. They market their mobile power wash services to managers and owners of warehouses, restaurants, service stations, and transportation companies. They also target real estate owners and mobile home occupants. After contracting assignments, Wash America consultants travel to the client's site to complete the power-washing service.

Wash America offers a range of investment packages to attract entrepreneurs of various financial capabilities. An investment of $4,995 purchases the Mini Hydrojet Unit, which contains all equipment, accessories, and chemicals needed to pursue a small-scale, power-wash business opportunity. These entrepreneurs usually target smaller companies or building owners. The equipment is easy to operate and transport from one customer location to another in a small van or station wagon. It also does not require a large storage area.

Part-time entrepreneurs are the chief investors in this package, and they usually establish their base of operations in their homes. Wash America encourages this practice because it eliminates the cost of leased office space. This package also allows entrepreneurs to test the waters before investing their life savings. Wash America welcomes part-time entrepreneurs, and all consultants can upgrade their equipment and expand their time commitment as their customer base grows.

For entrepreneurs with more capital to invest, Wash America offers a choice of seven other packages that range in price from $8,995 to $24,995. These packages contain more sophisticated equipment and cleaning chemicals than the $4,995 package. This equipment is mounted on single or tandem trailers, and it is used to power-wash large transportation vehicles such as ships, airplanes, and tall structures.

For this type of operation, business owners may need to hire at least one more technician to perform the cleaning contracts, and they may need to lease space for the trailer and equipment. The price of labor and storage is not included in the investment estimate because these costs vary greatly from area to area. As with the less costly package, these upgraded cleaning systems are mobile and travel to the customer's site.

The more expensive investment packages are for entrepreneurs establishing a full-service company. Full-time entrepreneurs may take on a managerial or sales role and hire technicians to complete the power-washing assignments.

Wash America requires all consultants to attend a training workshop at its home office. The workshop ranges from one to four days, depending on the investment package purchased. Wash America teaches consultants to operate, maintain, and repair machinery. The company also trains them in the proper use of the chemical cleaning solutions. Consultants participate in actual power-washing jobs, and they see how other consultants operate their businesses. Consultants learn to price out specific contracts, follow recommended retail pricing guidelines, sponsor effective advertising campaigns, and manage a full-time staff.

Future Outlook

Wash America attracts the entrepreneur with a detailed investment and training package that requires no franchise commitment. The company charges no ongoing fees, and investors can choose from a wide selection of mobile wash opportunities.

The company has recently introduced an optional acoustical cleaning program. Consultants who choose to offer it to customers invest an additional $2,500. This new service is geared for consultants who experience a business slowdown during the winter months. The interior ceiling cleaning service keeps income at a steady level throughout the year. Entrepreneurs who offer this service travel to a customer's location, inspect ceiling surfaces, and remove stains and dirt using Wash America equipment and methods.

Contact Information
Address: 943 Taft Vineland Road, Orlando, Florida 32824
Telephone: 1-800-331-7765 or 1-407-855-2215
Contact person: Robert Sorger

CARPET CLEANING

HOST DRY CARPET CLEANING SYSTEM
(Racine Industries, Inc.)

Initial investment: $2,000
Total investment: $2,000
Ongoing fees: None
Right to use trademark and logo: None

Expansion History
Company operating since: 1936
Offering business opportunities since: 1958
Number of business opportunities: 2,000+

Industry Focus
Dry carpet-cleaning services are less likely to damage a carpet than the standard steam-cleaning methods.

Carpet-cleaning businesses are usually simple to learn and operate. Business owners can do the carpet cleaning themselves on a full- or part-time basis, or they can become managers and hire workers to do the cleaning for them.

Company Advantages
Racine Industries, Inc., manufactures Host dry-cleaning machines and equipment at its company facility in Wisconsin. The machines come with a three-year guarantee, and Racine provides initial and ongoing support to Host owner operators.

Host uses a natural-ingredient, low-moisture cleaning process to extract dirt from carpets. The dry-cleaning process eliminates the deposit of sticky, detergent residue on carpets that can attract more dirt.

Racine Industries, Inc., educates the consumer on proper carpet care. Established in 1936, the Wisconsin-based company has long been a leader in this large service industry, which has spawned hundreds of independent and franchise carpet-cleaning companies. The company's exclusive Host machine and products have won recognition for their quick-drying agents, which allow people to walk on carpets immediately after they are cleaned. Racine oversees the Host network, which includes distributors and more than 2,000 independently owned Host cleaning service companies.

Host owners are carpet cleaners. Many are husband-and-wife teams that perform the carpet cleaning initially on a part-time basis. The cleaning process is not physically demanding. The Host machine in full operation weighs only 30 pounds. It is easy to cart to a customer's home, and it fits into the backseat or trunk of most cars. Host owners are responsible for all aspects of the business, including marketing and customer service. Racine encourages entrepreneurs to increase business volume at their own speed. Most Host owners operate their business from home.

An investment of $2,000 purchases the Host dirt-extracting machine and cleaning accessory products. As part of the initial package, Racine provides an operations manual, promotional material, training, and ongoing support. Entrepreneurs are permitted to say they feature or use the Host cleaning system, but they are not allowed to portray themselves as employees of the company.

As Host owners become more established, they can join Racine's Professional Cleaners Association, with annual dues of $150. The association provides comprehensive liability, vehicle, and workmen's compensation insurance to members at lower rates. Membership in the association also entitles Host owners to up-to-date technical data regarding the company and the industry, a quarterly newsletter, a 30 percent discount on promotional material such as magnetic truck signs, patches, and literature, and advanced training courses at discounted fees.

Racine encourages entrepreneurs to attend either a two-and-one-half-day training seminar in Wisconsin or the company's "Host School on the Road" two-day program. Training focuses on equipment operation and maintenance as well as marketing and customer service strategies. Host owners can also call Racine for assistance in technical and operational matters.

Future Outlook

Dry carpet-cleaning systems such as Host are becoming more common in today's marketplace. These systems offer consumers an alternative to the traditional steam-cleaning method, which requires more time for application and drying. The Host carpet system allows consumers to walk on their carpets immediately after cleaning. The Host equipment weighs only 30 pounds and needs only one person to tote it from site to site. These convenient features make this business opportunity attractive to part-time entrepreneurs who usually work from home as a one- or two-person operation. The portable equipment also draws professional home and commercial cleaning companies that want to add a carpet-cleaning system to their list of existing services.

Contact Information

Address: 1405 16th Street, P.O. Box 1648, Racine, Wisconsin 53401

Telephone: 1-800-558-9439 or 1-414-637-4491

Contact person: Mary J. Carbajal, professional cleaners association coordinator

ENTERTAINMENT/LEISURE

HARRIS MINIATURE GOLF COURSES, INC.

Initial investment: $100,000 minimum (approximately) plus purchase or lease of land

Total investment: $100,000 minimum (approximately) plus purchase or lease of land

Ongoing fees: None

Right to use trademark and logo: None

Expansion History

Company operating since: 1961

Offering miniature golf course designs since: 1961

Number of miniature golf courses: 100

Industry Focus

Recreational activities that are easy to play and provide family entertainment are in demand. Parents are looking for weekend and nighttime activities they can enjoy with their children.

Miniature golf is an activity that requires little skill or talent. The game is becoming increasingly popular. More than 50 million people play miniature golf annually.

Company Advantages

Harris Miniature Golf Courses designs and builds a variety of courses for entrepreneurs. The company can erect portable rooftop courses as well as multilevel courses with waterfalls, streams, and fountains. The company has more than 30 years of experience in the design and construction of golf courses.

Today's families want to spend time together, but it's hard to find an activity that everyone can enjoy. Harris Miniature Golf Courses, Inc., of Wildwood, New Jersey, designs courses that appeal to both the novice player and to the most experienced long-hole driver. Established in 1961, Harris is an expert in contoured putting courses, and the company uses flowers, water, shrubs, and other props to make the course an enjoyable place to play.

For an initial minimium investment of approximately $100,000, entrepreneurs can contract Harris to design an 18-hole miniature golf course that may contain as many as 60 obstacles for players. The size and complexity of the courses vary with the entrepreneur's investment, and Harris guarantees each hole against water damage.

Harris will work with investors to decide if a site is suitable for a miniature golf course in terms of traffic, accessibility, and competition.

For the entrepreneur who owns a tract of commercial land and is unsure what to build on it, or has a business with excess land and wants to expand, miniature golf may offer some advantages. The activity used to be associated with summertime fun, but advances in course construction and interior designs have opened up a full-time year-round business opportunity.

Consumers pay between $3.50 and $5 per game per adult for a round of miniature golf that lasts about 45 minutes. The peak hours for the business are between 7:00 and 10:00 P.M. on weekdays and all day Saturday and Sunday. Once the course is constructed, there are only minor maintenance and supply costs and personnel wages to consider.

Miniature golf owners are independent of Harris Miniature Golf

Courses—the company is primarily there as a building and design consultant. Harris does not require or suggest any method of operation, nor does it collect ongoing fees or royalties. The entrepreneurs are solely in charge of their own marketing and business strategies.

The company does supply interested investors with color promotional materials and information on the miniature golf industry. The company has also produced a video that teaches entrepreneurs about the design and building of a course. Harris supplies the independent operators with operation manuals that explain the course's structure and how it works. Telephone support is available in case of problems or questions, and Harris invites interested entrepreneurs to talk to other miniature golf course owners.

Future Outlook

Company president Richard Lahey helped revamp both the company and the miniature golf trade when he bought Harris ten years ago. Lahey's course designs emphasize aesthetic quality. He has experimented with courses to obtain the right mix of challenge and fun that keeps play moving and customers coming in the gates.

The initial investment does not include the purchase or lease of the land. This expense is difficult to estimate since real estate prices vary greatly in different parts of the country.

Contact Information
Address: P.O. Box 243, Wildwood, New Jersey 08260
Telephone: 1-609-522-4200
Contact person: Richard P. Lahey

LOMMA ENTERPRISES, INC.

Initial investment: $5,900 to $32,900 plus purchase or lease of land
or space
Total investment: $5,900 to $52,900 plus purchase or lease of land
or space
Ongoing fees: None
Right to use trademark and logo: None

Expansion History
Company operating since: 1955
Offering miniature golf design and construction since: 1981
Number of minigolf courses sold: 4,000+

Industry Focus
Miniature golf has been a part of American leisure time since the
early 1920s. Advances in course technology and improved building
materials have made this activity year-round family entertainment.

Golf is becoming America's favorite participation sport. The golf
industry now reports more than $12 billion in gross revenue.

Miniature golf is a low-maintenance and high-profit-margin
enterprise.

Company Advantages
Lomma Enterprises offers financing arrangements to qualified
applicants who purchase one or more of its courses.

Lomma Enterprises has a 36-year history in the design, construction, and operation of prefabricated and portable miniature golf
courses.

Loma Enterprises provides entrepreneurs with in-person training
in the operation and marketing of this type of business.

Miniature golf is a business concept that has survived and thrived
for more than 70 years. Lomma Enterprises, Inc., is one reason the
industry has remained strong. Based in Scranton, Pennsylvania,
Lomma Industries has built more than 4,000 miniature golf courses

throughout the United States. Founded in 1955, the company is the oldest and largest designer and builder of prefabricated and portable miniature golf courses.

The role of Lomma is that of manufacturer and business consultant. The company assists entrepreneurs in all aspects of establishing a miniature golf course and builds customized courses for each client. All fairways, obstacles, and course greens are manufactured at the company's facility in Scranton and shipped by trailer to the miniature golf site. Lomma also provides on-site supervision for the construction of the course, which usually requires only one day's work.

Those who purchase Lomma-designed courses are independent operators. Whether first-time entrepreneurs or experienced business owners, Lomma's clients rely heavily on the company's expertise in the construction and operation of their courses.

As part of their service, Lomma studies the miniature golf site's plot plan and designs a course that best suits the size and shape of the lot or space. The company recommends that entrepreneurs lease or purchase at least 2,500 square feet of interior or exterior space for a nine-hole course and 5,000 square feet of interior or exterior space for an 18-hole course. Courses should be in an area that has a residential population of at least 10,000 people.

The costs for a Lomma-built course range from $5,900 to $32,900, depending on the size and location of the site. These expense estimates do not include the costs of labor, supplies, maintenance materials, utilities, advertising, and promotion. Lomma estimates that golf course owners will need between $7,500 and $20,000 annually to cover these expenses.

According to Lomma, the courses usually can be run by one person, which can cut these expenses by almost 50 percent. For owners who wish to hire a staff to operate the course, Lomma suggests that owners budget $6 per hour for each employee.

Lomma does not provide earnings claims for entrepreneurs, but it estimates the potential profits from this type of enterprise. For course owners in northern states whose businesses are open only April to October, Lomma maintains that an $80,000 gross profit is more than reasonable. Owners in southern and western states who operate the entire year can produce a much greater profit.

As part of their consulting package, Lomma provides entrepreneurs with an owner/operator training program. These training meetings are held in various areas throughout the United States, and they are free to Lomma clients. During these two-day seminars, Lomma's public relations and promotions director teaches owners how to operate and promote their course in their community.

The company also supplies clients with its "Idea and Promotions" kit that contains Lomma's most successful promotion campaigns. Lomma continues its promotion support to clients and regularly supplies clients with advertising copy and promotion and give-away ideas.

The company also enrolls each client in the Lomma Championship Golf Association, which entitles them to discounts on balls, putters, pencils, score cards, new obstacles, and other supplies.

Future Outlook

Lomma has shown that it can prosper in both economic booms and busts. The company is a recognized leader in the golfing industry, and 50 percent of all its business comes from client referrals.

Lomma's sectional course design allows owners to move course holes and change their layout. The sections also give operators the freedom to move courses indoors when the winter months approach.

Lomma's support is never-ending for clients. The company updates its clients on promotional ideas regularly and is willing to offer technical advice as needed.

While Lomma is known for its portable miniature golf courses, the company also will customize and construct full-size permanent courses.

Contact Information

Address: 1120 South Washington Avenue, Scranton, Pennsylvania 18505

Telephone: 1-717-346-5559

Contact person: Gary Knight, executive vice president

MINI-GOLF, INC.

Initial investment: $13,000 to $30,000 plus purchase or lease of land
Total investment: $13,000 to $30,000 plus purchase or lease of land
Ongoing fees: None
Right to use trademark and logo: None

Expansion History
Company operating since: 1981
Offering business opportunities since: 1981
Number of Mini-Golf courses sold: 1,200+

Industry Focus
Prefabricated miniature golf courses have established miniature golf as a year-round, indoor-and-outdoor leisure activity.

Prefabricated courses greatly reduce the amount of capital needed to enter into this industry. The smaller courses can be placed indoors in malls or storefronts, eliminating the need to purchase or lease a large parcel of land.

Company Advantages
Mini-Golf, Inc., constructs a variety of golf courses at its 25,000-square-foot manufacturing facility. The courses are delivered ready-to-install and require only four to five people to set them up properly.

Mini-Golf also acts as a supplier for its clients. The company carries an array of support products, such as balls, clubs, score cards, and golf pins.

Manufacturing companies such as Mini-Golf, Inc., have turned the one-time, exclusively resort activity of miniature golf into a year-round, all-climate pastime. The Jessup, Pennsylvania-based Mini-Golf has built more than 1,200 golf courses for entrepreneurs throughout the United States.

Those who purchase a Mini-Golf course are independent business owners. Mini-Golf offers a variety of courses, and entrepreneurs' selections are usually based on the type of land or space they have purchased or leased. Outdoor courses may be more elaborate and consist of multilevel holes complete with "fairway" obstacles. Indoor golf course owners usually choose the more simply designed courses that can be erected in mall corridors or retail store locations. The courses may differ in creative design and degree of difficulty, but they are all constructed with two-feet-by-two-feet railroad ties on top of artificial turf.

Miniature golf course owners oversee the operation and maintenance of the course, but they usually hire one or more persons to handle admissions and supervise the playing customers. The operating hours depend on the course's location, but most owners will operate a seven-day a week operation with extended hours on weekends and during the summer months. Course owners establish their own prices, and it is their responsibility to investigate their area or community and determine what price range it will support.

The costs for a Mini-Golf prefabricated course range from $13,000 to $30,000. This does not include the lease or purchase of land or store space, nor the labor needed to assemble the course at the location. The investment range reflects the difference in course design and size.

Prefabricated courses save the entrepreneur course design fees. The bulk of the work is done at the Jessup, Pennsylvania, plant. Mini-Golf also sends a representative to the customer's location to assist in the assembly of the course.

Mini-Golf supplies entrepreneurs with a free training and maintenance manual that outlines the proper procedures for operating and maintaining the golf courses. The company is also available for unlimited telephone consultation and provides press releases for entrepreneurs at no extra charge. Mini-Golf is a full-service supply company that offers entrepreneurs a wide range of products including golf balls, tees, clubs, pins, turf, and other accessory items.

Future Outlook

Mini-Golf's prefabricated design greatly reduces the cost of building a miniature golf course. The company's maufacturing process allows entrepreneurs to enter the golf industry with a lower investment. The courses can be moved from location to location, and course owners can upgrade their courses at any time.

Contact Information
Address: 202 Bridge Street, Jessup, Pennsylvania 18434
Telephone: 1-717-489-8623
Contact person: Joseph J. Rogari, president

SGD COMPANY, INC.
(Commercial baseball/softball batting ranges)

Initial investment: $21,000 and up ($7,000 to $9,000 per batting stall; SGD's plans are designed for a minimum of 3 stalls; the average range has 6 to 8 stalls), plus purchase and lease of land
Total investment: $21,000 and up ($7,000 to $9,000 per batting stall), plus purchase and lease of land
Ongoing fees: None
Right to use trademark and logo: None

Expansion History
Company operating since: 1952
Offering business opportunities since: 1961
Number of business opportunities: Not available

Industry Focus
Commercial batting machines attract both the athlete and the customer looking for recreation.
Enclosed batting machines and stalls require little space, which reduces land lease or purchase costs.

Company Advantages
SGD Company, Inc., enjoys a solid reputation in the recreation industry. The company started with golf driving range designs and expanded into other sports activities. SGD now supplies equipment and designs for tennis courts, swimming pools, and campgrounds.
Entrepreneurs can establish one or more recreational facilities at

a time. They can elect to invest in all opportunities at once, or they can gradually develop their baseball business into a multiactivity recreational center.

Another business opportunity that SGD Company, Inc., of Akron, Ohio, offers entrepreneurs is commercial baseball and softball batting cage facilities. For independent business owners, SGD provides exclusive designs for its enclosed batting facilities, and the company supplies all equipment and ancillary products, including the coin-operated ball machines, bats, balls, and safety netting.

Entrepreneurs who purchase the SGD batting cage system must first select a site for the batting range before they hire local builders or contractors to complete the construction. Land can be leased or purchased, and SGD recommends entrepreneurs establish their batting range in an area with a minimum population of 25,000 people. Batting cage owners should also expect to adjust their construction plans to meet local zoning or planning ordinances concerning parking, lighting, the number of batting stalls, and the hours of operation.

Most batting range owners operate their businesses between 120 and 130 days per year, depending on the climate of the area. Most ranges remain open for 6 to 8 hours on weekdays and 10 to 12 hours on weekends and during the summer months. Entrepreneurs who own SGD batting ranges usually manage the facilities and hire part-time and full-time workers to handle extended operating hours.

The costs of building an enclosed batting range facility start at $21,000 for three batting stalls, not including the lease or purchase of the land. The average stall is made of an enclosed cage that is 75 feet in length and 30 feet in height at the center. Also included in this figure are all batting accessories, lighting, fencing, netting, plus estimates for outside construction fees for the construction of the ranges. SGD is a consultant, and the company requires no on-going fees from entrepreneurs who purchase equipment and designs. The company does not make claims on earning potential, but it does maintain that some ranges earn up to $200,000 per operating season.

Owners are responsible for all maintenance and repair for the equipment and machines, and SGD suggests regular inspections to avoid unnecessary breakdowns. The company stocks replacement parts for all its equipment, and these parts are sent out on a priority basis to batting range owners.

SGD provides instruction in the operation of the machines, but it does not formally train entrepreneurs. In its role as consultant, SGD maintains telephone and field support. The company will send out technicians to repair machines or instruct owners on their use.

Future Outlook
Batting cage facilities have been in existence for more than 30 years. Enclosed batting cages are efficient because they need little land or labor to operate effectively. Baseballs and softballs remain in the fenced area and are easily retrieved at the end of the working day. Many batting range owners begin with a minimum number of stalls and expand their business as customer interest increases. Other entrepreneurs branch out and install other recreational centers, such as miniature golf ranges or driving ranges.

Contact Information
Address: P.O. Box 8410, Akron, Ohio 44320-0410
Telephone: 1-216-239-2828
Contact person: Dennis McGregor, president

SGD COMPANY, INC.
(Golf Driving Ranges)

Initial investment: $30,000 to $100,000 plus purchase or lease of land
Total investment: $30,000 to $100,000 plus purchase or lease of land
Ongoing fees: None
Right to use trademark and logo: None

Expansion History
Company operating since: 1952
Offering business opportunities since: 1961
Number of business opportunities: Not available

Industry Focus

Golf driving ranges allow golf enthusiasts to practice their swing and techniques conveniently and economically. And entrepreneurs who choose to combine the range with a miniature golf course give those inexperienced in golf a chance to enjoy the sport on a less competitive and less costly level.

The sport of golf has grown impressively in popularity over the last decade. Enthusiasts look for alternative ways to practice without the expense of green fees at a full-size golf course.

Company Advantages

SGD Company, Inc., has a 40-year track record in the design of golf driving ranges and miniature golf courses. The company is a large supplier of equipment for recreational activities.

For the golf enthusiast, there is no such thing as enough practice. SGD Company, Inc., of Akron, Ohio, gives golfers the opportunity to test their skills frequently with the company's specially designed golf driving ranges and miniature golf courses. Established in 1952, SGD Company is one of the oldest golf design companies in the recreation industry.

Entrepreneurs who seek out SGD's consultation services are business professionals as well as sports enthusiasts. Their most important task is to determine a suitable site, and this may mean contending with local zoning boards and completing traffic and population studies. Owners need to determine the advantages and disadvantages of the area in which they want to establish their golf centers. Customers should spot the location easily from the road, and the surrounding area should contain a large family or tourist population.

The lease or purchase of the land for the golf center is the entrepreneur's responsibility, but SGD does lay out specific recommendations. For the range, the land should be at least 1,200 feet deep and 150 to 300 feet wide. Land requirements vary for the miniature golf courses, and they depend on the artistic design and materials used for its construction. SGD courses are permanent and made with concrete-based materials. SGD will sell the plans and a breakdown of costs to entrepreneurs, but entrepreneurs hire local builders to construct the course or range.

After construction of the golf center is complete, owners settle into a managerial role. Both courses and ranges require maintenance such as mowing, seeding, and artificial turf vacuuming. Owners may attend to these tasks initially, but they will eventually hire part-time and full-time employees to handle these duties on a regular basis.

Entrepreneurs need between $30,000 and $100,000 for the construction of the driving range and miniature golf course. SGD sells each business opportunity separately, giving entrepreneurs the opportunity to expand and add an activity as business volume grows. The investment includes all materials and equipment needed to build the range or course plus the construction of a 600-square-foot building, installation of high-intensity lighting, the purchase and installation of signs, and the grading and seeding of the range and area around the tees. The estimated costs also cover the purchase of equipment, such as the golf balls, tees, baskets, a tractor ball picker, rubber mats, and golf clubs.

SGD is a consultant only, and it does not require entrepreneurs to operate their business in any specified fashion. No training class is offered with either the driving range or miniature golf opportunity, but SGD provides telephone consultation and in-person assistance if needed. The company maintains contact and support with owners by supplying them with a wide array of products and supplies.

Future Outlook

The success of an SGD driving range or miniature golf course hinges on the site chosen. This business venture requires a great deal of advance study before any investment is made.

SGD estimates that income from this business opportunity ranges between $15,000 and $200,000, depending on site and area population. This type of business opportunity involves only cash transactions, which eliminates the hassle of credit card payment or accounts receivables but also requires owners to use a hands-on business approach to protect their interests.

Contact Information
Address: P.O. Box 8410, Akron, Ohio 44320-0410
Telephone: 1-216-239-2828
Contact person: Dennis McGregor, president

FASHION AND APPAREL

DONCASTER

Initial investment: $500
Total investment: $500
Ongoing fees: None
Right to use trademark and logo: Yes

Expansion History
Company operating since: 1942
Offering fashion and apparel business opportunities since: 1942
Number of Doncaster consultants: 3,000+

Industry Focus
Selling fashions and accessories through direct sales is convenient for consumers, who don't have time to search through stores for fine clothing.

Direct selling allows customers to see the fabrics and colors as well as try on clothes. Mail ordering clothes directly can result in wrong sizes and undesired fabrics and colors.

Company Advantages
Doncaster has sold clothing through direct sales for more than 50 years. The company sells both men's and women's clothes, and it offers customers either custom-made designs or ready-to-wear selections.

For more than 50 years, Doncaster of Rutherfordton, North Carolina, has respected individual fashion tastes when designing its lines of clothing for men and women. The company's reputation for quality merchandise has made it one of the leading direct sales fashion companies in the United States today. Doncaster markets hundreds of its exclusive clothing designs through a network of more than 3,000 independent fashion consultants.

A Doncaster fashion consultant is more than a salesperson. The consultant is an authority on color, fabric, and design, and Doncaster customers look for this expertise in the company's representatives. Doncaster consultants are independent entrepreneurs who sell the clothing lines as either custom-made apparel or ready-to-wear fashion separates.

Fashion consultants can be part-time or full-time entrepreneurs. Doncaster offers two sales programs, and each program depends on the amount of time a consultant wants to invest in the fashion business.

The first or "showing consultant" program is for those who elect to sell the Doncaster clothing line only one week out of the year. Consultants usually invite potential customers to their homes for a show. Doncaster recommends that consultants send invitations to at least 150 potential customers to ensure a show's success. Customers set up individual or group appointments with the consultants to view Doncaster clothing lines, and the company supplies an array of samples for each consultant's show. Most consultants try to schedule at least 40 appointments during that week.

The second program is the "season consultant," who works throughout the year. Doncaster gears this plan toward entrepreneurs who wish to work between 20 and 40 hours per week on a regular basis. Season consultants are more flexible in setting up their appointment schedules, and they have the option of showing their fashions in their home, in a rented showroom, or at their customers' homes or businesses. As with the first plan, Doncaster supplies sample designs for the season consultants.

No matter what selling plan a fashion consultant chooses, market investigation is vital. Doncaster recommends that consultants target members of women's clubs, private bridge clubs, volunteer and professional organizations, and PTAs as potential customers. The company believes strongly in customer referrals, and these organizations tend to lead to many referrals. Doncaster makes no earnings claims, but it maintains that fashion consultants can earn between $10,000 and $30,000 annually.

To become a Doncaster fashion consultant, entrepreneurs pay an initial investment of $500, which covers the cost of training plus the purchase of racks and mirrors needed to display the clothing samples. Doncaster trains consultants in fashion and selling techniques through workshops, manuals, practice workbooks, videotapes, and audiotapes. The company also assigns a Doncaster regional manager to each consultant. The company encourages frequent communication between consultants and managers, and managers provide in-field support to consultants as often as needed. The district managers set up preview fashion screenings and workshops with all consultants so they remain informed on all clothing line changes or developments.

Doncaster also advertises in national publications and magazines plus a variety of organization newsletters. The company is well known for its participation in charity fund-raisers that receive both print and broadcast media attention. Doncaster also sponsors for its consultants an annual national sales seminar.

Future Outlook
Doncaster has stood the test of time. The company has varied its product lines over the years and has offered quality products to the customer who desires personal service and attention.

Doncaster has also witnessed the need for convenient service in its customers. The company once sold only custom-made garments, but its clothing lines now include ready-for-sale outfits. Their suits are sold as separates to ensure each customer an accurate fit.

Contact Information
Address: P.O. Box 1159, Rutherfordton, North Carolina 28139
Telephone: 1-800-669-3662 or 1-704-287-4205
Contact person: Debbie Penson

FOODS/BEVERAGES

LIL' ORBITS, INC.

Initial investment: $625 to $9,471
Total : $625 to $9,471
Ongoing fees: None
Right to use trademark and logo: Yes

Expansion History
Company operating since: 1974
Offering doughnut-making equipment since: 1974
Number of machines and vending items sold: Not available

Industry Focus
Doughnuts have had a tradition of high sales in the fast food industry.

Doughnuts are still considered a breakfast, lunch, or snacktime treat. There is no slow season for this product, and doughnut-making equipment is usually mobile and easily transported.

Company Advantages
Lil' Orbits is both a manufacturer and distributor for its products. Entrepreneurs buy the equipment, not a business, from Lil' Orbits, but the company allows them to use the Lil' Orbits name in their displays at no extra cost.

The company has been in existence since 1974 and has sold thousands of doughnut machines. Lil' Orbits has adapted its machinery and ingredients to make doughnuts lower in fat and calories.

Lil' Orbits markets accessory items for entrepreneurs as well. Canopies, mobile carts, trucks, plus pancake and crêpe machines have made the Lil' Orbits name easily recognized.

■ ■ ■

Doughnuts of all shapes and sizes have long been a fast food favorite among Americans. Founded in 1974, Lil' Orbits is a manufacturer and distributor of mobile doughnut-making equipment and accessory items. The Minneapolis, Minnesota-based company is a well-recognized international leader in the food equipment industry with thousands of doughnut, crêpe, and pancake machines in operation in more than 51 countries.

Both part-time and full-time entrepreneurs invest in Lil' Orbits equipment packages. Entrepreneurs who want full-time businesses establish shops or carts in retail locations. Those who work to enhance their income generally concentrate their business efforts on craft shows, flea markets, bazaars, and other types of outdoor events.

Lil' Orbits equipment packages range in price from $625 to $9,471. An investment in a lower-priced package purchases machinery with a few accessory items plus a supply of doughnut mix. The higher-priced packages include modular cabinets, filtration devices, sinks with self-contained water systems, built-in cash and utility drawers, aprons, scales, glassine bags, and a larger supply of doughnut mix.

Those who choose to work part time usually purchase one of the less expensive Lil' Orbits packages. As they become more comfortable in their investment, they tend to upgrade their equipment and vary their product offerings. Entrepreneurs who elect to take on the food business as a full-time occupation usually invest in the higher-priced packages.

Lil' Orbits is a manufacturer and consultant. It does not charge entrepreneurs any ongoing royalty fees. Entrepreneurs who use the Lil' Orbits name purchase their mixes and recipes from the home office. Along with its regular mixes, Lil' Orbits supplies special glazing and flavoring recipes for special occasions and holidays.

Most entrepreneurs make their doughnuts on site to demonstrate their freshness to consumers. Investors who sell the doughnuts in supermarkets and stores make the doughnuts either at their homes or in a commercial site and then deliver them. No matter how they run their operation, full-time and part-time entrepreneurs must in-form their local health departments of their activities and adhere to their rules and regulations.

Lil' Orbits delivers all equipment and accessory items through regular mail routes or package delivery companies, although entrepreneurs can elect to pick up the equipment in Minneapolis. Investors who travel to the home office receive a free training session in the operation of the equipment. Lil' Orbits provides written instructions for the equipment to all investors.

The company warrants machines and equipment for defects in the materials and workmanship for 90 days. After this period, Lil' Orbits charges entrepreneurs a $50 fee for each damaged component. The company attempts to repair and return all equipment within 72 hours. Lil' Orbits also maintains a customer service line for all entrepreneurs, and the company will make field trips to assist entrepreneurs in need of assistance.

Future Outlook

Lil' Orbits has expanded to 51 countries in its 18 years of operation. Entrepreneurs can use their imagination in marketing these products, and they can also use the well-known trademark. All equipment is made to be mobile, which also adds to the flexibility in marketing the doughnuts.

The company has answered consumers' concerns for healthful snacks with its low-fat, low-calorie doughnuts. Lil' Orbits added more equipment to its product line, which allowed entrepreneurs to offer more treats. This variety gained investors more followers and increased name recognition for Lil' Orbits.

Entrepreneurs who sell at outdoor events should also investigate Lil' Orbits trailer concession stand. The stand is 10 feet to 14 feet long and contains more than 6 feet 7 inches in head room. The trailer is a mobile kitchen with two water tanks, electric hot water heater, and built-in cabinets. Outdoor vendors should also look into Lil' Orbits accessory items, such as canopies and fiberglass doughnut stands.

Contact Information

Address: 2850 Vicksburg Lane, Minneapolis, Minnesota 55447
Telephone: 1-800-228-8305 or 1-612-559-7505
Contact person: Department CC or sales department

NEW ORLEANS SNOWBALLS

Initial investment: $1,495 to $5,295
Total investment: $1,495 to $15,000
Ongoing fees: None
Right to use trademark and logo: Yes

Expansion History
Company operating since: 1985
Offering business packages since: 1985
Number of machines and vending items sold: 60+

Industry Focus
Shaved-ice "snowballs" have been a popular treat for more than 50 years.

Food and beverage treat items usually have a low-production cost and a high profit margin.

Shaved-ice treats can be oeprated as a seasonal or full-time business. Entrepreneurs can establish a retail location or work at special events such as flea markets, carnivals, and fairs.

Company Advantages
New Orleans Snowballs provide entrepreneurs with two business packages. Both packages provide entrepreneurs with the details they need to establish a business. The company provides ample pre-opening and postopening support.

The New Orleans machine can produce up to 400 snowballs an hour.

Shaved-ice snowballs made their name in New Orleans, and now a North Carolina company is bringing this thirst-quenching treat to the rest of the country. New Orleans Snowballs, Inc., uses the traditional Louisiana recipe to make its variety of shaved-ice snowballs with cream, freezes, gourmet snowballs, and snowshakes. The treats are available in more than 100 flavors of syrup with or without topping. Established in Boone, North Carolina, in 1985, New

Orleans Snowballs has helped more than 60 entrepreneurs enter this tasty segment of the food industry.

"We like to do business with families. This worked well with our family, and we want to help other families achieve what we have done," explains Monty Joynes, president. "Small business is the backbone of this country, and I think we should help to promote it as much as possible."

Entrepreneurs need no food or retail experience to invest in this type of business. The company provides business owners with step-by-step instructions in the establishment and operation of a snowball-making enterprise. Entrepreneurs can choose to run a part-time or full-time venture.

Those entrepreneurs who wish to have a full-time business need to locate and lease a retail store. As business owners, they must decide their days and hours of operation, and whether they will be open for business throughout the year. Warm-weather entrepreneurs usually remain open all year, as do owners who lease indoor mall locations. Owners of free-standing sites may not deem it necessary or profitable to remain open during the colder months.

Part-time entrepreneurs are those who sell the snowball products at carnivals, flea markets, fairs, or other outdoor events. These entrepreneurs usually work weekends and summer and warm-weather evenings. Some travel may be involved, especially if business owners plan to set up a booth or kiosk at local community functions.

Whatever the location, the price for snowballs averages $1.25 for the simple snowball to $1.75 or more for the gourmet treat or the snowshakes that are served in 12- or 16-ounce cups. New Orleans Snowballs makes no earning claims, but the company estimates that it costs operators only 13 cents to produce and serve a 12-ounce serving.

New Orleans Snowballs offers entrepreneurs three investment packages. Package A provides a complete offering with instruction plus an added option to use the New Orleans trademark and name. An investment of $5,295 purchases a 110-volt ice shaver, a drip pan, and a set of extra blades. This package also entitles the investor to personal classroom and hands-on training at the New Orleans retail store in Boone, North Carolina. During this half-day training session, entrepreneurs learn how to operate the business and maintain the equipment. New Orleans also teaches entrepreneurs the exclusive syrup and snowball recipes as well as tested marketing strategies. This package also includes a 120-page operations manual that outlines proper procedures for all aspects of the business.

Entrepreneurs who choose this package should also be prepared to invest an additional $10,000 for leasehold improvements on a store, purchase or rental of a mobile unit, utility and security deposits, and other business start-up costs, including working capital. New Orleans also charges a $500 annual fee for the use of the trademark and logo. This option is available to entrepreneurs who attend the in-person training workshop.

Entrepreneurs may choose to purchase Package B. For an investment of $1,495 plus shipping costs, New Orleans Snowballs provides basic recipes and product descriptions as well as a 110-volt ice shaver, a drip pan, extra blades, and access to the company's supply catalog, which includes necessary items needed to run the business efficiently and more than 100 snowball syrup flavors.

Investors in Package C are those already in the shaved-ice or food industry. For these clients, New Orleans supplies an assortment of extracts from its manufacturing facility and a full line of supplies. Investment varies on the specific order, but all customers must present a commercial tax identification number and credit references from other COD purchases.

New Orleans Snowballs owner and president Monty Joynes also maintains telephone contact with all clients. His office reserves 9:00 A.M. to 11:00 A.M. and 9:00 P.M. to 11:00 P.M. daily for telephone inquiries and assistance.

Future Outlook
New Orleans Snowball realized the popularity of its product and capitalized on it. The company maintains strict control over who uses its name and who receives its line of supplies. New Orleans offers business advice to those who request it.

Contact Information

Address: 11 Carriage Square, 207 Highway 105 Ext., Boone, North
  Carolina 28607
Telephone: 1-704-262-3952
Contact person: Monty Joynes, president

KEEPSAKE, NOVELTY, AND GIFT ITEMS

CASI—CREATIVE AMUSEMENT SERVICES, INC.

Initial investment: $8,000 to $20,000
Total investment: $8,000 to $20,000
Ongoing fees: None
Right to use trademark and logo: None

Expansion History
Company operating since: 1976
Offering computer portrait equipment since: 1977
Number of CASI independent contractors: 7,200

Industry Focus
  Computer portraits are popular gift items. Consumers are attracted to personal gifts that are both original and economical.

Company Advantages
  Creative Amusement Services uses its exclusive computer system to "take photographs." Company founder Sam Kendes designed and manufactured the state-of-the-art, portable computer system. Entrepreneurs can carry and set up the equipment in a variety of locations.
  Creative Amusement was one of the first companies to develop the technical expertise to transfer portrait images to T-shirts, coffee mugs, and other novelty items.

CASI employs engineers and marketing staff at its company head-quarters to update and improve its technology and products.

CASI, or Creative Amusement Services, Inc., of New York City combines technical and creative talents to bring consumers unique gifts of computerized photograph images. Established in 1976, CASI has grown from a one-man operation to more than 7,200 independent contractors throughout the United States.

As independent representatives for CASI, entrepreneurs set up their computer portrait studios in malls, retail stores, craft fairs, flea markets, trade shows, and charity fund-raiser events. The computer equipment is portable and compact, and it requires only a small kiosk or 10-foot-by-10-foot work area to operate effectively. CASI does not require operators to run the business on a full-time basis, and many contractors retain their jobs during the initial months of operation.

CASI entrepreneurs operate efficiently with one or two persons. The CASI contractors use photographs or live subjects to make the computer portrait. Customers pay between $2 and $30 for a portrait that takes only seconds to reproduce and frame. An additional 15 to 20 seconds is needed to heat-press the image to items such as shirts, posters, coffee mugs, buttons, watches, pendants, and tote bags. The company makes no earning claims, but it does maintain that contractors can make up to 700 percent profit on most items.

An initial investment ranging between $8,000 and $20,000 purchases all equipment and supplies needed to establish the computer portrait studios. Contractors have no geographic restrictions, and the company encourages operators to market the service in as many locations as they wish. CASI offers the independent contractors a choice of computer systems, and contractors can upgrade their equipment as business grows.

The less expensive computer systems produce a photograph-quality thermal picture that can be transferred to various surfaces, while the more expensive systems allow operators to perform more sophisticated services, such as superimposed images. CASI charges no ongoing royalty fees, and independent contractors can order supplies and novelty products from the company, which also manufactures the computer systems and more than 500 gift items.

CASI trains its independent contractors through manuals and videotapes at the home office in New York City, at designated training classes throughout the country, or at the contractor's base of operations. The company provides technical support and is available to assist contractors in any repair or adjustment of their equipment. CASI maintains a toll-free number for contractors in need of assistance, and in-field help is available if necessary.

Future Outlook
CASI has widened its market by offering customers a variety of products. The company is a family-run organization headed by Kenneth Kendes, the son of founder Sam Kendes. CASI maintains quality in its computer systems by producing them in-house.

Contact Information
Address: 156 Fifth Avenue, Suite 323, New York, New York 10010
Telephone: 1-800-457-2274 or 1-212-645-4770
Contact person: Marketing Department

NATIONWIDE SCREEN PRINTING

Initial investment: $9,000
Total investment: $9,000
Ongoing fees: None
Right to use trademark and logo: None

Expansion History
Company operating since: 1984
Offering screen-printing equipment since: 1984
Number of independent nationwide entrepreneurs: 500+

Industry Focus
Screen printing is a popular novelty item that appeals to schools, community and fund-raising organizations, athletic clubs, and retail consumers.
    This type of enterprise is generally simple to operate with one

person. The equipment is portable and easily operated in a small room or work area.

Company Advantages

Nationwide targets entrepreneurs who want to work from home. The company personally trains all independent contractors on the equipment at the home office.

Nationwide has an eight-year history in the screen-printing business. The company has received industry recognition for its support network for independent contractors.

Today's fashions literally make statements. For Nationwide Screen Printing of Charleston, South Carolina, these statements translate into business profits. Established in 1984, Nationwide is an equipment and materials supplier to more than 500 independent contractors throughout the United States.

As Nationwide screen-printers, entrepreneurs use a simple process to put designs, logos, and words on textile surfaces. Entrepreneurs sell an assortment of products such as T-shirts, caps, jackets, and other sportswear to individual consumers or organized clubs and associations.

Nationwide entrepreneurs can sell these products on a part-time or full-time basis. Most screen printers begin as part-time business owners who maintain their jobs and sell the designed clothing during the evenings and weekends. Part-time entrepreneurs usually forgo the expense of a retail workshop and use their homes as a base of operations. Part-timers market their products through home shows, craft fairs, flea markets, or prescheduled appointments.

As business demand increases, many entrepreneurs elect to turn their part-time endeavor into a full-scale business. Those who choose this route may spend the bulk of their time selling the specialized articles of clothing to churches, businesses, athletic organizations, and community clubs for fund-raisers or advertisement purposes. Full-time entrepreneurs can also establish retail locations at area malls or shopping centers.

Nationwide screen-printers are usually hands-on entrepreneurs who perform the screen-printing tasks themselves. One person easily operates the Nationwide screen-printing press, which can imprint a garment with as many as four colors simultaneously. Full-time screen-printers may purchase additional printing presses to meet the increased customer demand for their products. Nationwide does not make any earnings claims, but the company maintains that entrepreneurs can make a 100 percent profit or more on their merchandise.

Nationwide screen-printers need no art or design background. More than 90 percent of customers supply the artwork for the merchandise. If it is not supplied, the screen-printers can use computer software desktop publishing programs for designs. It is the screen-printer's responsibility to set prices for products, but each entrepreneur should investigate competitive rates before establishing retail pricing policy.

For an investment of $9,000, Nationwide screen-printers receive the screen-printing press, a speed dryer, cap printer and jacket printer attachments, cap and T-shirt screens, sample garments, squeegees, ink thermometers, and brushes. All equipment comes with a one-year warranty and technical assistance from Nationwide's office staff. Nationwide entrepreneurs also receive one day of training at the company's offices in South Carolina. Nationwide charges no royalty or renewal fees.

Nationwide trains entrepreneurs on an individual basis according to their needs. The company teaches first-time entrepreneurs to use the equipment and maintain it through actual "hands-on" demonstrations.

The company also teaches its entrepreneurs how to target and sell the products to the various markets. Nationwide sponsors a toll-free hot line for new and established entrepreneurs in need of technical assistance. If entrepreneurs feel they need a refresher course, Nationwide will retrain them at no extra charge.

Future Outlook

Screen-printing is an important part of fashion today. Consumers who want to wear a logo, advertise a club or business, or send a personal message use screen-printing. It is creative, personal, inexpensive, and durable. These qualities appeal to the consumer market as well as organizations caught in a tight budget. Nationwide provides ample support for this type of business opportunity. The company does not require its entrepreneurs to purchase additional supplies or materials from it and gives them lists of suppliers throughout the country.

Contact Information
Address: 8 Otranto Club Circle, Charleston, South Carolina 29406
Telephone: 1-803-863-8400
Contact person: Susan Priddy

N. B. NELSON CO.

Initial investment: $202.60 to $815.40
Total investment: $202.60 to $815.40
Ongoing fees: None
Right to use trademark and logo: None

Expansion History
Company operating since: 1979
Offering gift canning equipment since: 1979
Number of gift canning equipment sold: 2,500

Industry Focus
  Gift canning appeals to retailers and consumers alike. Gift canning is inexpensive, and gifts are secured safely within the can and are easily mailed.

Company Advantages
  N. B. Nelson supplies entrepreneurs with a variety of starter kits. Retailers can offer the canning service along with traditional box and paper wrapping. Entrepreneurs can offer canning service at holiday times in malls, flea markets, and craft shows.
  The canning wrap is reusable, and the company supplies personalized labels and colorized reusable lids. The can is also recyclable, which appeals to the environmentally conscious consumer.

  Signed, sealed, and delivered. N. B. Nelson Company of Whitefish, Montana, built its business network around these words. Established in 1979, N. B. Nelson provides retailers and gift purchasers with an alternative to conventional gift wrapping—can wrapping. For a price ranging between 25 cents and $5, entrepreneurs and retailers place a gift in an aluminum can, seal it, decorate it with personalized message labels, and prepare it for mailing.

The can-wrapping concept has gained popularity since the Nelsons first started promoting the service in national business publications. More entrepreneurs and retailers have bought the starter kits, and the company estimates that 2,500 entrepreneurs are actively selling the service.

This alternative has won over many retailers, who offer the gift-wrapping service in their stores, and part-time entrepreneurs, who sell the service on weekends at craft shows, flea markets, and malls.

For a minimum investment that ranges between $202.60 and $815.40 entrepreneurs receive a starter kit that includes all equipment and inventory needed to perform can-wrapping services. Starter kits vary in their contents, but all kits include a generous supply of cans, decorator labels, lids, mailing labels, and promotional materials.

Consumers and store owners are attracted to can-wrapping's simplicity as well as its durability. N. B. Nelson charges no ongoing royalties to those who sell or operate the canning kits. The company has little competition in its industry, and it earns most of its profits when entrepreneurs reorder cans and materials. Although N. B. Nelson makes no earnings claims, it does maintain that retailers and entrepreneurs can make up to 300 percent profit on each can-wrapping.

The company provides support to entrepreneurs with merchandising aids, printed materials, and telephone consultation. There is no prescribed method of business operation, and entrepreneurs are allowed to use their creativity to sell the products and service.

This business opportunity levies no restrictions, and entrepreneurs need little company support. N. B. Nelson maintains a toll-free number for questions, and the company encourages telephone contact.

Future Outlook

N. B. Nelson has tapped into the consumer's desire for originality. Gift giving is an arduous task for American consumers, who spend just as much time selecting the card and wrapping as they do buying the gift.

N.B. Nelson used ingenuity in directing its product at both retail establishments and part-time entrepreneurs. The inexpensive starter kit attracts entrepreneurs who are reluctant or unable to make large investments in business opportunities.

Contact Information
Address: P.O. Box 999, Whitefish, Montana 59937
Telephone: 1-800-552-8203 or 1-406-862-8115
Contact person: Neal or Karen Nelson

PERSONAL SERVICES

THE PROFESSIONALS, INC.

Initial investment: $6,990 to $9,990
Total investment: $6,990 to $9,990
Ongoing fees: None
Right to use trademark and logo: None

Expansion History
Company operating since: 1977
Offering business opportunities since: 1983
Number of business opportunities: 700

Industry Focus
Residential cleaning services are one of the fastest-growing industries in the United States. According to the U.S. Department of Commerce, this industry will gross more than $15 billion by 1995.

The increased trend in dual-income households has forced many people to rely on residential cleaning services to maintain their homes.

Company Advantages

The Professionals combines a turnkey operation without the commitment to a franchise organization.

The company offers entrepreneurs two opportunity packages. The higher-priced package includes personal training; the less-expensive package relies on manuals and telephone support.

The Professionals entrepreneur assigns the same maid to the same house for each cleaning session.

Entrepreneurs have the opportunity to expand their business and establish satellite offices for half the cost of the original package.

Established in 1977, The Professionals, Inc., of Ranger, Georgia, markets a complete, turnkey package that combines modern managerial skills with old-fashioned housekeeping standards. The Professionals' method rejects the widely known, team-cleaning concept that assigns four to five maids to one household at one time. Instead, the company enforces the "one-housekeeper-per-one-household rule" that sends a specific maid to the same house for each cleaning assignment. This method of operation has won support from more than 700 entrepreneurs throughout the country who have purchased the company's business opportunity package within the last nine years.

The Professionals' entrepreneurs are business managers. It is their responsibility to market this residential cleaning service through local advertisements, professional organization networking, direct mail campaigns, and other creative marketing strategies. Entrepreneurs purchase The Professionals' system of management, but they do not use the company's name in their daily operations.

It is also the business owners' job to hire maids to complete the cleaning tasks. The company makes no earnings claim, but it does estimate that entrepreneurs usually employ at least 10 to 12 maids by the end of the first year of operation. The maids work for a percentage of the gross revenue, which averages out to approximately $8 to $10 per hour.

"We are firm believers in the idea that an owner can't push the broom and run a business at the same time," explains Theresa Asano, founder and president of The Professionals. "We operated and still operate several offices, and we understand what the customers want to see. They feel more secure knowing that the same maid that cleaned their house last week is the same one that will clean their house this week."

The average cost to customers ranges from $40 to $45 for a typical three-bedroom, two-bathroom home. The Professionals' entrepreneurs tailor cleaning services to customers' needs. Customers choose the frequency of the cleaning service and the number of rooms they want cleaned.

For an initial investment of $6,990, entrepreneurs receive an instructional training manual and an original forms and invoice package that includes job proposals and estimate forms, expense reports, sales journal, and a client telephone log. This business opportunity package also contains an extensive marketing format kit with flyers, news releases, newspaper and Yellow Pages advertisement layouts, direct mail formats, plus real-estate agent and apartment manager promotional materials. The Professionals also includes a bookkeeping system, five videocassettes, a leadership program recorded on eight audiocassettes, and one year of consultation, guidance, and support.

The second investment package, priced at $9,990, includes all the features of the first package plus instructions and training for five additional business offerings: postpartum or motherly care services, moving and packing assistance, window cleaning, office cleaning, and floor refinishing. The investment in this second package also covers the costs for three days of training at the company's home office in Ranger, Georgia, and computer software designed to help manage all aspects of The Professionals' business system.

Entrepreneurs have the opportunity to expand their businesses and establish satellite offices. The Professionals insists that the offices be operated by business partners—not managers. The company does not offer exclusive territories, so entrepreneurs can establish offices anywhere throughout the United States.

Future Outlook

Theresa Asano believes strongly in the one-housekeeper-per-one-household rule. This method of operation allows entrepreneurs to keep close tabs on their maids, and it protects their maids from fraudulent claims of theft. Customers display more confidence in a company that maintains strict security controls.

Contact Information
Address: Route 1, Box 2400, Ranger, Georgia 30734
Telephone: 1-800-289-8642 or 1-404-334-4400
Contact person: T. A. Arsenault

TRAVEL AND LODGING

BUDGET HOST INNS

Initial investment: $2,500+ depending on motel and sign size
Total investment: $6,500 to $15,545 plus normal operating expenses of existing motel or lodge
Ongoing fees: $400 annual fee plus $10 per room over 30 rooms; $27 per room up to 150 rooms for advertising fees
Right to use trademark and logo: Yes

Expansion History
Company operating since: 1976
Offering Budget Host affiliation since: 1976
Number of Budget Host Inns: 200+

Industry Focus
Americans are value conscious when it comes to hotels, motels, and inns, especially if they are traveling as a family.
Travelers tend to trust nationally known lodge chains more than independent names.

Company Advantages
Budget Host Inns offers participants a national name and reputation.
Participants have the choice of retaining their motel name and

adding the Budget Host logo to their sign or becoming a full-fledged Budget Host Inn. The fees for participation in the chain are based on number of motel units. This translates to lower costs for smaller establishments.

Accommodations are the most important aspect of travel. Consumers want not only quality but value, and Budget Host Inns of Fort Worth, Texas, claims it can deliver both. Formed in 1976, Budget Host Inns is a national affiliation lodging chain that includes more than 200 independently operated motels throughout the United States and Canada.

Motel and hotel owners can become Budget Host members by paying an initial $2,500 membership fee. In return for the fee, motel owners purchase the right to use the Budget Host name and logo and share in the benefits of the national Budget Host directory service. Budget Host operators also participate in the chain's central toll-free telephone reservation system, which forwards customer inquiries from the central Budget Host office to a specific motel in the affiliation.

Along with the initial fee, Budget Host owners need to purchase a Budget Host sign, which ranges in price from $2,450 to $12,320, depending on size and content. There is also a one-time $50 fee for participation in the central toll-free reservations system. Annual fees to members include dues of $400 for the first 30 rooms of motels and $10 for each room thereafter, an annual charge of $27 per room up to 150 rooms to cover the affiliation's quality assurance and advertising fees, and an annual sign royalty of $275.

In order to become a Budget Host affiliation member, a person must either own an existing motel or be in the process of building a motel. Since most Budget Host operators know the motel business, they need little instruction in running a Budget Host establishment. The chain does conduct regular inspections to ensure customer quality, and owners are required to attend seminars and conventions. Operators have the option of retaining their original name and using the Budget Host insignia in conjunction with that name or eliminating their independent name and using Budget Host Inn instead.

As a central unit, Budget Host provides its motel operators with ongoing support through its national print and media advertising campaigns and its national account savings for the use of major credit cards. The company also holds several regional meetings per year to update operators on any changes in the Budget Host practices or requirements. Budget Host also provides in-field support to any operator in need of assistance.

Future Outlook

Budget Host Inns gives motel owners national name recognition. Travelers use hotel and motel chains they recognize. The Budget Host affiliation does not cut deeply into the profits of independent owners, and owners do not have to relinquish their names. The central reservation number and the national directory also work to make it easier for travelers to find and reserve Budget Host Inns rooms.

Contact Information

Address: P.O. Box 10656, Fort Worth, Texas 76114
Telephone: 1-817-626-7064
Contact person: Ray Sawyer

Dealerships

AUTOMOBILE MAINTENANCE

ENDRUST DETAILING SYSTEMS

Initial investment: $25,000
Total investment: $40,000
Ongoing fees: Minimum purchase of $1,800 supplies and
  equipment per year from Endrust Industries
Right to use trademark and logo: Yes

Expansion History
Company operating since: 1969
Offering dealerships since: 1970
Number of dealers: 50

Industry Focus
  Keeping a car well maintained adds to its life. Especially in uncertain economic times, car owners are not willing to purchase new
vehicles as often.

Company Advantages
  Endrust has weathered all types of economic conditions, and the
detailing business remains intact. Owners can make Endrust their
primary service or add Endrust to an already existing list of services.

  Established in 1969, Endrust has grown to a nationwide network
of 50 dealerships. Endrust dealers hand-wash and wax cars plus steam-
clean and vacuum interior upholstery and dashboards. As an additional service, dealers apply Englaze, the company's exclusive process
that protects an automobile's finish from natural elements. Endrust
dealers also design and apply pinstripes and other graphic work,
and they are trained to install sun roofs and tinted windows as well.
  Endrust dealers comprise two distinct groups. The first is the start-
up businessperson, who wants to sell Endrust products and services

only. The second group is the already established automotive service technician, who wants to add the Endrust detailing services to an existing business.

For both groups of dealers, Endrust charges an initial fee of $20,000, which covers the cost of all equipment, inventory, and on-site training. The initial investment also pays for the right to use the Endrust name and logo in the operation of the business.

Endrust charges no ongoing fees. The company requires all material and equipment used for the detailing services to be purchased from Endrust or an Endrust-approved vendor. Dealers who do not have an existing facility should expect to have in reserve an additional $20,000 for the rental and renovation of a 1,500-square-foot garage space and reception area. The additional funds also cover the costs of initial advertising, marketing, and insurance.

Endrust representatives train dealers at their site. Dealers as well as their employees are expected to be proficient at performing all detailing services. Although Endrust participates in national advertising programs, dealers promote their businesses locally through direct mail campaigns to the consumer and person-to-person selling to rental car agencies and new car dealerships.

Endrust does not require specific methods of business operation, but it does offer dealers advanced training in any new products or services developed by the home office. The company also produces newsletters that update dealers on new marketing trends in the automobile detailing industry.

Future Outlook

Endrust monitors its dealers carefully, paying special attention to the quality of service. The company is a family-owned business, and all officers are family members. Since it will remain a privately run organization, Endrust relies heavily on its reputation, and it has chosen to expand on a slower scale to guarantee quality services.

Contact Information
Address: 1725 Washington Road, #205, Pittsburgh, Pennsylvania 15241
Telephone: 1-412-831-1255
Contact person: Carol A. Griser, comptroller

END-A-FLAT TIRE SEALANT

Initial investment: $10,000
Total investment: $10,000
Ongoing fees: None
Right to use trademark and logo: Yes

Expansion History
Company operating since: 1980
Offering dealerships since: 1980
Number of dealers: 30

Industry Focus
Preventing flat tires can save consumers hundreds or thousands of dollars.
Well-balanced and inflated tires lead to better fuel mileage and less tread wear for any car or vehicle.

Company Advantages
End-A-Flat developed the preventive tire maintenance system more than 13 years ago. The system has proved effective on cars, trucks, and heavy industrial and farm equipment.
End-A-Flat's tire sealant material contains no flammable properties. This sets this company apart from other competitors that market aerosol sealant products that can ignite upon impact.

Preventive tire maintenance can save lives and money. End-A-Flat Tire Sealant offers consumers a protective hedge against the unpredictable tire blowout. A sister dealership of Endrust Detailing Systems, End-A-Flat was introduced to consumers in 1980. The tire sealant product has won over many automobile owners, farmers, and heavy equipment operators who use the End-A-Flat system to lengthen their tires' lives. The Pittsburgh, Pennsylvania-based company relies on its 30 national dealers to market the product.
End-A-Flat dealers come from two different entrepreneurial pools. Some incorporate this dealership into their already estab-

lished automobile repair or detailing shops, and others offer the
End-A-Flat product as their only service.

Initially, most dealers give "hands-on" attention to all aspects of
the End-A-Flat business, including sales, installation, and customer
service. Dealers try to market the product to individual car owners
as well as government agencies, farmers, construction companies,
or any other business or organization that uses vehicles in its daily
operation.

As business volume increases, many dealers turn their attention
to the marketing and customer service end of the business, and they
hire mechanics and technicians to handle the tire sealant installation.

The key to the dealer's success is the liquid polymer product that
is pumped into the tire by the exclusive End-A-Flat air pump system.
The durable, nonflammable, and nontoxic liquid material fends off
flats by forming an airtight seal on the inside of the tire when it is
punctured. The seal is permanent, and in most cases the tire does
not need to be repaired. The liquid polymer does not adversely
affect wheel balance, and it withstands extreme temperatures as
well as various traveling speeds. Compact car owners pay on the
average of $49 to have the End-A-Flat substance pumped into four
tires. Owners of trucks or heavy equipment vehicles that have more
than four tires can pay up to $155 or more for the End-A-Flat
service.

Entrepreneurs need $10,000 to buy an End-A-Flat dealership.
The investment purchases the rights to use the term End-A-Flat
dealer when marketing the product. Dealers also receive equipment,
inventory, and training with this investment. End-A-Flat assists dealers in finding a suitable site for their business. The company conducts on-site training for all dealers on the installation of the tire
sealant product. During this training period, dealers learn how to
market End-A-Flat to individuals, corporations, and government
agencies through direct mail campaigns, telemarketing programs,
and person-to-person sales.

Future Outlook

Like its sister company Endrust, End-A-Flat does not aggressively
search for dealers. Company representatives do attend trade shows
and occasionally business opportunity shows, but End-A-Flat is

comfortable with a slower growth rate. The company feels it can monitor and assist its dealers more effectively if it does not expand too quickly.

Contact Information
Address: 1725 Washington Road #205, Pittsburgh, Pennsylvania 15241
Telephone: 1-412-831-1255
Contact person: Carol A. Griser, comptroller

BUSINESS SERVICES

LASERCHARGE, INC.

Initial investment: $4,900 to $6,900
Total investment: $8,000 to $10,000
Ongoing fees: None
Right to use trademark and logo: Yes

Expansion History
Company operating since: 1986
Offering dealerships since: 1988
Number of dealers: 2,000 +

Industry Focus
Toner cartridges put the print in today's laser printers and copiers. Although the cartridges are disposable when the ink supply is finished, companies and businesses can save money by recycling these cartridges. New toner cartridges cost a minimum of $68. Recycled cartridges cost 50 percent less.

Company Advantages
   LaserCharge, Inc., is a leader in the toner cartridge recycling industry. The company and its dealers use its exclusive method to

recharge toner cartridges in almost all printer, copier, and fax machine models.

The LaserCharge dealer is a service and repair specialist. Dealers usually assess damage to a toner cartridge at the customer's site or in their retail or office locations. Dealers remove, recharge, and test the cartridge before reinstalling it in the computer or copier. The recharging process takes between 10 to 20 minutes to complete, and the dealer can earn up to $48 per recharge. Businesses either call the LaserCharge dealer when the toner cartridges fail, or they contract dealers to perform toner cartridge recharging on a regular basis.

LaserCharge offers entrepreneurs two dealership packages. Minimum investments range between $4,900 and $6,900. Both packages provide the same tools and supplies; the difference lies in the company-sponsored training. The more expensive plan includes expenses for a four-day training workshop at the home office in Austin. The less expensive plan provides manuals and tapes for home-study training. The dealers who choose not to attend the training workshop usually have some experience in copier and computer maintenance. LaserCharge also offers all dealers incentives to purchase the company's other high-technology service dealerships, LaserMaintenance, a copier and computer printer repair service, and MicroMaid, a preventive maintenance program for copiers and computers.

LaserCharge does not require its dealers to prescribe to any specific method of operation, but it does recommend that dealers invest an additional $2,000 to $3,000 to purchase a laser printer to test recharged toner cartridges. Most dealers eventually do establish a retail or warehouse location, but this is not mandatory. LaserCharge has no specific guideline that outlines store or office space, and many dealers prefer to start operations from home until their business volume warrants larger quarters.

LaserCharge emphasizes customer service and insists that dealers maintain a good rapport with customers. The company guarantees its products and processes, and it expects its dealers to do the same. LaserCharge allows dealers to set their own price standards, but the company suggests dealers investigate local markets for current fee rates before they open their LaserCharge dealerships.

Future Outlook

LaserCharge keeps a watchful eye on the computer industry and creates business opportunities that meet consumers' needs. The company has achieved success building dealerships on the LaserCharge recycling process with its LaserMaintenance and MicroMaid dealerships. Dealers can expand their businesses by purchasing these additional dealerships from LaserCharge at discounted prices. The company provides support to all dealers through its large equipment and supply network.

Contact Information

Address: 11130 Metric Boulevard, Austin, Texas 78758
Telephone: 1-800-299-8134 or 1-512-832-0079
Contact person: Janet Epstein

LASERMAINTENANCE

(LaserCharge, Inc.)

Initial investment: $6,900
Total investment: $10,000
Ongoing fees: None
Right to use trademark and logo: Yes

Expansion History
Company operating since: 1990
Offering dealerships since: 1990
Number of dealers: 100

Industry Focus

Laser printers and copiers are becoming essential business tools today. By 1995 there will be more than 9 million laser copiers and printers in use. That number can support a great many qualified repair and maintenance personnel.

Company Advantages

LaserCharge, Inc., co-sponsors LaserMaintenance dealership training with technology repair experts TRW. Dealers learn to repair and maintain the most popular laser printers and copiers.

Established in 1990, LaserMaintenance is the combined effort of LaserCharge, Inc., and TRW, one of the largest computer parts manufacturers and service companies in the world.

For a minimum investment of $6,900, LaserMaintenance dealers receive an exclusive territory plus a complete turnkey operation. LaserMaintenance dealers are repair specialists. They establish retail locations as a base of operations, and they service the most popular brands of laser printers and copiers.

As part of the dealership agreement, LaserMaintenance entrepreneurs have access to TRW's laser copier parts network, which is the largest parts network in the world. For the initial investment, dealers receive a laser printer tool kit and an instructional videotape and operations manual. That initial fee also includes travel and lodging expenses for the company's mandatory training course in Austin.

Most LaserMaintenance dealers are already established Laser-Charge dealers who have added laser copier and printer repair to their existing toner recycling business. This is not a prerequisite to purchasing a LaserMaintenance dealership, and the company views both dealerships as independent business opportunities.

As business volume grows, LaserMaintenance dealers may take on a managerial role and hire other employees to do the repair work. The company does not require dealers to conform to any kind of pricing policy, but it does recommend dealers investigate their territories before setting fees. On the average, dealers charge between $50 and $140 per hour for a maintenance call and $350 for repair service. The association with TRW allows dealers to enter large service contracts that they can refer to TRW's service network. For the referral, TRW pays LaserMaintenance dealers an immediate 10 percent commission and a monthly commission for the duration of the contract.

LaserMaintenance's four-day training class emphasizes both technical and business skills. Dealers learn through hands-on experience how to service the most popular brands of printers and copiers. The company also teaches dealers how to price and negotiate service and maintenance contracts. LaserMaintenance has a toll-free hot line for dealers in need of technical assistance. TRW will provide in-field assistance to dealers at discounted rates. LaserMaintenance also supplies marketing updates and newsletters to dealers on a regular basis.

Future Outlook
LaserCharge showed great foresight in establishing this business opportunity. The company has made a natural and logical evolution from its toner service dealerships to this high-technology dealership. LaserMaintenance allows LaserCharge dealers to increase their business volume, plus it opens doors for potential entrepreneurs.

Contact Information
Address: 11130 Metric Boulevard, Austin, Texas 78758
Telephone: 1-800-299-8134 or 1-512-832-0079
Contact person: Janet Epstein

MICROMAID
(LaserCharge, Inc.)

Initial investment: $6,995
Total investment: $6,995
Ongoing fees: None
Right to use trademark and logo: Yes

Expansion History
Company operating since: 1992
Offering dealerships since: 1992
Number of dealers: 4

Industry Focus
More than 60 million microcomputers exist in the United States alone. Computers are being used in every facet of life. Computer users need to maintain their machines regularly.

Company Advantages

MicroMaid is one of only a few companies that specialize in computer preventive maintenance.

LaserCharge has joined forces with Watson Information Systems of Austin, Texas, to develop this new and independent dealership opportunity. LaserCharge and Watson Information Systems provide a double support system for the MicroMaid dealers.

The MicroMaid opportunity is new to the computer market, but the name LaserCharge is not. Dealers have the advantage of a ground-floor opportunity combined with the experience of an established company.

MicroMaid offers businesses and computer users a regularly scheduled, comprehensive cleaning service that removes dust, lint, and other particles from the intricate workings of the computer before they cause permanent damage.

MicroMaid dealers are foremost computer-cleaning specialists. They travel to the customer's site to complete the 30- to 60- minute cleaning regimen that uses nontoxic solutions to clean everything from keyboards to floppy disk drives. MicroMaid dealers can also apply the cleaning solutions to printers, fax machines, and cable connectors. As part of MicroMaid's $69.95 maintenance fee, customers receive a diagnostic evaluation of the condition of their computer systems and an up-to-date virus-detection inspection. In addition to the cleaning service, MicroMaid also offers computer users a special 15-minute data backup service that copies important files to hard disk. The support service eliminates the tedious task of copying important data on floppy disks.

A $6,995 investment assures a MicroMaid dealer of an exclusive territory and the right to use the MicroMaid name and logo. Also included in this initial fee are the necessary equipment, tools, and cleaning supplies. A MicroMaid dealership requires only a small working space, and dealers carry all needed equipment in their tool case. Dealers do not need to rent professional office or warehouse space, and LaserCharge encourages MicroMaid dealers to operate the computer maintenance service from their homes.

LaserCharge requires dealers to attend a four-day training workshop in Austin. Training concentrates on cleaning and service techniques as well as marketing and management strategies. Laser-Charge calculates the costs of airfare, lodging, and meals into the $6,995 investment fee. LaserCharge and Watson Information Systems are available for post-training support. Dealers can call for assistance, and in-field help is available. LaserCharge also issues operation and technical manuals to all dealers as part of the training package.

Future Outlook
The computer service field has gained momentum over the past decade. There are many repair companies, but few have tapped into the preventive maintenance market. Computer users invest a great deal of money in equipment, and the costs for parts and repair labor can be staggering.

As with its other dealership divisions, LaserCharge has sought out expert advice in Watson Information Systems before launching this business opportunity. This dealership opportunity is relatively new, but the combination of these two companies may provide a solid support system for dealers.

Contact Information
Address: 11130 Metric Boulevard, Austin, Texas 78758
Telephone: 1-800-299-8134 or 1-512-832-0079
Contact person: Janet Epstein

PROFILES INTERNATIONAL, INC.

Initial investment: $10,000 to $15,000
Total investment: $10,000 to $15,000
Ongoing fees: $200 annual renewal fee and $10,000 annually in
    testing materials
Right to use trademark and logo: None

Expansion History
Company operating since: 1967
Offering dealerships since: 1991
Number of dealers: 100

Industry Focus

Evaluation tools can measure an employee's personality strengths and weaknesses. Corporations seek out scientific measuring devices when they compose their work forces.

Employees raise their performance levels if they are in a challenging and interesting job. Personality profiles direct management how to best use their employees' talents and reduce stress in the workplace.

Company Advantages

Profiles International has a team of technical advisors who assist the company in the development of personnel evaluation tests. Members of the technical team possess postgraduate degrees in psychology, education, and psychotherapy, and they maintain private counseling practices.

In today's competitive marketplace, corporations need more from their employees than eight hours of their day. Profiles International of Waco, Texas, helps corporations increase employee productivity with comprehensive evaluation surveys that identify the best personalities for a specific job.

Established in 1967, Profiles International was a pioneer in the personnel evaluations field. John Moore, a psychologist from Perdue University, first used evaluation tools in his work to prescreen U.S. government workers. In 1972 Profiles International founder John Shirley redesigned Moore's personality evaluation survey to meet business standards. The company has since changed owners twice, but each change resulted in more in-depth testing tools that have won support from both corporations and psychological professionals.

In 1991 new owners Jim Sirbasku and Bud Haney created Profiles International's marketing network, which includes 100 dealers and 50 area directors throughout the United States. Consultant dealers complete studies that focus on specific job classifications, employee stress levels, talents, and ethical directions. From these studies, they create for their clients a template that indicates what type person would best perform certain job functions. Clients use this information in two ways: They hire new employees who meet this template profile, and they retrain their current employees to improve their job performance.

Profiles International dealers are corporate consultants. They do not need a background in psychology or counseling, but they do need to be comfortable in a corporate atmosphere and possess a professional demeanor. Consultant dealers market the evaluation tools to human resource development departments, corporate management, or company owners. They either administer the evaluation tools themselves, or they teach corporate staff members to administer the tests. Consultant dealers then collect the tests, evaluate the scores using Profiles International's computer software programs, and return to clients a formal report detailing all results.

The cost of the tests for clients ranges between $25 to $135 per person, and dealers earn as much as a 200 percent or more profit on the sale and scoring of the tests.

Consultant dealers can and usually do start out as one-person operations. As business develops, many consultants take on other salespersons to promote the testing packages as well. The company encourages this practice, but all salespeople must be trained according to the company's standards.

Profiles International estimates that entrepreneurs need between $10,000 and $15,000 to purchase a dealership. The company does not offer any exclusive territories, so dealers are free to market their personnel evaluation tools to companies throughout the United States. Profiles International does have consultants who market their services outside the country, but the international push is still in its infancy. Along with the initial investment, Profiles International recommends that dealers keep an additional $2,000 in reserve for the purchase of office equipment, including a computer and fax machine.

For their investment, consultant dealers receive a one-year contract and an initial inventory package valued at $32,000 retail. This package includes written information and computer software for all evaluation surveys.

Also included in the intitial investment is a comprehensive training package containing sales and operational manuals as well as a promotional material packet including brochures, endorsements, test samples, and fee schedules.

As part of the company's contract, Profiles International offers dealers extensive training in sales presentation and test scoring. Appointed area directors hold at least one monthly training session that focuses on sales management and sales recruitment methods. The company encourages telephone contact with all dealers, and it sponsors an optional, monthly training class in Dallas. Profiles International also distributes periodic mailings to all dealers and newsletters to clients.

Dealers must purchase a minimum of $10,000 of testing materials annually from Profiles International, but they pay no royalty or advertising fees. Dealers also pay a $200 contract renewal fee annually.

Future Outlook

The company's owners have distinguished themselves in this industry. Both come from sales backgrounds and companies that have specialized in sales training and consultation.

The market for this type of service is vast. Industry research estimates that earnings have reached the $50 million mark, and this figure represents only 2 percent of the potential market. Profiles International's tests are simple to take and require only an hour of an employee's time. Results are computerized so dealers need no background in psychology to succeed. The company has installed a strong support system in its area directors, company-appointed independent entrepreneurs who are responsible for the training and supervision of dealers in their areas.

Contact Information

Address: 4525 Lake Shore Drive, Waco, Texas 76710
Telephone: 1-817-751-1644
Contact person: Jim Sirbasku, CEO, or Joe (Bud) Haney, president

ENTERTAINMENT/LEISURE

SPORT IT, INC.

Initial investment: $2,500 ($1,500 with a nonexclusive territory)
Total investment: $2,500 ($1,500 with a nonexclusive territory)
Ongoing fees: $25 monthly service fee
Right to use trademark and logo: Yes (private-labeled merchandise only)

Expansion History
Company operating since: 1984
Offering dealerships since: 1984
Number of dealers: 5,600

Industry Focus
The national sporting goods industry grosses more than $20 billion annually, according to the National Sporting Goods Association.

Sports play an important role in Americans' daily lives. Consumers not only enjoy watching professional teams, but they also participate in clubs and league sports through their local communities and places of employment.

Company Advantages
Sport It, Inc., has established for its dealers a network of national brand-name suppliers that provide quality merchandise and speedy delivery of sporting goods.

Sport It encourages entrepreneurs to operate their business from home initially, where they can develop their own marketing avenues in the community. Eventually many dealers choose to sell the national brands sportswear and equipment plus Sport It private-labeled merchandise through mail-order programs, home party plans, catalog retail operations, or sporting goods retail stores.

Sport It has developed into the largest sportswear and equipment distributor in the United States with its network of 5,600 dealers.

A Sport It dealer starts out as a home-based entrepreneur. Dealers market their sporting goods to individuals as well as clubs and leagues. Consumers can purchase anything from a bow and arrow, to golf clubs, to baseball team uniforms, jackets, hats, and gloves. Customers choose most of their merchandise from catalogs, but specially designed products are available as well. Sport It dealers market merchandise from more than 128 national companies, including Wilson, Converse, MacGregor, Coleman, Rawlings, and Spalding. Along with these national brand-name products, Sport It dealers also market their own private label sports products.

The core of the Sport It network revolves around the company's unique relationship with the national manufacturers. Sport It dealers work directly with the manufacturers in the placement and delivery of orders. This process cuts out the middleman and allows dealers to provide prompt and economical service to customers.

An initial investment of $2,500 purchases a Sport It dealership. The company has sponsored an investment rebate program that encourages entrepreneurs to act quickly when buying a dealership. Under this program, Sport It reduces the initial investment to $1,500 if a dealer purchases a nonexclusive territory within a certain time period. Dealers who participate in this program also are eligible to receive a rebate for the remaining $1,000 after they earn $15,000 in sales. Those who do not take part in the rebate program pay $2,500 up front.

For those who choose the rebate program, the dealership contract is effective for three years. Dealers who choose to pay the full $2,500 receive a five-year contract. Sport It assigns only nonexclusive territories, but the company protects dealers who are operating efficiently and profitably.

Most Sport It dealers begin as part-time entrepreneurs. Full-time dealers can choose to market the products through various methods. Some maintain their home-office status and sell the sporting goods through mail-order, direct sales programs, and fund-raising campaigns. Others choose to establish a catalog or full-service retail store. Sport It does not allow dealers to use the Sport It name as part of their business name. Dealers do pay a $25 monthly service charge to Sport It for the company's network and support services.

Sport It dealers do not need to attend any formal training workshop. The company provides all dealers with detailed manuals and video and audio training tapes. The instructional material explains how the Sport It network works and provides dealers with concrete marketing techniques. The company also publishes regular newsletters and sponsors conventions, seminars, and marketing workshops. Sport It maintains a toll-free hot line for dealers, and Sport It personnel are available to assist dealers whenever needed.

Future Outlook

Sport It's manufacturer network provides dealers with high-quality, brand-name merchandise. This system is unique because the manufacturers have agreed to work with home-based entrepreneurs, which is not a widely accepted practice among the larger sporting goods manufacturers. This network gives Sport It dealers an advantage over competition that needs to establish retail stores in order to sell these nationally recognized labels.

Contact Information

Address: 4196 Corporate Square, Naples, Florida 33942
Telephone: 1-800-762-6869
Contact person: Ron C. Eastman, president

THE WORLD ROBOTIC BOXING ASSOCIATION

Initial investment: $9,500 minimum for territory of 1 million people. (Add $1,000 for each 1 million additional people; some states are discounted if population does not reach 1 million.)
Total investment: $9,500 minimum plus $495 annual fee
Ongoing fees: None
Right to use trademark and logo: Yes

Expansion History
Company operating since: 1986
Offering dealerships since: 1986
Number of dealers: 120

Industry Focus

Robotic boxing provides organized activities at school social functions as well as public taverns, charity events, and fund-raisers.

Company Advantages

The World Robotic Boxing Association has attracted more than just bar owners and patrons with its mobile "boxing fights." The company has marketed itself successfully to charity organizations, colleges and universities, military installations, and corporations.

Organized tournaments can be established for the robotic matches. The home office will provide promotion for new dealers in their exclusive areas. Robotic dealers can sponsor tournaments that ensure long-term customer participation.

Established in 1986, the World Robotic Boxing Association now has more than 120 "Rocky-Bot" dealers throughout the United States that feature hand-controlled robots competing in 30-second, three-round matches.

Organizations and companies pay Rocky-Bot dealers a minimum of $350 for an evening at ringside. Corporations guarantee dealers a $750 contracting fee, and schools pay as high as $1,200. In return, dealers manage the robotic boxing event and supply all necessary equipment, including the four-by-six-foot portable ring and the two robotic figures. Individual customers pay the dealers $3 to sit at the controls of these robots. The goal of each player is to push the opponent robot's head off its shoulders. This feat wins the fight and advances the contestant in tournament action.

In this business opportunity, dealers perform many duties. They act as masters of ceremonies, announcing the Rocky-Bot matches and introducing the contestants. They conduct corner-side interviews with the Rocky-Bot players and supporters. The dealers encourage participation by spectators, and they award trophies and prizes to all winners. Depending on the event, dealers can also act as referees, but most hire and train referees for the matches.

Dealers can either focus on individual boxing bouts or can establish long-term league and tournament bouts. As business volume grows and customer interest increases, dealers may take on a managerial role and hire masters of ceremonies to cover the boxing matches.

An initial investment of $9,500 entitles a licensee to an exclusive territory that includes 1 million people. The fee also purchases all equipment, inventory, and promotional supplies needed to conduct the robotic contests effectively. The World Robotic Boxing Association charges no royalty fees, but there is an annual renewal fee of $495 to maintain an exclusive territory.

The World Robotic Boxing Association requires its dealers to attend a two-day training workshop that focuses on marketing the boxing matches and managing the tournaments. The company also supplies dealers with manuals and videotapes that outline the association's methods of operation. Dealers receive post-training support in the form of seminars and newsletters that update contests and other promotional ideas.

Future Outlook

Tavern owners are under pressure from government and consumer groups to downplay alcohol advertising. An organized sporting event that encourages participation can attract many customers. Participants need no special skills or strengths, and the bouts are considered safe, a feature that has drawn other customers, such as school and charity organizations.

This business needs a great deal of marketing and promotion. Dealers must be able to knock on doors and do demonstrations to promote this game. The company makes no earnings claims, and dealers are not required to hold a minimum number of bouts. Most fights take place in the evening, which allows dealers to start this venture as a part-time opportunity.

Contact Information
Address: 183 N. Main Street, Cumberland, Iowa 50843
Telephone: 1-712-774-2577
Contact person: Keith Namanny, president

HOME IMPROVEMENT/CONSTRUCTION

AMERIBRITE SYSTEMS, INC.

Initial investment: $3,975 to $9,975
Total investment: $3,975 to $9,975
Ongoing fees: None
Right to use trademark and logo: No

Expansion History
Company operating since: 1979
Offering dealerships since: 1986
Number of dealers: 200+

Industry Focus
This company is active in ceramic tile and grout restoration. Indirect competition comes from companies that paint or dye tile to hide dirt and mildew.

Company Advantages
Ameribrite Systems has launched a series of products that attract residential and commercial customers. The company offers two dealership packages. One is for those who want to start part time and build their business gradually, and the other is for those who want to make a full-time commitment right away.

Ceramic tile is durable, but the buildup of mildew or dirt in the grout can cause the tile to erode. Ameribrite Systems of Deerfield, Beach, Florida, uses its own patented cleaning and polishing products to remove these unsanitary menaces from counters, walls, and floors.

Established in 1979, Ameribrite consists of more than 200 dealers worldwide. Dealers determine the type of business they wish to build. Some pay the minimal investment of $3,975, which purchases equipment and materials needed to restore residential floors and bathrooms. Other dealers elect to purchase a multiuse cleaning system for $9,975, which includes additional equipment and cleaners to restore ceramic tile as well as brass, copper, fiberglass, cement, stainless steel, aluminum, and other materials. Those who purchase the larger system target commercial accounts, such as hotels, hospitals, restaurants, and retail stores.

Ameribrite uses manuals and videos to train dealers in the company's methods and products. Training seminars are offered at the home office for dealers who want personal instruction. Ameribrite has few rules for dealers. There is no formal agreement between the company and dealer, and no exclusive dealership areas are assigned. Ameribrite eventually hopes to build a network of dealers who will work with each other to develop cooperative advertising campaigns and job referral services.

Dealers are not authorized to use Ameribrite's various trademarks or logos, and they cannot depict themselves as employees of Ameribrite. However, they are permitted to say they are independent contractors for Ameribrite products. The company will supply each dealer with brochures, sales aids, and a television commercial developed for the geographical area where a dealer will operate. Ameribrite expects dealers to promote their businesses through telemarketing and direct mail campaigns.

The company charges no ongoing royalty or advertising fees, but dealers purchase all cleaning material products from Ameribrite.

Future Outlook

Ameribrite holds at least seven patents on restoration products that safely clean and restore many surfaces for less than 25 percent of what it would cost to replace the damaged floors or walls. The company gives dealers ample freedom to experiment with their business and build it at a comfortable pace.

Ameribrite will consult with dealers at their request at no charge. This business needs promotion and visibility in order to succeed.

Contact Information

Address: 180 E. Hillsboro Boulevard, Deerfield Beach, Florida 33441

Telephone: 1-305-481-2929

Contact person: Ray Hedin, president

CLOSET CLASSICS

(Laminations, Inc.)

Initial investment: $5,000 to $20,000

Total investment: $5,000 to $20,000

Ongoing fees: Minimum inventory purchase of $10,000 every 90 days

Right to use trademark and logo: Yes

Expansion History

Company operating since: 1987

Offering dealerships since: 1987

Number of dealers: 95

Industry Focus

Adequate closet space is one of the most important features in a home. Consumers look for practical and convenient ways to store their clothes and belongings.

The arrival of closet organizer systems gave consumers the opportunity to expand storage space without demolishing walls and reducing room size.

Company Advantages

Laminations, Inc., manufactures all Closet Classics components at its 97,000-square-foot facility in Holland, Michigan.

The company also supplies dealers with point-of-purchase advertising displays plus wholesalers and home builders with Easy Track self-installed closet systems.

Laminations maintains ongoing support for dealers and supplies free advertising and promotional material.

• • •

The Closet Classics dealers range from small, one-person operators to million-dollar-sales companies that employ a professional sales staff and installation crew. The size of the dealers may vary, but their goal does not. All dealers are to show, market, design, and install closet organizer systems to both residential and commercial customers.

Laminations manufactures and supplies dealers with all the systems and ancillary hardware. Most dealers lease commercial showroom and warehouse space in an industrial park or similar setting. Some also participate in home shows, mall demonstrations, or other specialty marketing programs to promote the Closet Classics systems.

Customers can select Closet Classics systems in white, almond, oak, pickled vinyl laminates, or cherry veneers with solid cherry doors. Dealers or their sales representatives go to the customers and evaluate their closet needs. The dealer then designs a storage system that meets the customer's specifications and budget.

Closet Classics systems range from the simple to the elaborate walk-in storage facility. Laminations also manufactures floor units for workshop or garage areas and in-home computer and office spaces. In addition to their residential customers, dealers cater to commercial clients who need special storage facilities for equipment or office supplies. Retail prices start from $95 and go up to $1,000. Laminations allows dealers to set their own prices, and the company makes no formal earnings claims. It does maintain that dealers can potentially make up to a 200 percent profit on closet system installations.

An initial investment of $5,000 purchases the mandatory minimum inventory that Laminations expects a dealer to carry. This inventory includes various-size doors and hanging vertical panels, support rails, brackets, and shelves, plus drawer fronts and bottoms. The company estimates that dealers will need an additional $15,000 to cover the costs of leasing, working capital, insurance, and other start-up expenses. Dealers are required to purchase from Laminations at least $10,000 in inventory every 90 days.

Laminations requires dealers to complete a mandatory training workshop that is held either at the dealer's site or the company's headquarters in Michigan. Dealers learn to design and install the various closet systems, plus they receive instruction in marketing and business management. As part of the company's ongoing support program, Laminations provides dealers with color advertising brochures and flyers at no charge. Dealers participate in co-op advertising campaigns, and Laminations initiates and passes on to dealers model home demonstrations, creative marketing programs, and new product development.

Future Outlook

Laminations, Inc., is also a dealer in the plastic and laminations industry. Dealers know who made their products, and the company maintains strict quality production controls.

Laminations does allow dealers flexibility in business operation, but it retains enough control to ensure dealer loyalty and reliability. Closet Classics dealers can sell only Laminations Closet systems, but they are allowed to sell competing accessory items.

Contact Information
Address: 3311 Laminations Drive, Holland, Michigan 49424
Telephone: 1-800-562-4257 or 1-616-399-3311
Contact person: Barry Walburg, director of marketing

EAGLE'S NEST HOMES, INC.

Initial investment: $25,000 to $125,000
Total investment: $25,000 to $125,000 plus interior furnishings and improvements
Ongoing fees: None
Right to use trademark and logo: Yes

Expansion History
Company operating since: 1983
Offering dealerships since: 1983
Number of dealers: Not available

Industry Focus

Factory-built housing accounts for more than 50 percent of new construction. During the 1990s, this percentage is expected to increase as the costs of on-site, traditional construction skyrocket.

Factory-built homes can be erected within four to five days. The houses are built in a factory and constructed to withstand the stress of relocation to a customer's lot.

Company Advantages

Eagle's Nest Homes, Inc., was one of the first entrants into the factory-built housing industry. The company offers consumers a selection of ten models that exceed building industry standards for materials and energy conservation.

Eagle's Nest Homes come with built-in computer systems that contain burglar, fire, and medical emergency alarm systems. Upgrades in the computer system, such as electronic banking and automatic controls for exterior and interior lighting, can also be added.

Eagle's Nest Homes, Inc., of Canton, Georgia, is one company that has contributed greatly to the growth of the factory-manufactured homes industry. Established in 1983, Eagle's Nest Homes uses its dealers across the country to market its selection of ten houses that range in size from 800 square feet to 4,000 square feet and come in one- and two-story models.

Eagle's Nest dealers are customers first. After they have purchased a home, customers can apply to Eagle's Nest to become dealers. Dealers do not need any experience in either construction or real estate sales, but they do need to have a firsthand knowledge of the Eagle's Nest product. Eagle's Nest promises delivery of the materials within 30 to 60 days. It will construct the house for the customer or deliver it in shell or unfinished form. Prices for the houses range from $25,000 to $125,000, depending on the model and the completion stage. Some dealers live in the house and use it as a showcase in their local communities. Others build the houses as "spec homes" or model homes, and live elsewhere. Whichever approach, dealers market the homes most effectively through real estate brokers. Dealers and brokers can negotiate a commission on the sale of one or more homes. The broker advertises the home, shows it to buyers, and completes all paperwork. As with normal real estate transactions, the broker is paid at the time of settlement.

Before house construction begins, dealers must secure a mortgage for the home as well as ground and all necessary building permits. Eagle's Nest requires a $5,000 down payment before it delivers the home to a dealer. No other money is due until the dealer takes possession of the home. Since there are different real estate prices in different areas of the country, Eagle's Nest allows dealers to set their own sales prices and their own profit margins. Other costs that dealers should take into consideration are legal, engineering, and contractor fees.

Eagle's Nest requests that all dealers attend a two-day seminar at the home office in Georgia. The workshop teaches dealers how to complete construction using local builders and contractors. The training seminar also focuses on obtaining mortgages and financing for projects and the correct ways to shop for and contract a realtor.

Eagle's Nest provides dealers ongoing engineering support for future projects. The company also issues brochures, videos, and other promotional materials to dealers. Dealers are invited to advanced seminars and workshops.

Future Outlook

Eagle's Nest Homes, Inc., delivers quality-built homes at affordable prices. In many parts of the country, new-home construction is out of the reach of many consumers, and companies such as Eagle's Nest make home ownership a possibility.

Consumers need to become versed in purchasing or leasing land when taking on this business opportunity. Eagle's Nest recommends using a well-established real estate broker to assist in the search for land and potential buyers. It would be well worth Eagle's Nest dealers' time to investigate the housing and real estate market in their area and evaluate the demand for factory-made housing.

Contact Information

Address: 5979 Highway 20 East, Canton, Georgia 30114
Telephone: 1-404-479-9700
Contact person: Greg Roubaud, president

NATIONAL SUPAFLU SYSTEMS, INC.

Initial investment: $2,500
Total investment: $20,000
Ongoing fees: None
Right to use trademark and logo: Yes

Expansion History
Company operating since: 1980
Offering dealerships since: 1980
Number of dealers: 91

Industry Focus
Chimney maintenance can prevent destructive fires. Home owners are often unaware of the dangers that exist in faulty chimney flues.

Chimney relining can be marketed to both consumers and insurance professionals directly. The relining systems can vary tremendously from company to company, and consumers need to investigate the various procedures.

Company Advantages
National Supaflu Systems uses a cast-in-place technique that pumps cementitious chimney relining material into the flue without major construction or demolition work. The cast material was developed in Great Britain and has enjoyed a 15-year successful track record there. Supaflu introduced the chimney relining system in the United States in 1980.

Supaflu provides a complete turnkey operation for dealers and maintains an ample support system.

A faulty or deteriorating chimney can lead to disaster. National Supaflu Systems, Inc., of Walton, New York, relines chimney flues before they have a chance to cause fire and catastrophe. The cementlike product forms a weather- and temperature-resistant cast material that seals leaks and cracks in chimneys.

National Supaflu markets its service to homeowners, insurance professionals, masons, entrepreneurs, historical preservation organizations, and fire experts through a network of 91 dealers throughout the United States and Canada.

The responsibilities of the dealers vary. Initially, most dealers handle all aspects of the dealership, from chimney evaluation to marketing. As business grows, dealers tend to take on a more managerial role, marketing the Supaflu service, scheduling chimney relining contracts, and contacting new customers.

As part of the contract with their customers, dealers perform chimney inspections to determine if any fire hazards exist. Before installing any relining material, dealers clean and brace chimneys and then insert an inflatable tube into the flue. The tube acts as a guide for the cementitious material that is pumped into the chimney. The material takes less than a day to set and dry, and the Supaflu process usually requires no demolition or reconstruction of chimney walls.

For an investment ranging from $2,500 to $20,000, National Supaflu dealers purchase the rights to an exclusive territory based on household populations. In addition, the fee buys all equipment and supplies needed to run the chimney relining service efficiently, including a variety of marketing materials and operation manuals. Dealers are free to use the Supaflu trademarks and logos. As part of the dealership contract, dealers enter into a national cooperative advertising campaign, plus the company's national referral network that automatically distributes customer requests to local dealers. National Supaflu charges no royalty or ongoing fees, and the company does not require dealers to establish offices or retail locations. Dealers need only a small space to operate the business effectively, and some dealers work out of their homes until they establish a customer base.

National Supaflu insists dealers attend a training seminar at the home office in Walton, New York. The workshop certifies dealers in the Supaflu process and covers in detail all aspects of the relining business, from marketing to installation. National Supaflu teaches dealers about the construction of chimneys and how to identify hazards.

National Supaflu offers dealers post-training support with regular seminars, workshops, and conventions. The company's 20-year guarantee on the relining product also helps market the system. National Supaflu maintains a toll-free hot line for dealers in need of assistance, and in-field technical support is available from the company's certified engineering staff. Supaflu also publishes seasonal newsletters for its dealers. The newsletters update technical and marketing strategies and allow dealers to share experiences and concerns with each other.

Future Outlook

National Supaflu's guarantee reflects this company's commitment to quality. The dealer support system is the backbone of National Supaflu, and the company's success is dependent on its dealers' success.

Dealers must wear many hats, including consumer educator. Insurance and fire professionals comprehend the value of the Supaflu service, but few homeowners know the hazards that lurk inside their chimney flues. Supaflu dealers need to reach the consumer before tragedy strikes. Preventive maintenance can open up a wide market for the Supaflu dealer.

Contact Information

Address: P.O. Box 89, Walton Industrial Park, Walton, New York 13856
Telephone: 1-800-788-7636 or 1-607-865-7202
Contact person: Wayne M. Hubbard

KEEPSAKE, NOVELTY, AND GIFT ITEMS

SENTI-METAL BABY SHOE BRONZING CO.

Initial investment: $99.95 starter kit
Total investment: $200

Ongoing fees: None
Right to use trademark and logo: Yes

Expansion History
Company operating since: 1934
Offering Senti-Metal business opportunities since: Not available
Number of Senti-Metal independent contractors: 450+

Industry Focus
  Bronzed baby shoes have become a staple in the baby gift and
novelty industry.

Company Advantages
  Senti-Metal is one of the oldest bronze baby shoe companies in
the world today. The company's origins are steeped in family tradition. The company guarantees all its work and does make potential earnings claims to its independent contractors.

  New parents look for ways to recall the precious moments of
their baby's first years. Senti-Metal Baby Shoe Bronzing Company
allows parents to capture at least one of these moments with a
process that preserves baby shoes, rattles, pacifiers, and other objects
in bronze or pewter. Established in 1934, the Columbus, Ohio-
based company is a family-owned business that has grown from a
part-time enterprise to a manufacturing company with a 44,000-
square-foot plant and 100 staff craftsmen. The company markets
its products through a network of 450 independent sales agents
throughout the country.
  Independent contractors, or "keepsake consultants," are the main
avenue of revenue for the company. Consultants work through
retailers to attract consumers to the bronzing service. For a small
fee, retailers place the Senti-Metal bronze samples on store counters
in the baby and children's departments. The display sample contains
inquiry cards that customers can fill out and leave with the retailer.
Keepsake consultants collect the cards and follow up with the customer directly.
  A $99.95 initial investment purchases a starter kit that contains

four retail store displays, brochures, and other bronze and pewter samples. Most consultants invest an additional $100 and purchase extra display samples to increase their marketing area. The keepsake consultant's primary role is that of order taker. The company provides each consultant with a full sales kit and a tested 15-minute sales presentation. If a customer opts for the service, the consultant takes the shoe or object and sends it to the manufacturing plant. All bronzing and pewter preservation work is completed at the plant within four to six weeks and then mailed back to the customer directly.

Senti-Metal recommends but does not dictate retail prices to its consultants. The company works on a wholesale basis with each contractor, and it is each contractor's responsibility to establish the profit margin. On the average, sales total $120 per item, which is approximately a 100 percent markup on the cost of bronzing or pewter service.

Most keepsake consultants begin this venture on a part-time basis and gradually build to a full-time commitment. Although retailers are the primary way to reach customers, consultants also attend craft shows, flea markets, and church bazaars.

Senti-Metal contractors do not have to attend any training classes, but they do receive a detailed sales manual that focuses on the presentation to the customer. The company is available for telephone support and encourages contractors to call with questions.

Future Outlook

New parents are eager customers for this service. As long as there are babies, this novelty service has the chance to thrive. This opportunity for investment attracts the entrepreneur who does not want to quit a secure job initially, and the company encourages part-time commitment.

Contact Information
Address: 1919 Memory Lane, Columbus, Ohio 43209
Telephone: 1-800-323-9718 or 1-614-252-0353
Contact person: Reid Romer

TOMORROW'S TREASURES

Initial investment: $100 sales kit deposit
Total investment: $1,100 including working capital
Ongoing fees: None
Right to use trademark and logo: Yes

Expansion History
Company operating since: 1980
Offering dealerships since: 1980
Number of dealers: 50+

Industry Focus
Photographs are an important part of everyday life. They capture not only significant events but daily life events as well.

Consumers want to see that a company has established photographic service credentials before they ship their prized negatives through the mail.

Company Advantages
Tomorrow's Treasures has a 12-year history in the photographic service industries. The company uses only state-of-the-art technology to complete its photographic services.

Tomorrow's Treasures maintains a computer linkup with Eastman Kodak's quality-control system facility in Rochester, New York. The computer link provides constant monitoring of Tomorrow's Treasures' photofinishing process.

Tomorrow's Treasures offers a variety of photographic services, from enlargements to restoration services. Dealers also offer customers a selection of keepsake gift items, which are marketed through catalogs.

Established in 1980, Tomorrow's Treasures is a full-service company that uses state-of-the-art equipment to enlarge, duplicate, improve, and restore photographs. The company completes all photographic services at its laboratory facility in Maryland. As an added service, Tomorrow's Treasures also sells special packaging programs, such as wedding albums and keepsake gift items. The company markets its services through more than 50 dealers.

Dealers are primarily salespersons. Their goal is to expose the consumer to the variety of photographic packages Tomorrow's Treasures offers and encourage a long-term relationship with the company. Dealers sell an introductory kit that contains colorful catalogs, a 35-mm camera, photographic samples, customer endorsements, and discount copies for all services offered by Tomorrow's Treasures. Customers order their specialized photographic services directly through the Maryland laboratory using the coupons and special promotions. Customers who place three or more orders receive a revolving credit card from Tomorrow's Treasures that entitles them to purchase at wholesale prices a variety of personal and household keepsake items.

Dealers receive commissions only on the kit's initial purchase. They do not receive commissions on any photographic order or any keepsake items. Tomorrow's Treasures refunds the $100 kit fee to all dealers who sell more than ten kits.

Those who choose to participate in the Tomorrow's Treasures' program receive their own kit from the company. They can use the kit to participate in Tomorrow's Treasures' services and promotions, or they can market the service to other consumers using the kit as a sales tool. Those who choose to market the kit to other consumers do so through direct mail campaigns, telemarketing, and person-to-person sales methods.

Dealers can build their commission base by encouraging other consumers to market the kits as well. As more consumers become dealers, dealers expand their role and become field dealers, district dealers, and finally regional dealers. Each step in the dealership ladder earns an override on all sales completed by dealers on the lower rungs of the ladder.

Tomorrow's Treasures charges no ongoing royalty fee, and the company provides telephone and field training especially in the area of sales presentations. The company also holds dealer meetings for all participating in the program, but these sessions are optional.

Future Outlook

Tomorrow's Treasures encourages part-time dealerships. The company's four-tier dealership ladder allows customers to try their hand at personal sales. Customers who do not want to sell the introduction kits still receive bonuses and discounts on all Tomorrow's Treasures photographic services.

Dealers must be willing to knock on doors to find a large target market. Consumers who appreciate the costs of special photographic services will not consider the $100 fee out of line. Other consumers may, and dealers must be able to educate potential customers on the advantages of this program.

Contact Information

Address: 111 N. Glassboro Road, Woodbury Heights, New Jersey 08097

Telephone: 1-800-899-5656 or 1-609-468-5656

Contact person: George W. Braun

UNITED BRONZE, INC.

Initial investment: $369.95 to $799.95
Total investment: $369.95 to $799.95
Ongoing fees: None
Right to use trademark and logo: None

Expansion History
Company operating since: 1977
Offering dealerships since: 1977
Number of dealers: 600

Industry Focus

There has been a strong demand for bronzed baby items since the first companies began offering these products back in the 1930s.

Mementos that can be passed from generation to generation have always attracted a large number of consumers. Consumers think of these keepsakes as sentimental investments.

Company Advantages

United Bronze dealerships are full-service businesses. Dealers are responsible for marketing and sales as well as bronzing the keepsake items.

Dealers have a choice of three investment packages. They can elect to start on a part-time basis with the most economical of introduction kits and gradually expand to a full-time business commitment that requires more equipment and materials.

The company stands behind its product and offers lifetime guarantees on all bronzing or preservation work completed by dealers.

Based on Rumford, Rhode Island, United Bronze, Inc., uses an exclusive metalcraft system that airbrushes liquefied bronze, porcelain, pewter, and copper finishes to children's accessory items and adult novelty items such as sports equipment, pet collars, and plastic statues. Founded in 1977, United Bronze markets its preservation process through a network of more than 600 dealers throughout the United States.

United Bronze dealers are salespersons, promotion specialists, bronzing technicians, and customer service representatives. Dealers do not have to possess any special background for this opportunity, and United Bronze supplies them with detailed marketing plans and strategies. Dealers are free to develop their own sales strategies, and the company encourages the use of direct mail and telemarketing campaigns, customer referral discount promotions, cooperative sales promotions with retail stores, and person-to-person sales.

It is the dealer's responsibility to apply the one-step metalcraft process to customers' keepsake items. United Bronze does not expect dealers to rent a professional workshop. The equipment takes up only a small amount of space, and most dealers use a section of a room in their homes as their workshop area.

For an investment ranging from $369.95 to $799.95, entrepreneurs receive an introductory kit containing all equipment and inventory needed to operate the dealership properly, including bronzing mixtures, novelty picture frames and wall mounts, and operation manuals. The kits differ in the amount of inventory and the type of equipment. The higher-priced Deluxe Master Bronzing Shop Kit contains both an airbrush compressor and a tabletop spray booth. These tools are not needed to run the business effectively, but they do make the work easier and less time-consuming.

United Bronze encourages entrepreneurs to invest what they can and upgrade their kits as business grows. United Bronze charges no royalty or ongoing fees. Dealers reorder inventory and bronzing materials from the company. United Bronze offers those dealers who purchase the $799.95 deluxe kit a full rebate when they reorder $2,000 in supplies. There is no time limit on reaching this goal.

The average cost to the dealer for bronzing ranges between $1 and $3. Depending on the object or order, customers pay between $39.95 and $59.95 for one unmounted bronzed object.

Dealers can start part time or full time. Many start with the smaller kits and add more equipment and inventory as their sales increase. For many dealers, their part-time commitments evolve into full-time businesses. Some hire other salespeople to contact customers and make presentations. Others prefer to sell, and hire one or two people to complete the bronzing work.

United Bronze requires no formal training of its dealers. The company supplies all instructions and operation manuals, and each dealer is required to study these materials. The company welcomes questions from dealers and maintains telephone contact.

Future Outlook

United Bronze offers a unique preservation system that allows dealers to complete the bronzing order themselves. The company has had a great deal of success in the novelty industry. Its plans to attract other customers besides the baby shoe market has helped the company's expansion over the last decade.

Contact Information
Address: P.O. Box 4799, Rumford, Rhode Island 02916
Telephone: 1-401-434-7312
Contact person: Order department

Multilevel Marketing, Distributorships, and Direct Sales Programs

ADVERTISING AND PROMOTION

DIRECT MAIL USA

Initial investment: $6,600
Total investment: $8,000 to $10,000
Ongoing fees: None
Right to use trademark and logo: Yes

Expansion History
Operating since: Not available
Offering distributorships since: Not available
Number of distributorships: Not available

Industry Focus
More than 72 percent of all coupons redeemed come from direct mail advertising campaigns. Direct mail advertising is the fastest-growing form of media advertising, and the industry has witnessed a 160 percent growth spurt in the last ten years.

More than 89 percent of households in the United States use discount coupons on a regular basis.

Company Advantages
Direct Mail USA is a turnkey operation. Distributors work with the home office to design and mail direct mail flyers and packages.

Direct Mail USA is primarily a sales business. All sales calls are completed either on the telephone or in person.

Direct Mail USA distributors contract with small and large businesses to complete direct mail campaigns in the customer's immediate service area. As licensees, distributors guarantee all phases of the mail campaign, from advertisement design, copy, and layout, to the actual mailing of the brochures or coupons themselves.

An initial investment of $6,600 purchases the right to an exclusive territory based on a residential population of 250,000 people. Distributors purchase the territory for three years, and Direct Mail USA allows distributors to expand their areas at no additional charge. In addition, Direct Mail USA will mail to 5,000 retail and service businesses in a distributor's area the distributor's name, business card, business reply card, and brochure. Distributors also receive a mailing map of their territories and a distributor supply list containing marketing brochures, stationery, complementary novelty items for customers, and an assortment of forms. Lodging costs for a required four- to five-day training seminar are also included in the initial fee, but airfare to the workshop in Eugene, Oregon, is not. The class teaches distributors sales techniques and instructs them in bookkeeping, management, and all advertising services offered by Direct Mail USA. Distributors should expect to spend an additional $1,200 on a fax machine, copier, office equipment, and a telephone hookup.

Direct Mail USA charges no ongoing royalty fees, but the company does charge distributors for printing and graphic art services supplied as part of the distributorship contract. Distributors do not need to be advertising or art experts, but they should be able to sell advertising space.

Future Outlook

Direct mail is an effective means of advertising, but the industry contains a great deal of competition, especially from franchise companies. Direct Mail USA may have an advantage in that it charges no royalty or franchise fees. The company makes money in its printing and graphics services ordered by distributors.

Contact Information

Address: 108 Main Street, New Paltz, New York 12561
Telephone: 1-800-634-2718 or 1-914-255-0547
Contact person: Stanley Kowalik

BOOKS AND EDUCATIONAL MATERIALS

USBORNE BOOKS AT HOME

Initial investment: $159.95
Total investment: $159.95
Ongoing fees: None
Right to use trademark and logo: None

Expansion History
Company operating since: 1989
Offering business opportunities since: 1989
Number of book consultants: 690

Industry Focus
Parents seek out books that interest and educate children. More and more consumers are seeking to purchase educational gifts for children.

Schools and parents are placing more emphasis on nurturing children's interest in reading. Schools encourage parents to read with children on a daily basis.

Company Advantages
Usborne Books at Home has only a three-year track record behind it, but already the company has 690 consultants throughout the United States.

The company sells only Usborne books. Usborne has been an internationally recognized publisher of children's stories, puzzles, and learning books for more than 20 years.

In 1992 Usborne Books at Home instituted a new bonus and rebate incentive program, which boosted company sales almost 170 percent.

. . .

Few possessions are as valuable as books. Usborne Books at Home designed its direct sales program around this belief. An Usborne consultant's main function is to schedule in-home parties or direct sales demonstrations. During these parties, consumers can view a sample of 50 books relating to education, art, science, crafts, and entertainment. The books are for children of all ages, and they range in price from $2.95 to $21.95.

Usborne Books at Home is a multilevel marketing opportunity. The first step on the ladder is that of consultant. For an investment of $159.95, consultants receive an introductory kit that contains samples, a listing of all Usborne products, and a training manual.

Consultants are independent contractors, and they can operate their business on a part-time or full-time basis. Usborne grants a $50 rebate to all consultants who sell more than $1,200 during their first 12 weeks of operation. Consultants who earn more than $2,500 in sales during this period receive the entire initial investment back. Usborne pays consultants a 25 percent commission on all books sold, and the company estimates sales of the average home party to range from $235 to $400. Usborne also awards bonuses and incentive prizes to consultants who reach certain sales milestones.

As consultants become more comfortable in their product line, they can recruit other entrepreneurs to become consultants as well. Usborne promotes consultants to supervisors after they have recruited five consultants and earned a minimum of $1,500 during one month of the most recent quarter in which they operated. Supervisors receive the customary 25 percent on all books they sell directly plus a 10 percent commission on any books sold by their recruits. As supervisors, they are also entitled to other bonus packages, contests, and incentive programs.

Neither consultants nor supervisors need office space or special telephone lines. All scheduling appointments can be accomplished from home, and Usborne encourages consultants to explore as many marketing avenues as possible. Consultants work well through nursery school and elementary school contacts as well as extracurricular clubs and church organizations. Usborne does not require consultants to attend any formal training seminars, but the company does assign a supervisor to each consultant as a local support system. Usborne also publishes newsletters and introduces new sales and bonus programs to bolster consultant activity. The Usborne home office is available for telephone consultation and encourages consultants to maintain regular contact.

Future Outlook

Usborne Books at Home experienced a dramatic increase in sales during 1992. The company credits its new incentive and bonus programs for the increased activity among its consultants. Usborne Books are recognized throughout the United States, so consultants do not have to offer proof of product quality.

Contact Information
Address: 10302 E. 55th Place, Tulsa, Oklahoma 74146
Telephone: 1-800-331-4418 or 1-918-622-4522
Contact person: Kathy Plecinski

BUSINESS SERVICES

BUTLER LEARNING SYSTEMS, INC.

Initial investment: $500
Total investment: $10,000
Ongoing fees: None
Right to use trademark and logo: Yes

Expansion History
Operating since: 1959
Offering distributorships since: 1980
Number of distributors: 45

Industry Focus

Sales techniques have changed drastically in recent years. Companies need to focus attention on training programs if they want to survive and prosper in the 1990s.

Company Advantages

Butler Learning Systems has been in existence more than 30 years, and the company has developed sales programs to meet the needs of businesses in different economic times.

Butler offers clients more than 30 sales and management training programs.

Established in 1959 by Harvard Business School graduate Don Butler, Butler Learning Systems has developed into a leading sales and management consultant company that includes 45 distributors throughout the United States.

A Butler Learning Systems distributor is a consultant to both managers and sales professionals. The distributor's main role is to contract companies and corporations to hold one or more of Butler's 30 management and sales training seminars. The seminars are a combination of state-of-the-art technology with audio and visual displays and group dynamics consisting of employee discussions and role playing. All seminars are tailored to the customer's personnel and financial needs, and distributors conduct extensive in-field research to determine the best program for a client.

Butler distributors run the seminars lasting from one to four days. The prices range from $95 to $3,000 per person or more, depending on the length of the program and materials used. As part of the initial customer contract, distributors also provide postseminar support through updated research and progress reports on both management and sales personnel.

An initial investment of $500 purchases a Butler Learning Systems distributorship. Butler grants distributors the right to use the company trademark, logo, and seminar materials. By contract, distributors must use only Butler workbooks and enrollment materials, and they must identify themselves as independent entrepreneurs for Butler—not employees. Butler estimates that distributors will need a total investment of $10,000 for training, promotion, and marketing. The $10,000 also includes other start-up expenses, such as office equipment and seminar enrollment materials, which Butler sells to distributors at a 40 to 50 percent discount.

Distributors have the option of using Butler's audiovisual materials in their seminars instead of workbooks and other written materials. For these seminars, Butler charges distributors a 10 percent royalty on all collected fees, and it is the distributor's responsibility to keep track of these fees.

Butler distributors are required to attend a one-week training course at the company's headquarters in Dayton, Ohio. Butler teaches distributors presentation and telemarketing skills to attract companies and corporations to the seminars. Butler also thoroughly trains each distributor in the various programs, and company representatives are available to help distributors during initial sales presentations and seminars. The company sponsors weekend training workshops regularly during the year and participates in national advertising and promotional campaigns.

Future Outlook

Don Butler perfected his seminar skills and programs over a 21-year period before he offered distributorships to independent business persons. Butler has a long list of clients, and he offers a variety of programs to attract many types of companies.

Distributors must be professional and comfortable in the corporate environment, and they must be able to communicate effectively.

Contact Information
Address: 1325 W. Dorothy Lane, Dayton, Ohio 45409
Telephone: 1-513-298-7462
Contact person: Don Butler

COLORFAST MARKETING SYSTEMS, INC.

Initial investment: $200
Total investment: $200 plus working capital
Ongoing fees: None
Right to use trademark and logo: Yes

Expansion History
Company operating since: 1986
Offering dealerships since: 1987
Number of dealers: 3,500

Industry Focus
Color-photograph business cards and promotional materials can add status and recognition to a company's image.

Company Advantages
Most photography and printing work is completed in the company's lab in California. The in-house processing reduces manufacturing costs, which in turn reduces distributor costs.

Colorfast Marketing Systems of Chatsworth, California, offers color-photograph business cards, magnets, greeting cards, laminated luggage tags, and other personalized promotional material.

A Colorfast distributor is foremost a salesperson. Person-to-person sales are the primary route to success, and distributors must be willing to knock on doors to win customer support.

For an initial fee of $200, Colorfast distributors purchase a starter kit that contains Promokard, the company's exclusive color-photograph business card, brochure samples, and other Colorfast products. Distributors are allowed to use the Colorfast logo in their sales presentations, and they can represent themselves as independent agents for the company. It is not mandatory that distributors take photographs for their clients. Colorfast can make company cards from already existing negatives or photographs supplied by the customer. The company does recommend that distributors have a 35-mm camera to service clients who do not have photographs available.

As independent entrepreneurs, Colorfast distributors set their own retail prices for the photographic cards and materials. The company recommends that distributors maintain a 30 to 100 percent profit margin, depending on the type and volume of the order. The company does not enforce any method of operation, as long as high-quality products and services are provided. Colorfast encourages distributors to begin on a part-time basis until they feel ready to expand their business. Distributors do not have to open a professional office, and most elect to run their distributorships as home-based operations.

Colorfast does not require distributors to attend any training seminars. The company supplies training manuals and videos. The training materials teach distributors how to price and sell the business cards and other products. The company encourages telephone contact, and it urges distributors to call with questions and concerns. Colorfast sends out periodic newsletters and marketing updates to all distributors.

Future Outlook

Colorfast has survived while other companies in the color-photograph business card industry have perished. The company had the foresight to change from having its own salaried sales staff to offering distributorships.

Competition in the promotional marketplace has sent many companies looking for ways to attract customers. First impressions mean a great deal, and professional-looking business cards and brochures can impress a potential customer.

Contact Information
Address: 9522 Topanga Canyon Boulevard, Chatsworth, California 91311
Telephone: 1-818-407-1881
Contact person: Mike Elk

CAR MAINTENANCE

AIR-SERV, INC.

Initial investment: $50,000 to $250,000
Total investment: $50,000 to $250,000

Ongoing fees: None
Right to use trademark and logo: None

Expansion History
Company operating since: 1981
Offering distributorships since: 1981
Number of distributorships: 90

Industry Focus
Air vending machines and vacuum cleaners have become commonplace at both service stations and convenience stores. Today's machines are easily accessible to consumers, and they are simple to use.

Company Advantages
AIR-serv, Inc., holds six patents on various air machines. Distributors have the option of selling, renting, or leasing the machines to service station and convenience store owners. Distributors can also negotiate an arrangement whereby owner and distributor share the profits generated by the machines.

Contrary to popular belief, air is not a free commodity. AIR-serv, Inc., of Mendota Heights, Minnesota, provides coin-operated air dispensers, air/water dispensers, and vacuum cleaners. Established in 1981, AIR-serv uses its 90-member distributor network to install these self-service machines on the parking lots of service stations, convenience stores, and car washes.

An initial investment ranging between $50,000 and $250,000 purchases the rights to an exclusive territory for an AIR-serv distributor. Territories vary in size, depending on the distributor's investment. This investment also includes the purchase of all equipment and inventory needed to run the distributorship effectively.

Most distributors begin as part-time entrepreneurs. They purchase 15 machines or less at a cost of $1,000 each, and they run the distributorship from their homes. There is no need for warehouse space or vehicles, since all the air machines fit into the trunk or backseat of a car. As business develops, distributors can purchase more machines and expand their territories. At this stage, distributors take on a more managerial role, and they hire workers to transport, install, and maintain the equipment. Most distributors eventually leave their home-based offices and lease professional office and warehouse space for equipment and vehicles.

Distributors develop customers through person-to-person sales and direct mail campaigns. Customers either buy or lease the machines from the distributors. Often distributors and customers will enter into a joint agreement whereby they share the profits generated by the air dispensers.

AIR-serv charges no ongoing royalty fees to distributors, and the company enforces no quota system. The company has six federally registered trademarks, which are prominently displayed on all machines. Distributors can use the trademark on vehicles and uniforms as long as they identify themselves as independent contractors for AIR-serv—not employees. AIR-serv guarantees its products against breakage and vandalism for 18 months, and the company expects its distributors to offer this same guarantee to their customers. All distributors have the benefit of the company's national marketing campaign, which includes direct mail programs, trade show exhibits, and advertising in business magazines and trade journals. AIR-serv provides its independent contractors with color brochures and promotional material at the start of their distributorship. The company also supplies its distributors with a list of service stations and convenience stores in their territories.

AIR-serv requires distributors to attend a one-day meeting at the home office in Minneapolis before they can become approved independent contractors. The company sponsors regional meetings as well as seminars, and AIR-serv schedules regular field visits with distributors.

Future Outlook
AIR-serv currently has 40,000 machines throughout the United States located on the same lots as major oil company self-service stations and nationally recognized convenience store chains. There are more than 185 million cars, each equipped with five tires (four regular and one spare), on the road today. Also in need of air are bicycle tires, swimming pool equipment, and athletic gear such as basketballs and footballs.

Contact Information

Address: 1370 Mendota Heights Road, Mendota Heights, Minnesota 55120

Telephone: 1-800-247-8363 or 1-612-454-0465

Contact person: Steve Vollmer

PRO-MA (USA) SYSTEMS, INC.

Initial investment: $15 registration fee plus a $20 literature kit with training manuals

Total investment: $135 wholesale cost of a case of automotive products for use in demonstrations

Ongoing fees: $15 annual renewal fee

Right to use trademark and logo: Yes

Expansion History

Company operating since: 1983

Offering distributorships since: 1983

Number of distributorships: 45,000 + (combination of PRO-MA Systems and Grace Cosmetics)

Industry Focus

Car performance products can help consumers increase the life of their vehicle. If the product proves itself, customers form a long-lasting relationship with the manufacturer.

Car performance products direct sales programs bring an assortment of products to the customer that eliminate time-consuming trips to automobile stores for products that may not be effective.

Company Advantages

PRO-MA (USA) Systems is part of an international company headquartered in Australia that includes more than 45,000 independent contractors selling its products throughout the world.

PRO-MA Systems guarantees all of its products to retail customers. Independent contractors can increase their commission earnings by sponsoring other contractors and becoming managers, supervisors, and directors in the marketing network.

· · ·

Longwood, Florida-based PRO-MA (USA) Systems equips consumers with products that can keep their cars on the road and reduce the potential for high-priced repair. Established in 1983, PRO-MA Performance Systems is the sole distributor of the company's line of fuel additive products, diesel treatments, metal-base lubricating sprays, engine performance boosters, and waterless car wash products. The company maintains its world headquarters in Queensland, Australia.

A PRO-MA distributor uses direct sales marketing techniques to sell the car performance products. PRO-MA does not dictate any specific marketing technique, and it encourages distributors to find their best sales presentation. Independent contractors use contacts with friends, office colleagues, and community organizations to schedule home shows or private demonstrations. Contractors can sell PRO-MA products on a part-time or full-time basis. They can market the products alone, or they can form partnerships. PRO-MA estimates that more than 80 percent are husband-and-wife or family-member teams who initially become PRO-MA contractors to earn extra income. Eventually most contractors convert the part-time effort into a full-time business commitment as they learn more about the products and the direct sales marketing method.

PRO-MA distributors receive commissions of 25 percent or more on all products they sell. This commission rates increases as sales increase and distributors climb the management ladder. Consultants can become managers, supervisors, and directors by recruiting other distributors and selling a minimum amount of products.

As managers, contractors must prove to the company that they have sold a minimum of $180 in retail value of products. Managers should also sell at least two cases of the PRO-MA performance products every two months to retain active status. Managers also have the responsibility of training and supervising personally sponsored product representatives. As managers, contractors earn a 30 percent commission on items.

Managers reach supervisor and director status by increasing the number of subrepresentatives and product sales. Supervisors and directors order the merchandise from PRO-MA for their representatives, and they also provide initial and general training sessions for their personally sponsored contractors. Supervisors earn a 30 percent commission plus a 10 percent bonus on volume purchases, and directors earn in addition 20 percent commission plus bonuses on orders made by the managers and contractors beneath them.

An initial investment of $35 registers an entrepreneur as a PRO-MA representative and purchases an introductory kit with operating instructions and promotional material. Contractors also have the option of buying one case of the PRO-MA automobile and performance products valued at $180 for the discounted price of $135. The case allows the representative to use the products and demonstrate them to potential customers.

All PRO-MA representatives receive personal training either from their managers and supervisors or from the home office leadership program. The training focuses on product knowledge as well as sales techniques, goal identification, and marketing skills. The company also is available for telephone support, and PRO-MA conducts seminars, international conventions, and award ceremonies on a regular basis.

Future Outlook

PRO-MA has developed an immense international following in less than ten years. The company has secured the exclusive distribution rights to all of its car-care products. PRO-MA also introduced a skin care and cosmetic line in 1983, Grace Cosmetics, which can be sold along with the car performance products or alone. The two product lines help to attract both men and women into the network and as customers.

Contact Information

Address: 477 Commerce Way, #113, Longwood, Florida 32750
Telephone: 1-407-331-1133
Contact person: Gene Rumley, vice president

CHILDREN'S SERVICES

DISCOVERY TOYS, INC.

Initial investment: $220
Total investment: $220
Ongoing fees: None
Right to use trademark and logo: Yes

Expansion History
Company operating since: 1978
Offering business opportunities since: 1978
Number of independent consultants: 25,000+

Industry Focus
Children's toys have come under closer scrutiny in the last ten years. Educators and parents insist on toys that encourage imagination and curiosity.
Children's toys need to be durable and safe. Parents look for these features when they purchase a toy for their child.

Company Advantages
Discovery Toys has grown from a one-woman, home-office business to an $83 million corporation that employs more than 170 people in only 14 years of operation.
Discovery Toys' success stems from the company's variety of products as well as its well-organized direct sales program that rewards sales revenue as well as consultant recruitment.
Discovery markets approximately 130 toys at one time. The company has exclusive distribution contracts on more than 75 percent of this merchandise. Discovery's design team also develops products.

A child's toy should enhance the imagination, not destroy it. Discovery Toys, Inc., has worked successfully to bring this theory to consumers. Established in 1978, Discovery Toys began as a part-time endeavor of Lane Nemeth, a former educator and day-care center director. Today she heads an $83 million company that relies on more than 25,000 independent contractors or educational consultants throughout the world to distribute a wide selection of books, games, and toys.

The Discovery Toys educational consultant markets a selection of toys person-to-person through home and office shows. The shows are designed to give parents a hands-on opportunity to view and handle some of the toys and games. In addition to the samples, each consultant also carries a 52-page glossy order book filled with products Discovery offers.

Educational consultants are mostly women who begin on a part-time basis setting up a schedule for shows and demonstrating the products. Toys, books, and games vary in price, but 85 percent of the products sell for under $15. Consultants earn a 22 to 25 percent commission on each sale.

Consultants can increase their income potential by recruiting other educational consultants. Discovery maintains a multilevel sales structure with educational consultants working with upline managers. As consultants recruit other salespeople, they progress to manager, advanced manager, senior manager, and sales director. Managers receive a 1 percent commission on each sale completed by the educational consultants under them.

A $220 investment purchases a professional sales kit and support materials and turns an entrepreneur into a Discovery Toys consultant. Discovery will rebate most of this investment as consultants achieve a designated sales volume within a specified period of time.

Consultants need no background in sales or toys. Discovery managers train all consultants in product knowledge and sales presentation. The company sponsors bonuses and incentive programs for consultants not only to sell products but to recruit new consultants as well.

Future Outlook
Discovery combines quality products with convenience. The toys and games are durable, safe, and economical. The company undertakes a worldwide search for new products each year, and accepts

the rights to maket, on the average, 130 toys, games, and books annually.

The company has little direct competition. Other person-to-person marketing companies sell toys but on a smaller scale than that of Discovery. Toy manufacturers rely mainly on retail outlets for their goods, and their average prices are generally higher as a result.

Contact Information
Address: 2530 Arnold Drive, Martinez, California 94553
Telephone: 1-800-426-4777 or 1-510-370-3400
Contact person: Helen Johnson, spokesperson

COMMERCIAL MAINTENANCE PRODUCTS AND SERVICES

ABSOLUTE SYSTEMS, INC.

Initial investment: $900 to $3,000
Total investment: $900 to $3,000
Ongoing fees: None
Right to use trademark and logo: No

Expansion History
Company operating since: 1988
Offering distributorships since: 1988
Number of distributorships: 1,000

Industry Focus:
Ceiling cleaning costs 50 percent less than ceiling replacement and painting.

Dirt, mildew, and fungi can contribute to an unhealthy environment.

Ceiling cleaning is a specialized, detailed service not offered by many companies. This market has great growth potential.

Company Advantages

Absolute Systems uses a network of more than 8,200 area distributors and subdistributors to sell products and accessories to the cleaning contractors. The contractors are independent entrepreneurs who invest in the Absolute Solutions cleaning system. The network provides easily accessible support for contractors in the field.

Ceilings trap dirt, smoke, grease, and other unhealthy contaminants. Absolute Systems, Inc., of Clearwater, Florida, eliminates these problems with its nontoxic, biodegradable, enzyme system that removes pollutants from both porous and nonporous ceiling surfaces.

Contractors are the key players in the Absolute Systems network. As independent entrepreneurs, contractors target administrators and owners of hospitals, businesses, schools, stores, hotels, apartment complexes, and private homes. Some contractors sell the ceiling service through retail locations. Others rely on direct sales, telemarketing, and person-to-person sales programs.

During the initial months of operation, many contractors are ceiling cleaning technicians and business owners. As business volume increases, many contractors hire technicians to handle actual cleaning assignments. They move to commercial or retail space to accommodate the addition of marketing staff and equipment. When contractors reach this point, they assume a management role, dedicating their time to the administrative and marketing needs of their businesses.

An initial investment of $900 purchases the Absolute Systems start-up package that includes a self-contained sprayer, pump, and a supply of cleaning solutions. The portable, 36-pound plastic sprayer is the heart of the operation. It holds extension poles, a 5-gallon solution pail, a 5-gallon rinse pail, a 25-foot electrical cord, a 20-foot hose, a trigger handle with single and double sprayer tips, and a separate compartment for the cleaning pump.

For a larger investment of $3,000, a contractor receives the company's full-service Tetronic system, which cleans not only ceilings and walls but carpets and upholstery as well. This system holds a 5-gallon solution tank and a 5-gallon recovery tank as well as a vacuum motor, a 10-foot vacuum and solution hose, a stainless steel floor tool, upholstery tools, and a ceiling and wall cleaning wand.

Absolute Systems encourages contractors to become area distributors. Even while acting as distributors, however, contractors can accept cleaning assignments. However, distributorships do provide opportunity for contractors to earn more profit by selling the company's equipment and supplies to other contractors within a 100-mile radius. Distributors are not responsible for finding new contractors, and the home office approves any new contractor who would operate within the distributor's area. The distributor is responsible for training new contractors through videos, manuals, and seminars in the Absolute Systems methods of cleaning and deodorizing. Absolute Systems also offers contractors telephone support in the sales and application of the company's products. The company will contact prospective customers for contractors and provide in-field assistance.

Future Outlook

Absolute Systems operates an efficient network that allows entrepreneurs to advance. The company still keeps a hands-on approach to its contractors and demonstrates this through a companywide support system.

Ceiling cleaning is only beginning to gain customer attention. Concerns about the workplace environment have forced business owners and managers to look into cost-effective procedures to remove health hazards and pollutants. Ceiling cleaning is an economical way to do this.

Contact Information
Address: 1555 Sunshine Drive, Clearwater, Florida 34625
Telephone: 1-800-762-5326 or 1-813-449-1776
Contact person: Charles Carnes III

CHEMMARK INTERNATIONAL

Initial investment: $20,000
Total investment: $20,000 plus working capital

Ongoing fees: None
Right to use trademark and logo: Yes

Expansion History
Company operating since: 1960
Offering distributorships since: 1963
Number of distributors: Not available

Industry Focus
Safe working and living environments are of key importance to employers, employees, and customers. Businesses and restaurants have revamped their policies concerning smoking, air circulation, and cleanliness. Stricter governmental regulations exist for employers, and they must provide a healthy and safe working atmosphere for personnel.

Company Advantages
ChemMark has been in the environmental health industry since 1960. The company has developed from selling sanitizing equipment for restaurants and bars to an international network that sells a full range of interior environmental safety products.

ChemMark first marketed its patented SwingMark valve system, which cleaned and sanitized bar glass materials, in 1960. The company now consists of an international network of distributors who market not only restaurant sanitizing equipment but air purification and odor control products as well.

ChemMark distributors pay an initial $20,000 fee, which purchases the rights to an exclusive territory based on population for five years. The fee also entitles distributors to use all ChemMark trademarks and logos in the development of their sales routes, and it purchases all inventory and equipment needed to operate the distributorship. Distributors should also have in reserve at least $10,000 to cover the costs of insurance, marketing, and other miscellaneous start-up expenses.

Distributors operate as independent contractors for ChemMark, but the company requires them to attend and complete training either at the home office in Orange, California, or at the regional office in Kansas City, Missouri. Training is extensive and educates distributors on all ChemMark products and their maintenance.

All distributors are expected to sell, install, maintain, and service ChemMark equipment, which includes restaurant sanitizing and washing machines, flying insect and odor control devices, a power glass-washing brush and cleaning chemicals, and air purification systems. Distributors sell the products mainly through person-to-person sales calls with business and restaurant owners.

The company requires distributors to guarantee equipment and services they have sold and installed, and it also requests that distributors adhere to the sales and marketing methods outlined in its operations manual.

ChemMark contractors must purchase ChemMark products from the home office. Any substitution of products is in violation of the contract. The contract also requires distributors to view this opportunity as a full-time commitment. All operators must establish a commercial office and ChemMark telephone listing no later than 45 days after signing the distributorship agreement.

ChemMark develops its own products and updates distributors on new products and services through regional meetings and in-field visits. The company maintains regular telephone contact with all distributors and encourages them to call if problems or questions arise.

Future Outlook

ChemMark's success is due to the company's watchful eye on government health and safety regulations. The company continues to develop up-to-date products for businesses and the restaurant industry. This foresight has enabled distributors to expand their customer network.

Contact Information

Address: P.O. Box 1126, 635 E. Chapman Avenue, Orange, California 92268

Telephone: 1-714-633-8560

Contact person: Darol W. Carlson

GARDENING

WORLD GARDEN SOCIETY
(Living Well Gardens)

Initial investment: $200 to $300
Total investment: $200 to $300
Ongoing fees: None
Right to use trademark and logo: Yes

Expansion History
Company operating since: 1992
Offering distributorships since: 1992
Number of distributorships: 5 +

Industry Focus
   Gardens designed for small spaces such as apartment balconies
are very much in demand. Approximately 50 percent of Americans
live in apartment buildings and condominiums.
   In the past, apartment and condominium dwellers were limited
to window box gardening kits. Few buildings offer tenants or occupants free ground space for vegetable and flower gardens.

Company Advantages
   The World Garden Society is an offshoot of the 15-year-old
company Living Well Gardens. Living Well Gardens was founded
by F. Wesley Moffett, an inventor who has diligently worked to
develop growing methods and products that would supply food for
third-world countries. Moffett's zealous research led him to this
gardening program, which requires only a small amount of land in
which to grow flowers, herbs, and vegetables. Moffett has set up
manufacturing facilities in India, Africa, and Russia.

The secret of the company's success is in its special silica-based growing medium and its garden containers, which can be stacked in different configurations. These stackable gardens eliminate much of the need for land space and arable soil.

Moffett experiments with all of his growing methods at his Naples, New York, home and laboratory facility. He continues to research all types of gardening methods in hopes of being able to teach people to become self-sufficient in their food needs.

The stackable gardening system allows the disabled and elderly to enjoy gardening again. Consumers do not need to bend or go down on their hands and knees to dig or maintain their crops.

No weeds grow in this gardening system. This reduces the amount of work consumers must undertake to maintain their gardens.

Home-grown vegetables are a source of pride for many amateur gardeners. Unfortunately, not all Americans have ground space to grow their own plants. World Garden Society eliminates this problem with its garden kits, which need only a small amount of land. The company introduced this product to the United States in 1992, and it has attracted hundreds of gardening enthusiasts. The company plans to market its system through independent distributors throughout the United States.

World Garden Society distributors are independent contractors who are responsible for the sale of the gardening system and for the education of consumers to its many uses. Distributors best achieve this goal through demonstrations at home shows, garden clubs, women's clubs, lodge meetings, and private parties. As independent contractors, distributors can explore larger commercial accounts as well, including greenhouse owners and professional landscaping companies.

Consumers can grow vegetable and flower gardens using this system of stackable containers. The containers can be set horizontally or vertically, whichever is more convenient for the gardener. All or most portions, including the top, bottom, and sides, can be used for planting and holding vegetable and floral seedlings.

The container takes up a small amount of ground space, which frees up an area for other plants. Consumers then stack the containers in a variety of formations, thus allowing elaborate gardens in the most cramped quarters.

The soil used for the gardens is also a key to this gardening system. It is an exclusive silica-based medium developed by Living Well Gardens. The medium has proven effective in many parts of the world, including desert environments, and it can accommodate most vegetation needs. The gardening kit containers are portable, and gardeners can move their crops, indoors or outdoors, whenever they please.

For an initial investment of $200 to $300, distributors receive at least one complete gardening kit that they can use for demonstration purposes. The investment also purchases the rights to use the World Garden Society name. Distributors can work full time or part time, and they have the right to establish their own retail prices on the gardening kits and set their own profit margins, which can vary greatly for residential and commercial accounts.

World Garden Society is in the process of setting up a four-tier multimarketing system that will allow and encourage distributors to recruit other distributors into the network. The sponsoring distributors can be promoted to managerial levels as their recruits sponsor new network members. Management level distributors receive bonus commissions on their recruits' sales.

World Garden Society offers in-person training for all distributors at no charge. The company views product education and promotion as important tools, and training will focus on these points. The company teaches distributors sales presentation techniques as well as business management through seminars at the home office.

Future Outlook

The World Garden Society was born because of consumer interest. Living Well Gardens had not planned to market these kits to hobby gardeners in this country, but demands made the company realize that a multibillion-dollar market potential existed.

World Garden will work to improve its products and kits. The company continues its research and views feeding the world's hungry as its primary directive.

Contact Information
Address: 2044 Chili, Rochester, New York 14624
Telephone: 1-716-247-0070
Contact person: F. Wesley Moffett

HEALTH AND BEAUTY

AMERICAN HORIZONS, INC.

Initial investment: $40 plus optional purchase of inventory
Total investment: $40 plus $20 annual newsletter subscription fee
Ongoing fees: None
Right to use trademark and logo: With written permission

Expansion History
Company operating since: 1987
Offering distributorships since: 1987
Number of distributorships: Not available

Industry Focus
Natural products that promote health and beauty attract today's consumer, but many products are too expensive for the average consumer.

The average consumer is taking more care in choosing products that do not contain harmful chemicals or ingredients.

Company Advantages
American Horizons combines the popularity of natural products with the convenience of home shopping.

Distributors have many options in selling their products, which makes the American Horizons line attractive to both part-time and full-time entrepreneurs.

■ ■ ■

Based in Jacksonville, Florida, American Horizons markets natural foods, beverages, and cosmetics made from herbs, vitamins, and minerals through a national network of independent distributors. The products can be sold individually or in kits, and they are moderately priced.

For an investment of $40, a distributor receives a starter kit that contains an operations manual and videotape as well as brochures and literature on all products sold by the company. Distributors can also purchase samples of American Horizons' trademark products, which range from Stop Drops, a hunger-reducing tablet, to the Isometric Facial Lift, a system containing an herbal mixture that tightens and rejuvenates skin.

The initial investment attracts many entrepreneurs who want to test the waters before jumping into a full-time business commitment. They usually start selling on a part-time basis, including nights and weekends. Distributors establish customers through telemarketing campaigns, shop-at-home sales, flea markets, home shows, and charity fund-raisers. Distributors can increase their business volume and profit margin by recruiting new distributors to sell products in their areas.

The company will permit its distributors to use their product trademarks and logos, as long as contractors do not represent themselves as employees. American Horizons believes in creating marketing, but it does enforce two strict rules. Distributors cannot place the products in any retail store, and they cannot promote the products as any kind of medical cure or treatment.

American Horizons does not charge any ongoing fees, but distributors must reorder products from the company. American Horizons, which is privately owned, does not disclose how many distributors are actively selling its products, but it does attract an equal number of men and women. The company does not do a great deal of advertising to attract distributors. Instead, it relies on current contractors and customers to recruit new distributors.

American Horizons conducts training and local meetings regularly for distributors, and the company maintains a toll-free hot line for assistance. It also publishes a regular newsletter that introduces new products or corporate changes to distributors.

Future Outlook

American consumers looking for the healthier choices in weight control, nutritional supplements, and cosmetics have welcomed American Horizons' commitment to natural ingredients. Distributors do not need to have nutrition or cosmetic experience. American Horizons gives in-depth training on all products.

Contact Information

Address: 11251 Phillips Parkway Drive East, Jacksonville, Florida 32256

Telephone: 1-800-248-5249 or 1-904-260-4911

Contact person: Ronnette Bird, director of sales

FINELLE COSMETICS

Initial investment: $275 + $100 for skin scanner (optional)

Total investment: $275 + $100 for skin scanner (optional)

Ongoing fees: None

Right to use trademark and logo: Yes

Expansion History

Operating since: 1971

Offering business opportunities since: 1971

Number of independent consultants: 5,000+

Industry Focus

Personal-care products, especially cosmetics, sell well in all types of economic conditions.

Men and women are paying more attention to skin care. Consumers want to preserve a youthful appearance. Cosmetics and skin-care products provide a way to achieve this goal.

Company Advantages

Finelle Cosmetics uses direct sales to reach customers. Distributors or independent consultants can use a variety of methods such as home parties, flea markets, and personal referrals to sell the products. The direct sales structure also allows entrepreneurs to increase the percentage they receive on sales by climbing up the network ladder. Consultants can become managers or executive managers. Each link in the chain increases earning potential.

The desire to look younger and more attractive keeps consumers searching for the ultimate cosmetic system. Finelle Cosmetics meets this need with its collection of color-coordinated cosmetics and skin-care products. Established in 1971, Finelle reaches consumers through a network of 5,000 independent entrepreneurs who sell these products to consumers directly without having to keep backup inventory.

Finelle independent contractors are sales consultants, analysts, and teachers. They not only introduce the Finelle products to consumers, but they evaluate skin, eye, and hair color to determine the best products and colors for an individual. Last, the Finelle consultant uses the company's "Fun With Color" program to teach consumers how to coordinate makeup, skin undertones, and wardrobe.

Finelle gives its consultants ample room in marketing the cosmetics. Consultants can start on a part-time basis and sell the products and programs to co-workers, friends, and family. Most part-time consultants work weekends and evenings, sponsoring home parties or lessons. As business develops, many consultants choose to make a full-time commitment.

To increase income, consultants can recruit other entrepreneurs into the Finelle network. Consultants receive commissions on new recruits' sales. The Finelle multilevel program continues until managers become elite executive managers. Throughout the program, Finelle offers consultants increased profit percentages, prizes, and bonuses. The company makes no earning claims, but it does say one home party or lesson on the base consultant level should result in sales of at least $200, with the consultant receiving 40 percent of the revenue.

For an initial investment of $275, consultants receive an introductory sample kit that contains all Finelle cosmetics and beauty aids. The company also supplies a skin scanner, an instrument that looks closely at the skin's composition to determine its flaws and strengths. There is no money-back guarantee for consultants, but Finelle will refund the $100 deposit for the skin scanner.

As part of their initial training, Finelle consultants attend seminars and workshops conducted by other consultants at the home office. The company also supplies videotapes and operations manuals for each consultant. Finelle invites all consultants and managers to regularly scheduled company-sponsored seminars and conventions. Finelle is available for telephone consultation, and managers will assist consultants if questions and concerns arise.

Future Outlook
Many cosmetic companies have found success using the direct sales method, which rewards the most ambitious salesperson with bonuses and prizes without taking away revenue from the least ambitious.

Finelle's "Fun With Color" program goes beyond the cosmetic sale. It teaches consumers how to use products correctly. This may translate into smarter buying on the consumer's part, and it also makes satisfied customers.

Contact Information
Address: P.O. Box 5200, Lawrence, Massachusetts 01842-2808
Telephone: 1-800-776-9889 or 1-508-682-6112
Contact person: Mark Feigenbaum

GRACE COSMETICS
(PRO-MA [USA] Systems, Inc.)

Initial investment: $35
Total investment: $135 (optional purchase of skin care and cosmetic products)
Ongoing fees: $15 annual renewal fee
Right to use trademark and logo: Yes

Expansion History
Company operating since: 1983
Offering business opportunities since: 1983
Number of independent consultants: 45,000 + (combination of PRO-MA Performance Systems and Grace Cosmetics)

Industry Focus

Consumers search for products that promise to nurture and preserve their skin's natural beauty. While consumers take cost of these products into account, it is not the main factor in the decision to buy cosmetics and skin-care products.

Skin care is becoming increasingly important to both sexes. The industry is researching and developing products that appeal to men's special skin needs.

Company Advantages

Grace Cosmetics is part of the direct marketing giant PRO-MA Systems, which is well recognized for its sale of automobile performance products. Many husband-and-wife and family teams join the distributor network and sell the full range of PRO-MA products.

Grace Cosmetics products contain only natural, botanical, or water-soluble ingredients. The products combine natural herbal mixtures, vitamins, aloe vera, RNA, and eucalyptus.

Grace Cosmetics manufactures its own line of skin-care products. The company contracts out its cosmetic line and its new line of natural nutritional products that includes vitamin-fortified, weight-reduction products and energy enhancers.

PRO-MA Systems launched its line of natural skin-care products and cosmetics to attract educated consumers who are hesitant about using chemicals and artificial ingredients in their daily personal regimen. First marketed in 1983, Grace Cosmetics appeared to be an odd complement to PRO-MA Systems' automobile performance products, which have achieved great sales success for more than nine years. The company applied the same direct marketing strategy to its sister division, and Grace Cosmetics blossomed into a worldwide network that includes more than 45,000 PRO-MA distributors or independent consultants.

A Grace Cosmetics distributor can sell the natural cosmetics in a variety of ways. Many independent contractors use home demonstrations as their key distribution method. Others perform skin-care and cosmetic demonstrations at local community centers, churches, schools, or motel meeting rooms. Consultants also hold "Women on the Move" seminars that let consumers watch a makeover demonstration on three models before they enjoy a five-minute "quick" makeover themselves. PRO-MA encourages consultants to participate in trade shows, charity events, and fund-raisers as well.

The role of Grace Cosmetics consultants is to educate the consumer on proper skin care and cosmetic use. Consultants perform color-imaging services, which teach consumers to match the appropriate cosmetic shade to their own skin tone.

Distributors can work one hour a week or 40 hours a week. PRO-MA encourages consultants to start out on a part-time basis until they become comfortable with the product and consumers. Most consultants do eventually turn the sale of Grace Cosmetics into a full-time career. Grace Cosmetics consultants are usually part of a husband-and-wife or family team who market both the cosmetics and automobile products.

Independent consultants earn a minimum of 25 percent commission on each order placed with Grace Cosmetics. The earning potential increases if consultants sponsor other entrepreneurs in the Grace Cosmetics network.

Consultants who have other independent contractors working under them are managers, supervisors, and directors. The level of management depends on the number of consultants recruited as well as the volume of orders. PRO-MA promotes consultants as they reach certain sales milestones. The managers receive added commissions plus volume bonus awards for orders secured by their sales force.

PRO-MA also expects managers, supervisors, and directors to maintain certain sales volume level. Management is also required to participate in the training of new sales consultants with PRO-MA's leadership training team. Managers should also conduct regular meetings and workshops for their sales teams.

An initial investment of $35 registers an entrepreneur as a Grace Cosmetics consultant. Along with a $15 registration fee, the $35 also includes the purchase of a sales kit that contains promotional literature about Grace Cosmetics and its products. Consultants are free to purchase a case of cosmetics at the wholesale price of $135.

PRO-MA educates Grace consultants in product knowledge, sales techniques, and personal development skills. The company assigns a leadership team to train all new consultants, and it sponsors bonus and award incentive programs. PRO-MA also conducts international conventions and regular workshop meetings for consultants on all levels.

Future Outlook

Grace Cosmetics has the advantage of being a part of an expansive direct sales company. PRO-MA participates in the development of this product line and manufactures its skin-care products at its plants in Florida and Australia. The company has also broadened its customer base for Grace Cosmetics with its new nutritional line that includes a weight-loss program, energy products, and vitamins.

Contact Information
Address: 477 Commerce Way, #113, Longwood, Florida 32750
Telephone: 1-407-331-1133
Contact person: Gene Rumley, vice president

NAIL TECHNOLOGY, INC.

Initial investment: $500
Total investment: $500
Ongoing fees: None
Right to use trademark and logo: Yes

Expansion History
Company operating since: 1989
Offering distributorships since: 1989
Number of distributorships: 40+

Industry Focus

The cosmetic fingernail industry grosses more than $1 billion annually.

Consumers pay between $40 and $60 per salon visit for a manicure or special nail service.

Many consumers do not want to spare the time for a professional manicure, nor do they want to wait days or weeks for an appointment at an established salon.

Company Advantages

Nail Technology, Inc., has developed a new nail system called Diamond Ice, which eliminates the need and cost of professional salon manicures. In 1992 the company decided to market this new product through a distributorship method.

Nail Technology manufactures its own Diamond Ice products in its facility in Nebraska. The products contain no harsh acid base primers or acrylics, and there is no need to use dangerous ultraviolet light in the application and drying process.

Nail Technology was established in 1989, and the company succeeded in marketing its own line of fingernail products. In 1992 Nail Technology's new nail program, Diamond Ice, prompted the company to refocus its goals and concentrate totally on this revolutionary nail-care system. Nail Technology has determined to market this system through a customized distributor and direct sales program.

It is the distributor's main goal to teach consumers about the advantages of the "do-it-yourself" nail-care system. Distributors have the flexibility to employ their own marketing techniques, and many use home demonstrations or nail-care workshops as a means to market their products. Nail Technology is also willing to negotiate private labeling agreements with distributors. The company has granted permission to distributors to advertise in various media including television. All advertising must portray the distributor as an independent contractor for the company and not as an employee or agent.

The Diamond Ice system contains no acrylics and no ingredients harmful to the environment and does not have an offensive odor. The system is a complete step-by-step process for strengthening natural nails or extending natural nails' length with artificial nail tips. Nail Technology observes that the major advantage of its program lies in the ingredients of the company's products, especially its Diamond Ice Glaze Freeze. The Glaze Freeze strengthens and smoothes a nail's surface. It is easily applied with a brush, and it does not contain the commonly used, ozone-depleting chemicals found in many other nail products. Intead, the Glaze Freeze uses a liquid found naturally in bananas, strawberries, apples, and pineapples to secure a nail's strength with a hard-gloss finish that dries within 60 seconds of application.

Along with the Glaze Freeze, the Diamond Ice system contains an assortment of products that can repair broken or cracked nails, strengthen natural nails, and extend nail length. Nail Technology markets the products as a complete kit encased in a vinyl bag that fits easily into most purses.

Nail Technology requests that distributors purchase a minimum of $500 in inventory to begin their nail-care business. The investment supplies distributors with enough nail kits to operate their business effectively. Nail Technology estimates that distributors can earn up to a 50 percent profit on each nail kit.

Nail Technology offers consumers two kits. One sells for $49.95 and contains a total nail-care system, including Diamond Ice Adhesive, the Glaze Freeze, Diamond Ice Sanitizer, Diamond Ice Glaze Melt, and Diamond Ice Tip Melt. This kit also comes with the vinyl travel bag, a pair of folding scissors, a dust brush, adhesive silk, nail clippers, nail pads, neon nail files, assorted nail tips, an instruction booklet, and video. The $29.95 kit does not include the scissors and other accessory items, but it does contain the vinyl bag and the instruction video and booklet as well as all the Diamond Ice products.

There is no formal training for selling this product. The company encourages telephone contact, and it will assist distributors with problems or questions.

Future Outlook

Nail care is a thriving industry, but many consumers cannot afford the time or money for regular manicures and nail treatments. This do-it-yourself home kit is easy to apply, and, once applied, the nail products are long-lasting.

Contact Information
Address: P.O. Box 626, North Platte, Nebraska 69103
Telephone: 1-308-534-0616
Contact person: Matt Ackerman, president

SASCO

Initial investment: Distributor determines the amount of inventory
   he or she wishes to purchase
Total investment: Individually determined
Ongoing fees: .0983 percent minimum processing fee for all orders
Right to use trademark and logo: Yes

Expansion History
Company operating since: 1978
Offering distributorships since: 1978
Number of distributorships: 7,000 +

Industry Focus
   Natural health, beauty, and household products attract consumers who want to avoid products that contain artificial or hazardous chemicals.
   Direct sales marketing such as home presentations places the
consumer in a relaxed shopping environment. Consumers tend to
purchase more when they are in comfortable surroundings.
   Approximately 75 percent of North American households purchase $20 billion in goods and services offered by direct sales
marketing.

Company Advantages
   SASCO manufactures and sells natural skin-care products, nutritional supplements, herbal blends, personal care products, aloe
health drinks, and home-care products.
   The company retains the service of consultants who are renowned
experts in the health, nutritional, legal, and business fields.

   Since its inception in 1978, SASCO has utilized direct sales marketing techniques to educate consumers on its natural product lines
that use aloe vera and other herbal blends as their base ingredients.
The company relies on more than 7,000 distributors to conduct

home shows, small group presentations, grand opening promotions, and workshops as a way to promote the SASCO products.

SASCO distributors are independent contractors. Distributors can work alone or form partnerships or corporations. Many distributors begin as part-time entrepreneurs who choose to retain their jobs while learning to market the SASCO product line.

SASCO does not make earning claims, but the company does maintain that the average home demonstration yields $180 in sales. On the average, distributors earn a 50 percent profit on the retail sales price of each product. Distributors make their own schedules, but the company recommends that the independent contractors hold a minimum of two presentations per week.

Distributors network in their own communities to find and establish a customer base: community and school organizations, women's clubs, and fellow office workers are all potential customers. SASCO does not require any contractor to have experience in sales or health and beauty aid products.

A $40 investment purchases a full starter kit for new distributors, who can also purchase inventory at wholesale prices and use the products for personal demonstrations. To assist in the ordering process, SASCO attaches to each product a Royalty Value, or RV, rating. The company and distributors use the RV rating for orders and purchases. Higher RVs reflect larger orders, and these result in further discounts and bonuses for distributors.

Distributors or sales representatives can increase their earning potential by becoming sales directors and sponsoring other individuals to become distributors as well. As new distributors sell more products, sales directors receive a bonus commission of 10 to 20 percent of the RV value of the sale. Sales directors who attain the status of managing sales directors receive additional bonuses and commissions from the sales directors and distributors under their supervision.

SASCO conducts two training programs for new distributors. They are held regionally throughout the United States. It is not mandatory for distributors to attend, but SASCO encourages their participation. Leaders and sales directors also work with their sponsored distributors to teach them about the product, presentation skills, marketing, and operating their business. SASCO provides a detailed manual that outlines all products, their ingredients, and their uses as well.

Future Outlook

SASCO is a part of the versatile and growing direct sales industry. The company manufactures and develops its own line of natural products. Expert consultants hold graduate degrees in nutrition and health fields, and have led research in the uses of aloe vera and other herbs and minerals.

Contact Information

Address: P.O. Box 819053, Dallas, Texas 75381-9053
Telephone: 1-800-969-7474
Contact person: Jack Shuford, president

SHAKLEE CORPORATION

Initial investment: Based on purchase of starting inventory
Total investment: Based on purchase of starting inventory
Ongoing fees: $5 membership fee
Right to use trademark and logo: Yes

Expansion History

Company operating since: 1956
Offering Shaklee distributorships since: 1956
Number of Shaklee distributors: Not available

Industry Focus

Using and consuming natural products such as protein drinks and multivitamin and mineral products can help lower a person's risk of developing cancer, diabetes, and heart disease.

Consumers are increasing their awareness of environmental issues and how they can affect their health and quality of life. Consumers are gravitating toward natural products for personal and home care, passing over products that contain artificial or chemical ingredients.

Company Advantages

Shaklee Corporation has been in existence since 1956. The company is built on the principle: "The health of the environment is intertwined with the health of every person who inhabits it."

Shaklee was purchased by Yamanouchi Pharmaceutical Co., Ltd., in 1989. The Japanese company is an international leader in its industry. Shaklee is a member of the New York Stock Exchange and ranked as a Fortune 500 company.

Shaklee manufactures its nutritional supplements in its manufacturing facilities in Norman, Oklahoma. The company adheres to strict production controls, and it performs more than 262 separate quality-control tests on each product.

Shaklee maintains a full-service research and development facility in Hayward, California. At this 52,000-square-foot facility, a staff of scientists, researchers, and technicians develop products that work in harmony with nature.

Many multilevel marketing companies look to Shaklee Corporation as an example of success. A Shaklee distributor is a direct sales professional. The distributor uses a variety of marketing strategies to sell Shaklee products, including home demonstrations, community events, shows, and direct mail campaigns. The key for success of many distributors is the well-known Shaklee name. Distributors market the products by focusing on the company's attention to quality control and product development. All products come with a 100 percent guarantee from Shaklee's home office, and all are made with only natural, environmentally safe ingredients.

Shaklee also provides consumers with a variety of merchandise, such as protein drinks, multivitamin and multimineral products for adults and children, diet plans, and fiber supplements. The company also markets natural cosmetics, perfumes, and personal-care items. Its BestWater water purification system and a number of household cleaning products have won recognition by private and government environmental groups.

Shaklee distributors can work full or part time. As independent business owners, they map out what they want to sell and how they want their business to grow. Distributors begin by paying a $5 membership fee to Shaklee. This entitles an entrepreneur to a 15 percent discount on all products. Distributors can begin sponsoring or recruiting friends and relatives into the Shaklee network immediately. Shaklee's multilevel marketing program includes eight levels of distributors and then supervisor and coordinator management levels. As distributors climb the career ladder, they receive higher discounts on products as well as bonuses and awards.

Shaklee distributors receive training from their sponsors or sales leaders in their area of operation. Sales leaders use promotional and instructional aides supplied by Shaklee. Supervisors and coordinators may also hold sales workshops, and Shaklee conducts advanced training sessions as well. As part of the company's ongoing support system, Shaklee publishes a monthly magazine for all distributors and produces audio and video instructional tapes. Conventions and award ceremonies are held regularly, and Shaklee provides distributors with promotional material and camera-ready copy and artwork for local newspaper advertisements.

Future Outlook

Consumers are affected by the environmental concerns of the planet. Products that use environmentally safe ingredients will hold consumers' attention.

Shaklee has won awards for its work and research on environmental issues. The company's mission is to educate consumers in how they can contribute positively to the planet's environment while maintaining and enhancing their own personal health.

Shaklee has expanded its target market with its ownership of Bear Creek Corporation and Jackson & Perkins. Bear Creek is the nation's largest direct mail marketer of fine fruits and gourmet foods, and Jackson & Perkins is known as America's leading supplier of roses and other plants.

Contact Information

Address: 444 Market Street, San Francisco, California 94111
Telephone: 1-800-Shaklee or 1-415-954-3000
Contact person: Chuck Healy, vice president of sales administration
and strategy

VITAMIN POWER, INC.

Initial investment: $100 to $150
Total investment: $100 to $150
Ongoing fees: None
Right to use trademark and logo: Yes

Expansion History
Operating since: 1975
Offering distributorships since: 1975
Number of distributorships: 11,750

Industry Focus
Health and fitness are an American obsession. Consumers seek out products that can help them maintain healthy bodies and high energy levels naturally.
The health and fitness industry is diverse and allows a great deal of room for competing companies to grow and prosper.

Company Advantages
Vitamin Power manufactures the health and skin-care products purchased by distributors. The company offers all products at reduced costs to distributors.

Vitamin Power, Inc., of Freeport, New York, offers an array of natural vitamin, nutritional, and skin care products. Established in 1975, Vitamin Power manufactures these natural products in its 20,000-square-foot facility and then markets them through 11,500 independent distributors throughout the world.
Vitamin Power distributors are independent salespeople. They use a variety of marketing techniques to attract consumers. Some distributors use the direct sales approach, such as home parties or trade shows to sell their goods. Other distributors establish retail locations, and some choose to market the products through mail-order catalogs and advertisements. Distributors are independent contractors for Vitamin Power, and they cannot represent them-

selves as agents or employees of the company. The company insists that distributors use every product trademark or logo when offering them for sale. The company holds a number of registered trademarks, including its diet aid, Nutra Trim 7, and its Great Way Skin-Care Product line.

Vitamin Power gives distributors a free hand in the operation of their business. Most distributors start out on a part-time basis, hosting home parties in the evening or traveling to health fairs and various trade shows or expositions on the weekends. Eventually, as business volume increases, many distributors take on the sale of these products on a full-time basis.

For an initial investment ranging between $100 and $150, distributors purchase all support material, literature, and order forms needed to sell the nutritional and skin-care products. Distributors do not have to purchase any Vitamin Power products until a customer orders them. At that time, the distributor buys the products from the manufacturer at wholesale or 50 percent (or more) below retail prices. Vitamin Power makes no claims on what distributors can earn, but the company maintains that distributors can make up to a 100 percent profit on each product.

Distributors do not pay any ongoing royalty fees to Vitamin Power, and the company does not demand any sales volume quotas. Vitamin Power does not elicit exclusive territories, and it encourages distributors to explore as many sales avenues as possible.

Selling Vitamin Power requires no formal training, but all distributors are expected to read the literature kit provided in the initial distributorship package. The literature contains educational materials, sales catalogs, individual product brochures, and nutritional information. All sales aids have room for the individual distributor's own imprint or logo.

Vitamin Power updates all literature regularly and supplies distributors with new catalogs and sales promotions and special incentive programs.

Future Outlook

Fitness plays an important part in many consumer's lives, and the health and fitness industry has grown greatly over the past decade. Consumers are also interested in the ingredients in health and nutritional products. American consumers want nutrition and fitness without the dangerous side effects of chemicals.

Its large manufacturing facility gives Vitamin Power an advantage over other companies. Distributors know who made the products, and they can relay that information to their customers easily.

Contact Information

Address: 39 St. Mary's Place, Department CV, Freeport, New York 11520

Telephone: 1-800-645-6567 or 1-516-378-0900

Contact person: Bob Edwards

WECARE, INC.

Initial investment: $19 registration fee

Total investment: Based on purchase of Rose Marie skin-care line

Ongoing fees: None

Right to use trademark and logo: Yes

Expansion History

Company operating since: 1982

Offering distributorships since: 1982

Number of WeCare distributors: 5,000+

Industry Focus

Consumers are very particular about skin-care products. They look for merchandise that is made without harsh chemicals.

Companies that choose to merchandise their products through direct sales programs and multilevel marketing must assure consumers of these products' quality. A quality product that comes directly to the consumer and promises positive results can capture customer loyalty.

Company Advantages

WeCare offers consumers skin-care products that have a mink oil base. Mink oil is fragrance free and most similar to the body's natural oils.

WeCare's product line, called the Rose Marie Collection, offers consumers a complete skin-care system, plus shampoos, perfumes, cosmetics, sunblock, and after-shave products as well.

WeCare does not conduct any laboratory testing on animals.

WeCare, Inc., of Charlotte, North Carolina, has developed a series of products that preserves, protects, and enhances the body's most visible organ—the skin.

At the center of this skin-care line is its most important ingredient, mink oil. More than any other natural product, mink oil most closely resembles the natural oils in human skin. WeCare reaches its customer market directly through its 5,000 independent distributors throughout the United States, Canada, Europe, Australia, the Bahamas, and the Caribbean.

The WeCare distributor is a personal skin-care consultant. Distributors must not only know about the products, but must recommend which product is best for individual customers. Distributors work one-on-one with customers through home parties, individual direct selling, and skin-care demonstrations.

Sales consultants are independent contractors who are free to work full or part time. No sales background is necessary, but the company looks for individuals who can portray enthusiasm to potential customers and can make a commitment to WeCare.

WeCare has established a multimarketing program that allows distributors to earn commissions through personal sales, the recruitment and sales orders of other distributors, and customer purchases. The company rewards customers who purchase large volume orders with several membership packages that offer coupons, discounts, and special promotion bonuses.

Entrepreneurs pay a $19 registration fee to become a registered distributor. This first rung on the marketing ladder grants entrepreneurs the right to sell the Rose Marie line of products to consumers. For their efforts, distributors earn a 25 percent return on product orders, and they become eligible to subscribe to the company's networking order. This program automatically ships products and training materials, such as literature and brochures, to a distributor on a monthly basis.

Registered distributors graduate to become qualified distributors when they place a one-time order of $300. This level allows distributors to receive a 5 percent commission on customer orders and a 5 percent override on sales earned by any other personally recruited distributor. The qualified distributor can again rise to the level of key distributor and master distributor. Key distributors need minimum sales earnings of $1,500 in a one-month period, while master distributor status requires a distributor to earn at least $3,000 gross sales in one month. Entrepreneurs at these upper distributor levels also receive percentage overrides on personal sales and those completed by personally sponsored distributors.

WeCare also promotes distributors to seven management levels. As with the distributor levels, each promotion depends on the individual distributor's performance as well as the performance of personally sponsored distributors and their recruits underneath them. Management-level distributors earn overrides on each sale made by sales consultants in their individual networks.

All sales consultants can receive training at the home office in North Carolina, through periodic workshops held locally, and through individualized sessions with distributor sponsors. Distributors learn how to present and demonstrate the company's products, set personal goals, and implement marketing strategies to achieve those goals. WeCare conducts regular workshops and seminars for all distributors in its network, and publishes promotional and educational material on its products.

Future Outlook

The direct-sales industry records more than $40 billion in gross sales annually throughout the world. Many consumers want to purchase quality products, but they don't want to sacrifice the time to go find them. Companies such as WeCare satisfy the consumer's need for convenience and personal service.

The WeCare skin-care line consists of high-quality, well-researched products. None of the products is tested on animals, an important factor to both consumers and entrepreneurs alike.

Contact Information

Address: 10701-A South Commerce Blvd., Charlotte, North Carolina 28273

Telephone: 1-704-587-0400
Contact person: Richard H. Dickens, president

HOME ACCESSORIES AND APPLIANCES

ARTISTIC IMPRESSIONS, INC.

Initial investment: $99 to $200
Total investment: $99 to $200
Ongoing fees: None
Right to use trademark and logo: None

Expansion History
Operating since: 1986
Offering business opportunities since: 1986
Number of independent consultants: 700+

Industry Focus
Art and home accessory items benefit from the personal approach of in-home or party-plan sales.

Consumers want to improve and add to their existing homes. Art offers them a way to improve their home and change its appearance inexpensively.

Company Advantages
Artistic Impressions was founded by Bart Breighner, a veteran in the direct sales industry. He is the former director of North American sales for World Book Encyclopedia Company, and he established a successful financial planning and consulting firm as well.

Artistic Impressions offers sales consultants advancement potential and business-operating flexibility. Consultants can work part or full time, and they can decide the number of home parties they wish to contract during the work week.

• • •

Artistic Impressions, Inc., has redefined shopping for art with its direct sales program that brings oils, prints, and other art media to the consumer's home. Founded in 1986, Artistic Impressions sells more than 2,500 works of art per week through a chain of 700 independent consultants throughout the United States. The company commissions artwork from artists across the country and stores and frames the paintings and prints in its 20,000-square-foot facility in Lombard, Illinois.

Artistic Impressions consultants are salespeople who need no background in art or interior design. The goal of the consultants is to conduct at least one home party per week. At this party, consultants display approximately 80 unframed canvases that range in price from $64 to $300; the average sales price is $100, and average gross receipts total $725. Consultants usually earn a 22 to 30 percent commission on each sale.

Artistic Impressions consultants can increase their commissions by recruiting other independent contractors to work with them. As consultants rise to supervisory and management levels, they receive a commission of 4 to 7 percent on the sales made by their consultant team members.

Artistic Impressions makes no earnings claims, but the company maintains that consultants who work one night a week can earn $10,000 annually. This figure increases as the number of weekly shows and consultant recruits increases. Consultants can rise from a solo contractor, to sales director, to regional manager, to area manager, and finally to zone manager. Each management level requires a minimum number of consultants under a supervisor. Artistic Impressions estimates that the middle- and upper-level managers can easily earn a high five-figure income annually.

The initial investment to become an Artistic Impressions consultant ranges from $99 to $200. This fee allows the consultant the use of all standard sales equipment, including frame samples, easels, portfolios, paperwork, and consigned oils or prints. The canvases are owned by Artistic Impressions and offered to consultants on consignment. Customers purchase the artwork at the show, but they do not take their paintings home immediately. The canvases are sent to the company headquarters and framed, and then returned to the consultant who delivers them to the customers.

Artistic Impressions provides training to all consultants through professional video programs and training sessions. Local management and corporate headquarters instruct new consultants in sales presentation and product knowledge. Artistic Impressions also conducts regular sales meetings, management training classes, and conventions. The company sponsors bonuses, contests, and incentive programs to consultants on all levels, and it welcomes consultants' feedback and questions.

Future Outlook

Company president Bart Breighner has used his expertise in the direct-sales method of marketing to establish Artistic Impressions. The company has commissioned original work from artists. Customers are eager to purchase their favorite artwork at home demonstrations because they know these paintings are not carried at retail stores or galleries.

This type of business opportunity generally attracts young mothers who are looking to enhance their income without sacrificing their home life. These consultants tend to advance with the company as their children reach school age.

Artistic Impressions has a loyal consultant following. Many of the consultants who started with the company seven years ago are still in the program as regional and top-level zone managers.

Contact Information

Address: 240 Cortland Avenue, Lombard, Illinois 60148
Telephone: 1-708-916-0050
Contact person: Bart Breighner

REXAIR, INC.

Initial investment: $15,000 minimum
Total investment: $15,000 minimum
Ongoing fees: None
Right to use trademark and logo: Yes

Expansion History
Operating since: 1936
Offering distributorships since: 1959
Number of distributorships: 927

Industry Focus
In-home sales of vacuum cleaners and accessories have proved to be the best method of selling these products. Consumers want salespeople to prove the durability and performance of a vacuum on their own carpets and floors.

Company Advantages
Rexair has sold Rainbow vacuum cleaners and accessory products for more than 50 years. The company has grown successfully using its multilevel distributorship organization that transforms commissioned Rexair salespersons into top-level distributors and entrepreneurs.

Established in 1936, Rexair is the manufacturer of the Rainbow vacuum cleaner system. The company began as a small sales and service outlet in Michigan, but now it includes an international network of 927 distributors who sell and service the Rainbow products.

Rainbow distributors, or R.G.D. distributors, are managing business owners. They occupy the top level on the Rexair multilevel distributor chain. Their role is to hire and finance subdistributors and area distributors to sell and service Rainbow products. Subdistributors and area distributors are independent entrepreneurs who receive commissions from the R.G.D. distributor on each machine or accessory item sold. Subdistributors also work to establish their own offices and become R.G.D. distributors.

Rexair selects its R.G.D. distributors with great care. All must have sales and managerial background. Sales experience does not have to include Rainbow or competitive vacuum product knowledge, but it does have to include a successful record.

R.G.D. distributors supply the funds to keep their areas functioning properly. Rexair does not promise exclusive territories, but the company does try to maintain certain area borders. A minimum investment of $15,000 covers the cost of equipment, inventory, and start-up office expenses. As a rule, distributors must supply at least one Rainbow cleaning system for each subdistributor hired to sell in that territory. R.G.D. distributors are also responsible for leasing warehouse space. Rexair stocks each distributor's warehouse with Rainbow equipment, and the company maintains an open account with the distributor for the merchandise in the warehouse. Distributors purchase the machines and accessories at wholesale prices from Rexair and then sell them to customers at retail prices.

As part of the contract, distributors establish storefront offices for the sale and service of Rainbow equipment. These offices are the headquarters for subdistributors, area distributors, and service technicians. The company also expects R.G.D. distributors to furnish the office with appropriate equipment, including telephone lines, a fax machine, copier, and furniture. Rexair allows R.G.D. distributors to use the Rainbow trademark and logo, but they must emphasize that they are authorized distributors for Rexair and Rainbow products—not employees.

R.G.D. distributors are responsible for the training, activity, and support of all subdistributors and area distributors in their regions. They personally teach subdistributors the various functions of the Rainbow vacuum cleaner. R.G.D. distributors also teach successful sales techniques, including setting up appointments, demonstrating and selling the product, and educating the consumer on its use.

Future Outlook

The Rexair multilevel chain takes care of training new "recruits." Each level builds on the previous level, so most R.G.D. distributors are experts by the time they reach the top marketing position. Those who come in as distributors from the outside receive training from fellow R.G.D. distributors.

The company's warehouse policy allows distributors to have easy access to products and accessories. Although distributors pay for the warehouse space, they do not incur the expense of its contents until they purchase the merchandise to fill customer orders.

Direct, in-home sales is not an easy job, but the Rexair system claims successful salespersons receive lucrative earnings.

Contact Information
Address: 3221 W. Big Beaver Road, Suite 200, Troy, Michigan
  48084
Telephone: 1-313-643-7222
Contact person: Kenneth A. Hook

HOME SAFETY/ALARMS

U.S. SAFETY & ENGINEERING CORPORATION

Initial investment: $5,000 (negotiable for qualified distributors)
Total investment: $5,000 (negotiable)
Ongoing fees: None
Right to use trademark and logo: Yes

Expansion History
Company operating since: 1962
Offering distributorships since: 1962
Number of distributorships: Not available

Industry Focus
  Residential fire alarms can save hundreds of lives and thousands
of dollars in property damage. Fire departments throughout the
world endorse the use of fire and smoke detectors in private
residences.
  Insurance and mortgage companies look to see that homes are
protected with fire and smoke detection devices before they agree
to write policies or finance a mortgage.

Company Advantages
  U.S. Safety & Engineering has a 30-year track record in the fire
alarm industry.
  The company's alarm system is composed of two separate prod-

ucts: a heat detector guaranteed for 25 years and a smoke detector guaranteed for life.

U.S. Safety & Engineering Corporation teaches the importance of fire alarms to homeowners through its nationwide, independent distributor network that markets the company's residential fire alarm system.

U.S. Safety & Engineering views the role of its distributor seriously. The company essentially sells safety and consumer trust, and it expects its distributors to live up to that commitment. As a way of ensuring this trust, U.S. Safety & Engineering screens all distributor candidates carefully.

Interested entrepreneurs first complete a detailed application that focuses on their background and work history. This step is followed by an in-depth telephone interview. If the company is satisfied with an entrepreneur's qualifications, it will assign an exclusive territory.

At the heart of this company and its distributor network is the dual-sensor fire alarm system, which is composed of heat detectors and smoke detectors. Both detectors are contained in a round unit that is 7.5 inches in diameter. Homeowners mount the unit on any ceiling or wall surface. The U.S. Safety & Engineering product meets National Fire Protection Association standards.

The role of the distributor is that of educator, consultant, and salesperson. It is the distributor's responsibility to explain the alarm system and its capabilities in detail to homeowners. As independent business owners, distributors are free to explore many marketing avenues, including direct mail, telemarketing, and local media campaigns.

U.S. Safety & Engineering allows distributors free rein in establishing their businesses. Many distributors begin marketing the alarms on a part-time basis, usually during the evening and weekend hours. This allows first-time entrepreneurs to retain their jobs while they build their own business. Distributors tend to increase their time commitment as customer requests for the fire alarm system develop.

U.S. Safety & Engineering asks for a minimum investment of $5,000. The company refers to this as a "soft" minimum, which means it can be lowered for qualified distributors who do not have enough investment capital. The initial investment purchases alarm system inventory, an exclusive territory, and the right to market the U.S. Safety & Engineering product and name.

U.S. Safety & Engineering provides new contractors with personal training from an established distributor. Most of the training involves observing the established distributor's sales presentation and product explanation. New distributors also learn how to follow up on client leads, advertise the product, and gauge their inventory. U.S. Safety & Engineering offers the observation training free of charge. As part of its ongoing support program, the company also sponsors seminars and clinics that are designed to enhance sales and presentation skills.

Future Outlook

The company believes its success lies in the customers' trust for its product and its representatives. U.S. Safety & Engineering's belief in its distributors and their commitment is illustrated in its flexible policy with the initial investment.

The company's alarm system is well-known throughout the country, and U.S. Safety & Engineering backs it up with its long-term warranties.

Contact Information

Address: 2365 El Camino Avenue, Sacramento, California 95821
Telephone: 1-916-482-8888
Contact person: Robert D. Boyd

KEEPSAKE, NOVELTY, AND GIFT ITEMS

AMERICAN NAME JEWELRY

(Lasting Impressions, Inc.)

Initial investment: $299 to $599
Total investment: $299 to $599
Ongoing fees: None
Right to use trademark and logo: Yes

Expansion History
Company in business since: 1980
Offering distributorships since: 1980
Number of distributors: 1,000

Industry Focus
Personalized costume jewelry has always had a successful following from consumers.

Company Advantages
American Name Jewelry operates efficiently as a part-time business endeavor.

Dealers can market their customized products in a variety of places, including flea markets, craft fairs, and auto shows.

For entrepreneurs who want to purchase both Chain-by-the-Inch and American Name Jewelry dealerships, the company offers a $50 discount on the initial investment fee.

Another division of Lasting Impressions, Inc., is American Name Jewelry. American Name sells beaded, custom-designed necklaces, bracelets, earrings, and pins. For an initial investment ranging from $299 to $599, American Name dealers receive an initial inventory consisting of a variety of beads and bead containers, pins, bead string, velvet display pads and easels, a tape measure, tool set, sample bead bracelet, and a step-by-step instruction booklet.

Most dealers choose to market the American Name products on a part-time basis, which usually involves weekend travel to flea markets, craft fairs, automobile and flower shows, and charity events. Those who elect to market the personalized jewelry on a full-time basis usually have established retail stores or kiosks in malls and shopping centers.

American Name dealers do not pay any ongoing fees nor do they have to adhere to any company operating policy. The company does require that jewelry made with the material be advertised under the American Name trademark and logo and be purchased from the home office.

Lasting Impressions does not require any formal training for this dealership. Dealers are responsible for reading the company's training booklet. As with its sister company, Chain-by-the-Inch, American Name Jewelry comes with a money-back guarantee.

Future Outlook
Dealers can make up to a 1,500 percent profit on most jewelry sales. Lasting Impressions will refund the initial fee to unsatisfied dealers.

Contact Information
Address: 4407 Vineland Road, Suite D-5, Orlando, Florida 32811
Telephone: 1-800-843-7165 or 1-407-876-0341
Contact person: Bruce Mandleblit

CHAIN-BY-THE-INCH

(Lasting Impressions, Inc.)

Initial investment: $399 to $699
Total investment: $399 to $699
Ongoing fees: None
Right to use trademarks and logos: Yes

Expansion History
Company operating since: 1980
Offering independent distributorships since: 1980
Number of distributors: 1,000

Industry Focus
Jewelry never goes out of style, but as it is a luxury item, consumers look for the best possible bargains.

Company Advantages
Lasting Impressions, Inc., markets two distributor opportunities: Chain-by-the-Inch and American Name Jewelry. For entrepreneurs who want to purchase both dealerships, the company offers a $50 discount on the initial investment fee.

Chain-by-the-Inch distributors can market custom-sized chains, earrings, and other jewelry items in a variety of ways through retail stores, flea markets, house parties, and mail-order catalogs.

Dealers do not need a background in jewelry. All products have a quality guarantee and are certified by Lasting Impressions, which is a member of the Jewelers Board of Trade.

Chain-by-the-Inch, one division of Lasting Impressions, Inc., of Orlando, Florida, offers consumers custom-cut costume and 14-carat gold-layered jewelry.

Established in 1980, Chain-by-the-Inch stocks its gold chain merchandise in 25- and 50-foot spools. The easily stored and portable merchandise has attracted many entrepreneurs, who either sell the jewelry directly to the consumer through house parties and flea markets or add the jewelry line to already existing retail stores.

Entrepreneurs become Chain-by-the-Inch dealers with an investment ranging from $399 to $699. Lasting Impressions requires no waiting period or screening process, and the company accepts Visa, Mastercard, and C.O.D. orders for the payment of the initial investment fee, which covers the cost of inventory. For the initial investment, Chain-by-the-Inch dealers receive nine 25-foot rolls of various gold and crystal-styled chains. Also included is a mirrored Lucite chain display, a jeweler's tool set, a metal chain ruler, a laminated counter sign, an instruction booklet, and written guarantees for the jewelry.

Chain-by-the-Inch dealers do not attend any formal classroom training, but each operator is expected to read the company's instruction booklet carefully. The company charges no ongoing royalty fees, but it does require dealers to purchase their jewelry advertised as Chain-by-the-Inch merchandise from Lasting Impressions.

Lasting Impressions is available for telephone consultations with dealers who have concerns or questions. The company has a money-back guarantee for dealers who are unsatisfied with the results of their Chain-by-the-Inch enterprise. Lasting Impressions does not guarantee income for its dealers, but it claims that dealers can make up to a 1,500 percent profit on many of the jewelry items.

Future Outlook

Direct selling to consumers through house parties and flea markets can result in high profits. Chain-by-the-Inch dealers are free to market their merchandise as they see fit, and the company encourages sales creativity. House parties and flea markets are usually evening and weekend activities, so dealers should be prepared to give up this time for the sake of business.

Contact Information
Address: 4407 Vineland Road, Suite D-5, Orlando, Florida 32811
Telephone: 1-800-843-7165 or 1-407-876-0341
Contact person: Bruce Mandleblit

CRADLEGRAM, INC.

Initial investment: $95
Total investment: $99
Ongoing fees: 40 percent on first $300 gross; 50 percent on gross above $300
Right to use trademark and logo: Yes

Expansion History
In business since: 1988
Offering distributorships since: 1988
Number of dealerships: 139

Industry Focus
Novelties, especially personalized novelties, have always been a great attraction to consumers. Novelty items usually coincide with happier events, which makes the consumer more apt to spend on these products.

Company Advantages
Cradlegram concentrates on birth and religious announcements such as baptisms and bar mitzvahs. The products are marketed to the consumer directly, to institutions such as hospitals, health maintenance organizations (HMOs), and retail outlets as well.

Cradlegram maintains strong dealership support, and its $95 initial investment fee is affordable to most potential dealers. The company, whose product consists of parchment with personalized messages, fills all dealer orders quickly, usually within 72 hours.

The novelty industry often provides an inexpensive route into business ownership. Cradlegram, Inc., of Miami, Florida, demonstrates this point with its personalized birth and religious announcement dealerships, which require no more than a $99 initial investment.

Established in 1988, Cradlegram offers customers a choice of 22 verses, written in various languages and printed on either pink or blue parchment. Owned and operated by a husband-and-wife team, Sylvia and Henry Cronin, Cradlegram has grown to more than 139 dealerships in 48 states.

Dealers pay a total investment of $99, which purchases all sample books and brochures needed to sell the personalized announcements. Cradlegram charges $4 to those who inquire about the dealership program, and they get a Cradlegram information kit that includes a dealership agreement, samples, a brochure, plus other promotional information. When entrepreneurs decide to invest, they send the home office $95 along with the signed dealership agreement, and the company returns to them a start-up kit that includes supplies, price sheets, and sample books. Dealers also receive a how-to manual that outlines company marketing and sales techniques.

A Cradlegram dealer's main responsibility is to take orders for the personalized announcements. Customers choose the verse and color of each announcement from samples and a four-color brochure. Prices range from $24 for 10 announcements to $40 for 25 announcements, and they are delivered to customers usually within four to five days. Dealers are not responsible for any printing. All orders are sent to Cradlegram, which uses its own network of printers to fill the announcement requests. The company works closely with Florida International University's Small Business Institute. The institute directs Cradlegram to printers and language experts, who translate the verses into the requested language.

Dealers can either market the announcements to customers directly, or they can sell the Cradlegrams through hospitals and their gift shops, HMOs, and other insurance companies that give complementary gift items to policyholders. Some dealers also sell the personalized announcements to retailers who offer the personalized service to customers.

Cradlegram dealers receive a 40 percent commission on sales totaling $300 per month or less. Any sales above $300 are awarded a 50 percent commission. Cradlegram allows dealers to deduct their commissions immediately, and the company does not ask to see any financial statements reflecting dealers' earnings. Cradlegram does not allocate exclusive territories, but the company will not place another dealer in an area that is being developed successfully.

Cradlegram dealers range from part-time workers who want to earn a second income, to full-time entrepreneurs. The company is operated as a home-based business in Miami, and it advises its dealers to work from home. Dealers use the Cradlegram trademark and logo, which are registered with the U.S. Patent Office. Cradlegram does not meet each dealer in person, but it does maintain telephone and mail support. The company plans to implement a dealer "checkup" program in the near future to monitor dealers' sales productivity.

Future Outlook

Cradlegram maintains that dealers can earn a solid income if they are willing to sell these products aggressively. The company works with dealers to establish individualized business plans. Cradlegram's close ties with the Small Business Institute at Florida International University has aided in the development of the company.

Contact Information

Address: P.O. Box 16-4135, Miami, Florida 33116-4135
Telephone: 1-305-595-6050
Contact person: Sylvia Cronin

JIM SCHARF HOLDINGS, LTD.

Initial investment: $200
Total investment: $200
Ongoing fees: None
Right to use trademark and logo: Yes

Expansion History
Company operating since: 1986
Offering distributorships since: 1986
Number of distributorships: 20 +

Industry Focus

Mounted kitchen appliances save valuable counterspace, and they can be conveniently placed within a consumer's grasp.

Company Advantages

Jim Scharf Holdings, Ltd., has been recognized by the Canadian government for its entrepreneurial opportunities. The Scharfs have a successful history in T-shirts and other novelty items. Operations for the E-ZEE plastic wrap dispenser have been moved into a larger facility.

The patented E-ZEE plastic wrap dispenser from Jim Scharf Holdings, Ltd., is a 4-by-13-inch appliance that is attached to the underside of kitchen cupboards and dispenses plastic wrap. The dispenser's blade is designed to leave two inches of plastic after each tear, so consumers can easily grab hold of the plastic wrap the next time it is needed.

Scharf's original dispenser was constructed of metal and retailed for $50. Scharf invested $300,000 in the dispenser and developed a plastic version that now sells for $40. The new product in combination with a national print and television advertising campaign has put the company in full-production mode.

Scharf sells the product through retail stores and to the consumer directly through a network of distributors in Canada. Scharf also plans to import the product into the United States. The company encourages part-time and full-time distributors to explore all marketing routes, including selling the dispenser at retail stores as well as home shows, trade shows, and flea markets.

For an initial investment of $200, a distributor receives 10 dispensers. Scharf guarantees this investment and will return the money to the distributors if they fail to sell the original order. Distributors can make 100 percent profit on the dispensers, which they buy wholesale from the company for $17 to $20 each. Distributors also sell refill rolls of plastic wrap. The dispenser holds all brands of plastic, but most customers choose to buy the wrap in bulk form from the E-ZEE Wrap distributor. Distributors need no special training to sell this product, but they do need initiative and determination.

Scharf charges no ongoing fees, but distributors still benefit from the company's advertising campaign that will continue in Canada and expand into the United States. Scharf has also recently hired an American firm to handle public relations in the United States.

Future Outlook

Scharf Holdings, Ltd., has researched this product thoroughly. The dispenser eliminates the need for cardboard dispenser boxes, which fits in well with today's environmentally concerned consumers.

Contact Information

Address: Box 305 Avenue K and 9th St., Perdue, Saskatchewan,
   Canada, SOK 3CO
Telephone: 1-800-MOR-WRAP or 1-306-237-4365
Contact person: Jim or Bruna Scharf

NOVO CARD PUBLISHERS, INC./
MODERNE CARD, INC.

Initial investment: $1,000
Total investment: $1,000
Ongoing fees: None
Right to use trademarks and logos: Yes

Expansion History
Company in business since: 1929
Offering distributorships since: 1929
Number of distributors: 200+

Industry Focus
   Greeting cards are a convenient way of communicating with
friends and family. Consumers rely on greeting cards to relay their
feelings to people.

Company Advantages
   Novo Card Publishers, Inc., has a 63-year record in the greeting-
card industry. The company has staff artists and creative personnel
who design the cards.
   Novo/Moderne distributors do not need to lease office space.
They conduct sales calls at retail establishments that sell the cards
to the public.

   Novo Card Publishers, Inc., and its sister trademark, Moderne
Card, Inc., create a variety of greeting cards for all occasions and
life events. The Chicago, Illinois-based company markets its products through more than 200 independent distributors.
   Novo distributors are independent sales contractors who sell

greeting cards to gift shops, party stores, drugstores, and super-markets. Distributors need no sales experience, and they can take on the distributorship on a part-time or full-time basis.

The key to success for Novo distributors is a good rapport with retail store managers and owners. It is the distributor's responsibility to introduce products to retailers, take their orders, and deliver the merchandise. As independent contractors, distributors set their own sales prices for the cards. Novo does not offer any earnings claims, but the company maintains that distributors earn from 50 to 70 percent profit on each order.

Entrepreneurs need approximately $1,000 to become a Novo distributor. This includes $250 for the Novo sample kit and the right to use the Novo and Moderne trademark and name in the sale of the merchandise. Novo refunds the cost of the kit to distributors after they place their first order. Also included in the initial invest-ment are the wholesale purchase of starting inventory and allow-ances for marketing, advertising, and working-capital expenses.

Novo does not require distributors to attend any formal training classes. The company will provide initial and ongoing telephone and in-person support if needed.

Future Outlook

Novo and Moderne Card, Inc., are recognized trademarks to retail shops that sell greeting cards. The company has more than half a century of experience in designing and marketing.

The company does expect distributors to show enthusiasm when selling its product. The company offers distributors a great deal of flexibility in how they manage their business.

The greeting-card industry has a great deal of competition, and entrepreneurs may have to work with retailers to get enough shelf space for their products.

Contact Information

Address: 4513 North Lincoln Avenue, Chicago, Illinois
Telephone: 1-800-624-2426 or 1-312-769-6000
Contact person: Kris Chae, president

WATER PURIFICATION SYSTEMS

AQUA-FLO, INC.

Initial Investment: $5,000 (minimum working capital)
Total Investment: $5,000 (minimum working capital)
Ongoing fees: None
Right to use trademark and logo: No

Expansion History
Company operating since: 1981
Offering distributorships since: 1981
Number of distributorships: 80

Industry Focus
Water-conditioning systems can save building and business owners thousands of dollars in fuel and water costs.

Lime scale buildup and hard water can greatly reduce or destroy boiler and air conditioning equipment efficiency.

Government, industry, and everyday consumers have relied in the past on chemical treatment for water systems. Environmental concerns have caused us to utilize alternative forms of water conditioning.

Company Advantages
Aqua-Flo's exclusive manufacturing design uses a magnetic filter rather than chemicals to descale boiler, air-conditioning, and water systems.

Much of the equipment manufactured by Aqua-Flo meets National Sanitary Foundation standards.

Aqua-Flo is a leading manufacturer of ozone-generating equipment, which is used as a primary disinfectant and biocide in lieu of chemicals in drinking-water systems and industrial waste water improvement programs.

Aqua-Flo's water-conditioning system is self-contained and has a 10-year warranty with an unlimited life expectancy.

Hard water deposits corrosive and damaging material into heating, air-conditioning, and plumbing systems. Aqua-Flo, Inc., virtually eliminates hard-water damage with its self-contained water treatment system that removes and prevents lime scale buildup. First manufactured in 1981, the Aqua-Flo system uses a permanent magnetic chamber to dissolve minerals such as calcium and magnesium carbonates. The revolutionary design of this water-conditioning product has transformed Aqua-Flo into an industry leader, and the company has more than 80 distributors for its products worldwide.

Aqua-Flo distributors market the water treatment system to residential consumers as well as commercial and industrial customers such as motels, hotels, condominium and apartment complexes, mobile home parks, restaurants, medical offices, hospitals, swimming pools, and processing plants. Prices for the Aqua-Flo products range from $300 to $5,000 for residential units and $2,000 to $20,000 for industrial units.

Aqua-Flo assigns distributors exclusive territories that are determined mainly by population. The distributors are responsible for the sale and installation of the Aqua-Flo unit, but they do not need a background in the plumbing industry.

Aqua-Flo grants distributors flexibility in the operation of their business. Distributors can establish a retail location to market the system, but most choose direct mail, telemarketing, and aggressive advertising campaigns. Many distributors also participate in trade shows, industry conventions, and direct sales methods.

Distributors are not allowed to portray themselves as employees of Aqua-Flo, but they are permitted to say they are independent distributors for the company. There is no initial fee to become an Aqua-Flo distributor. The company does not expect distributors to purchase any equipment, but it does require them to have enough capital to market the Aqua-Flo products effectively. Aqua-Flo recommends that distributors have on hand a minimum of $5,000 to cover the costs of advertising, establishing a home or commercial office, the installation of a telephone line, and the purchase of any other needed office equipment.

The company also charges a $500 fee for a two-day training seminar, which takes place at Aqua-Flo's factory in Baltimore, Maryland. The fee includes food and lodging, and its goal is to instruct distributors in the technical aspect of the Aqua-Flo products, including the testing of water quality, which helps distributors prescribe the right Aqua-Flo product. The training also educates them in the installation of the product.

Aqua-Flo provides ongoing support for distributors. The company supplies operation and product manuals, advance training on any new product developed by Aqua-Flo, and a toll-free number for technical assistance.

Future Outlook

Aqua-Flo, Inc., has redefined the standards for water-conditioning treatment. The product treats water by electromechanical means rather than chemicals, and it also aids in the elimination of algae and bacteria in water and air-conditioning systems. The Aqua-Flo system provides a more sanitary and environmentally sound water product.

Company founder Alden Coke is a chemist who owned a research and development company before developing the Aqua-Flo system. He is widely respected throughout the water-conditioning industry.

Contact Information

Address: 6244 Frankford Avenue, Baltimore, Maryland 21206
Telephone: 1-800-368-2513 or 1-410-485-7600
Contact person: Alden Coke, president

MULTI-PURE DRINKING WATER SYSTEMS

Initial investment: $375
Total investment: $375
Ongoing fees: None
Right to use trademark and logo: None

Expansion History
Company operating since: 1970
Offering Multi-Pure distributorships since: 1982
Number of Multi-Pure distributors: 85,000

Industry Focus
Water is our most important natural resource. Consumers' trust in municipal water supplies has deteriorated, especially when there is evidence of harmful toxins such as lead, bacteria, and chemicals.

The water purification industry has developed several methods of reducing harmful substances in drinking water. The United States government has approved carbon block filtration as an effective means of water purification.

Industry research estimates that by 1994, consumers will spend more than $12 billion on improving their water quality.

Company Advantages
Multi-Pure Drinking Water Systems was the first company to introduce the carbon block filter purification system, which is made with materials approved by the Federal Drug Administration (FDA).

Multi-Pure Drinking Water Systems costs consumers approximately seven cents per gallon, and the company maintains that consumers who use bottled drinking water can save up to $600 a year by converting to a Multi-Pure System.

Established in 1970, Multi-Pure's success stems from its exclusively designed, disposable, solid, carbon block filter. This filter strains solid, semisolid, and other contaminants from drinking water while simultaneously reducing the levels of chlorine, lead, odors, asbestos, trihalomethanes, and other potentially harmful elements.

A Multi-Pure distributor is a direct salesperson. Distributors market the Multi-Pure system and accessory products to homeowners and businesses throughout their area. Multi-Pure offers a variety of filtration systems, including a countertop model and an under-the-sink model. Consumers pay an average of $329.95 for the system itself plus an additional $34.95 annually for replacement filters.

Independent distributors can explore many marketing routes. Most participate in telemarketing, direct mail, and person-to-person sales campaigns. The distributor contacts potential customers and schedules appointments at the customer's home. The in-home sales presentations consist of product demonstration as well as water tests that identify the presence of chlorine and other chemicals in the drinking water.

To become a member of the Multi-Pure network, an entrepreneur must be sponsored by an existing distributor. The company's distributor system is a ten-level marketing organization. Distributors climb the ten levels by sponsoring new distributors into a sales team and forming a subdistributor network. It is not uncommon for these subnetworks to include hundreds of members.

Distributors earn commissions through their own personal sales, from sales of their own sponsored distributors, from sales made by distributors in their immediate subnetwork, and from sales on the replaceable carbon filters.

First-level distributors earn an initial $49.95 commission on their first sale plus a 20 percent commission on all additional sales. As distributors reach sales milestones, they improve their level status and earn up to 35 percent in commissions plus bonus awards.

A $375 investment purchases the rights to market the Multi-Pure Drinking Water System. Included in this investment is a $25 registration fee plus a $280 (distributor discount) purchase of a drinking water system for demonstration. Multi-Pure also estimates that distributors should have in reserve an additional $70 for initial advertising expenses.

Multi-Pure does not require any minimum sales quota for a distributor to retain active status. The company also allows distributors to advertise the water system, but all artwork and copy must be approved by the home office. Distributors are free to use the Multi-Pure name in advertising, but they must present themselves as independent distributors for the company.

All Multi-Pure distributors receive an operations manual plus audio and video instructional tapes as part of the training program. Upper-level distributors conduct personal training for their sponsored distributors in their local area. Sponsoring distributors also maintain telephone contact, and they conduct workshops and seminars as well. Multi-Pure holds monthly training and recruiting meetings for all distributors, and the company has a toll-free number for assistance.

Future Outlook
The increase in public awareness of environmental issues has made drinking-water improvement into a multibillion-dollar industry. Multi-Pure has outlasted many of its competitors because of its solid carbon filter. This design has won the support of government and private agencies that promote water filtration systems as a means for improving water quality.

Contact Information
Address: 21339 Nordhoff Street, Chatsworth, California 91311
Telephone: 1-818-351-5275
Contact person: Donald V. MacCrossen

TRANSWORLD INDUSTRIES

Initial investment: $1,000
Total investment: $1,000
Ongoing fees: None
Right to use trademark and logo: Yes

Expansion History
Company operating since: 1968
Offering distributorships since: 1968
Number of distributorships: 1,800 domestic; 570 foreign

Industry Focus
Consumers invest in purification systems that will provide contaminant-free water.

Competition in this industry comes not only from rival purification systems but from bottled water companies as well.

Consumers can judge the effectiveness of water-purification systems by researching the product and its components. The federal government has also conducted studies on the various methods of water purification, and data can be retrieved from government sources and consumer organizations.

Company Advantages

Transworld Industries is the only company that uses the KDF-55D water purification system. Transworld claims that it is the most reliable method of removing contaminants from water systems.

Company owner George Busca possesses a degree in research design from MIT and an MBA in sales from Harvard University. He designed the water-filtration products and distributed the products throughout the United States and 137 additional countries. Transworld Industries is in a joint venture with another company that manufactures all the filtration products.

Transworld Industries makes water safe for drinking with its energy-saving, water-purification products. In existence since 1968, Transworld Industries markets its elite line of products to residential and commercial customers with assistance from more than 2,370 distributors throughout the world.

The core of this company's success is the distribution of products that contain the patented filter material KDF-55, which works alone or in conjunction with sediment and Carbosyl filters to eliminate harmful elements and bacteria growth from drinking water.

The goal of distributors is to sell and install the filtration products, which include trademarks such as Filtaflo, Waterquest, and Carbosyl. The models vary according to the type of water supply available to consumers. For municipal water customers, the Filtaflo canister unit is installed either on top of the kitchen or bathroom counter or underneath. Most consumers can install the canisters themselves, but the distributor will complete this task if necessary. The unit contains a meter that monitors the filtering process, and most cartridges last for approximately 3,000 gallons of water.

Transworld Industries markets its Waterquest system to rural consumers who use well water. The system is a four-foot-tall container that is installed in a basement or storage shed area. Well-water consumers also benefit from the Triple Deal filter system that drains water through a sediment cartridge, KDF-55D cartridge, and finally a Carbosyl cartridge.

Distributors are independent contractors who operate and run their own business. They can be part-time entrepreneurs or full-time business owners with a retail showroom and a sales staff. Transworld Industries encourages distributors to start slowly and focus their attention on gaining volume sales. Volume sales allow the distributor to purchase the purification systems for less money.

Transworld also advises distributors to structure a business plan that attracts commercial and larger accounts, such as builders and architects. Distributors can obtain multiple water-purification sales installing the systems in new housing or office developments. As independent entrepreneurs, distributors are free to use any marketing avenue that they feel will attain results. Most distributors do subscribe to Yellow Pages displays as well as newspaper and magazine advertisements. Transworld Industries encourages the use of promotions, displays, gift certificates, and trade-in programs to attract customers. An initial investment of $1,000 establishes an entrepreneur as a Transworld Industries distributor. Distributors are assigned exclusive territories with a minimum population of 300,000 residents. The initial investment covers the cost of sample purification units as well as initial marketing and promotion. Distributors should also purchase a fax machine and maintain a separate telephone line for its operation. Distributors can either work from home or lease office space.

Distributors are not required to attend any formal training class, but Transworld Industries provides detailed and illustrated manuals and other literature to educate distributors on the product and the market. The company also supplies its independent contractors with free water tests for customers plus color advertisement materials and brochures.

Future Outlook

Transworld Industries has a competitive edge with its line of products featuring the KDF-55D. The company claims the products are more effective and less expensive than competitors' products that contain plain carbon filters. Transworld has received a great deal of international recognition for its cost-effective products.

Contact Information
Address: 2961 W. Glenlord Road, Stevensville, Michigan 49127
Telephone: 1-616-429-8706
Contact person: George Busca

Licenses

ADVERTISING AND PROMOTION

FIESTA CARTOON MAPS

Initial investment: $6,495
Total investment: $7,500
Ongoing fees: None
Right to use trademark and logo: None

Expansion History
Operating since: 1979
Offering licenses since: 1985
Number of licensees: 103

Industry Focus
Cartoon maps are not a novelty item, but a sophisticated advertising medium for local businesses and organizations.

This type of business emphasizes person-to-person contact. No equipment or inventory is needed to operate the business successfully.

Company Advantages
Fiesta Cartoons developed its product line and marketing strategy for seven years before it began offering licenses to entrepreneurs.

The simplicity of this business attracts first-time entrepreneurs. Fiesta releases to interested parties actual bank statements that show the company's revenues and expenses.

Fiesta Cartoon Maps of Tempe, Arizona, designs and prints caricature maps of towns and cities throughout the United States and Mexico. The maps, available in many sizes, are colorful and exaggerated depictions of an area, and they serve as useful advertising tools. Businesses and community organizations pay to have their names and addresses appear highlighted on the finished product. Fiesta sells the area maps through a network of 103 licensees throughout the United States and Mexico.

Fiesta licensees are salespeople. They solicit "map space" from 100 business owners and civic associations in their territories. Advertisers pay between $200 and $700 to have their names and addresses boldly marked on the area map along with community landmarks and well-known streets and waterways. When the 100 advertising spaces are sold, licensees send the order to the company's facilities in Arizona. Fiesta Cartoons produces the maps in quantities of 10,000 or more, and the licensee distributes them throughout the territory. The company estimates production costs for 10,000 maps to total approximately $6,550. Fiesta does not make earnings claims, but it does maintain that licensees can net up to $29,075 or more on one area map the first year. Each map is updated on a yearly basis, which regenerates income for the licensees.

An initial investment of $6,495 purchases the rights to an exclusive territory or one area map. Fiesta works with licensees to determine which community organizations will lead to the most advertisers, and then licensees target those organizations.

The initial fee also covers traveling and lodging expenses for the company's training workshop as well as all promotional materials, sales, and operations manuals needed to conduct business properly. As part of this fee, each licensee is entitled to the company's in-house art and production facilities, which guarantee a six-week delivery of all orders.

Licensees pay no ongoing royalty or advertising fees to Fiesta, and they can purchase additional territories for $1,500 per area. The company estimates that licensees will need an additional $1,000 in working capital to cover miscellaneous expenses.

Most Fiesta licensees actively run their businesses themselves. The company does allow absentee ownership, but the licensee must be prepared to pay a professional salesperson a commission of 20 percent or more to sell the advertising space. As licensees add more territories to their businesses, they will find it necessary to hire sales teams to sell advertising space in the expanded areas.

Fiesta Cartoon Maps requires all licensees to attend a three-day training workshop at its offices in Arizona. The training focuses on initial and follow-up sales techniques as well as management and personnel recruitment methods. Fiesta maintains telephone and in-field support for all licensees as needed.

Future Outlook

Fiesta maintains an ongoing support program for its licensees. The company works with licensees to determine the best avenue for the promotion of the map, and it conducts an extensive sales work-shop to ensure a licensee's success. The in-house production facilities in Arizona simplify the operation of this business opportunity for licensees and eliminate the need for equipment and an art staff.

The company markets its products nationally through advertising campaigns and exhibitions. The cost for this service is included in the licensee's initial investment.

Contact Information

Address: P.O. Box 3137, Tempe, Arizona 85281
Telephone: 1-800-541-4963 or 1-602-966-4639
Contact person: Ron Beckman
Contact person: Donald V. MacCrossen

CHILDREN'S SERVICES

CREATE-A-BOOK, INC.

Initial investment: $5,995 to $12,000
Total investment: $5,995 to $12,000
Ongoing fees: $300 annual license fee
Right to use trademark and logo: Yes

Expansion History
Operating since: 1980
Offering licenses since: 1981
Number of licensees: 600+

Industry Focus
Parents and teachers are stressing the importance of developing children's interest in books.

Few bookstores can commit the space for a large selection of children's books.

Company Advantages
Create-A-Book books are personalized for each individual child. When children see their names in print, they become more interested in the story, and they look forward to further reading.

Create-A-Book has a 12-year history in this personalized book industry. The company has been recognized for its fund-raising work with literacy groups and the Give-A-Book programs sponsored by business and industry across the United States and Canada.

Create-A-Book's founder, Karen Hefty, earned a master's degree in reading specialization and taught reading for more than 16 years. She is the author of the Create-A-Book series. Each book within this series is designed to teach children the value of self-esteem.

Create-A-Book received a patent in 1992 for its proprietary hard-binding process.

Create-A-Book calls their licensees "dealers." These dealers market their books through retail locations or through special programs such as fund-raisers and community literacy campaigns. Dealers who choose a retail avenue set up displays in larger department stores, or they operate their own store, kiosk, or cart in shopping centers, malls, and hospital gift shops. Some dealers combine the two marketing tactics: They set up a store or kiosk during the holiday seasons only and concentrate on the special marketing campaigns the remainder of the year.

The Create-A-Book dealer's main tools for this trade are a computer and laser printer. Customers choose a story from a list of more than 18 titles. They supply the dealers with a child's name and other pertinent information. Dealers enter the information into the computer, print it out, and produce a hard-bound book within seven to ten minutes. Dealers offer the books in both regular lettering and Braille, and book prices average $14.95.

An initial investment of $3,995 purchases a software licensing agreement and the right to use the Create-A-Book name. As part of this license agreement, dealers receive a training videotape and an operations manual that teaches licensees how to set up the equipment and run the software correctly. Create-A-Book offers no exclusive territories, and licensees are free to market their products throughout the United States and Canada. Create-A-Book charges no royalty fees, but the company does charge licensees an annual $300 renewal fee.

Create-A-Book estimates that dealers will need an additional $2,000 to $6,000 to establish their business. All dealers must purchase an IBM-compatible computer system with a hard drive as well as a laser printer.

Additional capital for lease arrangements will also be needed. The amount depends on the type and size of business the Create-A-Book dealer wants to operate.

Dealers may also buy Create-A-Book special posters, brochures, stationery items, holiday promotional material as well as novelty items such as pop-up displays, banners, decals, mobiles, and display books at discounted prices.

Create-A-Book requires no formal in-field training, but the company does maintain an ongoing support system through newsletters and telephone consultation. The company also sponsors an annual convention. Create-A-Book uses this forum to introduce new story lines, products, and methods of operation and distribution.

Future Outlook

Create-A-Book, Inc., has its roots in education. The personalized books combine lessons with entertainment. The books become keepsake items for children who see themselves as the main characters in these stories.

The company has made marketing advancements to capture other audiences. The introduction of Braille print and the drive toward literacy programs throughout the United States has increased the company's name recognition dramatically. Dealers gain from the company's fund-raising programs.

Contact Information
Address: 107 S.W. Caroline Street, Milton, Florida 32570-4717
Telephone: 1-800-392-READ or 1-904-623-9833
Contact person: Bruce Carpenter, director of marketing

FIT BY FIVE

Initial investment: $5,000
Total investment: $50
Ongoing fees: None
Right to use trademark and logo: Yes

Expansion History
Operating since: 1969
Offering licenses since: 1977
Number of licensees: 12

Industry Focus
All children need to become physically fit. Programs that stimulate children's interest in exercise are uncommon in the United States.

Not all children are natural athletes. If children feel uncomfortable or frustrated in athletics, they may reject exercise and physical fitness indefinitely. Children need programs that will bolster their self-esteem and make them eager to try physical fitness activities.

Company Advantages
Fit By Five provides children with physical and mental stimulation. The company was founded by Barbara Perkins-Carpenter, a former Olympic diving coach and member of the President's Council on Physical Fitness.

Fit By Five is the first program of its type in the United States. The programs focus on building children's self-esteem and interest in physical fitness.

Fit By Five licensees hold their classes in community centers, schools, or other facilities, but they can run the business from home.

Licensees do not need to be physical education teachers or exercise specialists. Fit By Five supplies all programs and lessons to the licensees.

Physical fitness is as important for children as it is for adults. Fit By Five of Rochester, New York, has delivered this message to thousands of preschool children throughout the United States for more than 23 years.

Geared toward nursery school–age children, Fit By Five uses planned physical activities to help children develop physically, mentally, and emotionally. Fit By Five now sells license agreements to those entrepreneurs interested in teaching the company's programs and concepts.

Fit By Five licensees are dual-role business owners. Initially most licensees are instructors as well as administrators. It is their responsibility to establish class schedules and locations, teach classes, advertise the programs, and hire and train other teachers. As interest in the programs develops, many licensees prefer to handle the administrative end of the business and hire instructors to teach the classes. Fit By Five licensees market the programs through nursery schools, day care centers, and community organizations.

Children ages two and one-half to five attend the three-hour classes up to three days per week. The semesters usually last 19 weeks, and the average tuition depends on how many days a child participates in the program.

Fit By Five has also recently developed a sister program that licensees can teach as well. "Perky Kids" is designed for the two- and three-year-old, pre–toilet-trained toddler. The classes average 90 minutes in length, and they also focus on physical play to boost self-esteem and discipline.

An investment of $5,000 purchases the rights to a Fit By Five license along with all programs, lessons plans, and operational manuals and videos. Fit By Five trains all licensees in the programs either at the home office in New York or at the licensee's location. Travel and lodging expenses are not part of the license agreement. Often licensees opt to have a representative come to their locations and teach the programs to all instructors. Fit By Five charges no ongoing or royalty fees. The lesson plans can be mixed and matched, and this gives licensees two years of programs for their initial investment. The company does offer additional programs and lessons for licensees and charges $5 for each additional set.

Fit By Five licensees are free to run their businesses on a part-time or full-time basis. As class enrollment grows, so does the need for time commitment. It is up to the licensees to determine what size business they wish to operate.

Future Outlook

Fit By Five's founder is an expert on physical fitness. She and her staff have developed programs that emphasize challenge not competition. There are few competitors in this industry.

Betty Perkins-Carpenter still operates and teaches in her original Fit by Five location. She maintains that her hands-on work keeps her in touch with the work of her licensees in other areas.

Fit By Five has not aggressively sought out new licensees. The company had originally used franchising as a means of expansion, but abandoned that route because it attracted too many investors at once. Perkins-Carpenter felt she could not give adequate attention to all franchisees. The company turned to licensing and reduced its exposure to investors. This change allowed the company to grow slowly and assist licensees in the establishment and maintenance of their programs.

Fit By Five still maintains a quiet profile, and Perkins-Carpenter remains involved in all programs and areas of licensee support. She also has developed programs for adult cardiovascular fitness and manages these as well from Fit By Five's home office.

Contact Information
Address: 1606 Penfield Road, Rochester, New York 14625
Telephone: 1-716-586-7980
Contact person: Betty Perkins-Carpenter

SIMPLICITY KIDS CAN SEW

Initial investment: $299
Total investment: $299 + purchase of sewing materials
Ongoing fees: $35 monthly license fee
Right to use trademark and logo: Yes

Expansion History
Company operating since: 1983
Offering licenses since: 1990
Number of licensees: 217

Industry Focus
Sewing is an economical and creative outlet for both children and adults. Any children's activity that emphasizes imagination and promotes self-esteem usually attracts parents and teachers.

Company Advantages
Simplicity Kids Can Sew uses simplified patterns and language to keep children interested in a sewing project. The sewing classes are geared for children from age 6 to 16.

The Kids Can Sew license agreement provides a turnkey operation that most licensees can run from home on a part-time basis.

Children are most proud of the things they make themselves. Simplicity Kids Can Sew recognizes this trait and has developed a sewing program around it. Established in 1983, Kids Can Sew uses the well-known Simplicity patterns plus its own exclusive patterns to teach children to sew.

The primary role of the licensee is that of teacher. Licensees use direct mail, flyers, and newspaper promotion to advertise the classes. Most Kids Can Sew licensees conduct classes in their own homes. Licensees tend to start teaching on a part-time basis. Kids Can Sew makes no earnings claims, but the company estimates that licensees can earn between $200 and $2,000 per month.

Kids Can Sew does not dictate class size for licensees, but the number of children should depend on the number of sewing machines available. Classes usually meet for one hour weekly, and tuition ranges from $25 to $45 per month.

Kids Can Sew licensees should have a basic knowledge of sewing skills. For an initial investment of $299, licensees purchase the rights to an exclusive territory that includes one zip code area. Licensees who wish to have a larger territory can purchase additional areas for $199 per zip code. Licensees can also become master licensees by recruiting other entrepreneurs into the Kids Can Sew network. For these efforts, master licensees receive a $50 immediate commission from the company and a $10 monthly commission as long as both the master and the new licensee remain active sewing instructors.

Kids Can Sew charges licensees with one zip code a $35 monthly renewal fee. For those who purchase a larger territory, the company charges an additional $25 fee per extra zip code. In addition to the initial investment, licensees may need additional capital for the purchase of sewing machines or other supplies. As part of the initial agreement, licensees receive one year of liability insurance, a comprehensive pattern package with patterns for all sewing levels, plus instruction videos and manuals. Licensees are permitted to use the Kids Can Sew trademark and logo in the everyday operation of their businesses as well, and they can purchase fabric and additional patterns from the home office at wholesale prices. Kids Can Sew licensees can also be distributors for the company, selling the Kids Can Sew products and patterns directly to the consumers.

Kids Can Sew licensees do not have to attend a formal training class. They are required to view the instruction video and read the operation manual, which focus on teaching, management, and record keeping as well. The company publishes regular newsletters for all licensees and enrolls licensees in the Kids Can Sew National Student and Teacher Referral Programs.

Future Outlook

Parents look for organized activities that teach children something valuable without sacrificing enjoyment. The costs for Kids Can Sew lessons are far less than other organized children's activities on the market today.

Carolyn Curtis, the founder of this company, began Kids Can Sew as a way to teach her own daughters to sew. Curtis first built her educational concept through mail-order sewing patterns, and now the company is focusing on its licensing agreements.

The initial success of this company is based on Curtis's ability to simplify sewing instructions for children. The company's foresight in entering into a formal agreement with Simplicity has also enhanced its growth.

Contact Information
Address: P.O. Box 1710 St. George, Utah 84771
Telephone: 1-800-I-MADE-IT or 1-801-628-7505
Contact person: Kathleen Egbert or Carolyn Curtis

Vending Machines
Mobile Vending

PROTOCOL, INC.

Initial investment: $15,000
Total investment: $15,000 to $18,000
Ongoing fees: None
Right to use trademark and logo: No

Expansion History
Company operating since: 1987
Offering distributorships since: 1987
Number of distributorships: 200+

Industry Focus
There is a great demand for discreetly placed vending machines that dispense personal-care and hygiene products such as Tylenol, Bayer aspirin, Maalox antacid tablets, perfume, cologne, and condoms.

The personal-care dispensing machines can be installed at any location where crowds gather, such as restaurants, bars, colleges, military bases, airports, and sport facilities.

Company Advantages
Protocol offers distributors a full business package, including equipment, marketing plans, and an ongoing support system.

Protocol's vending machines are compact and virtually vandal-proof, and the company offers a one-year protection plan on each dispenser.

Consumers do not always have on hand needed personal-care items. Protocol, Inc., offers patented vending equipment that dispenses a variety of brand-name merchandise including aspirin, feminine hygiene products, condoms, cologne, perfume, and antacids. Founded in 1987, Protocol markets its dispensing equipment and merchandise through an international and independent sales force of 200 distributors.

Protocol distributors are full-service businesspeople. With the company's help, they contact business owners and secure locations for the vending equipment. Distributors also install the units and monitor them to make sure they are stocked sufficiently.

Business owners who agree to have the units installed in their establishments play no part in the maintenance or stocking of the equipment. Their role is to decide how many vending units they want and what products they want to dispense. For their cooperative effort with Protocol distributors, business owners earn between 10 and 15 percent on the gross revenue generated by the vending equipment.

Protocol markets two vending units. Both are compact and easily installed on a small area of blank wall space. The two-column unit measures 4.5 inches by 11 inches by 34 inches, and can hold and dispense 320 individual packets of merchandise. This vending machine is divided into two adjustable dispensing columns that can each accommodate 160 Protocol packages. The three-column unit measures 4.5 inches by 17 inches by 34 inches and stocks 480 individual packets. All dispensing columns are adjustable, which allows distributors to interchange and vary merchandise.

Protocol allows distributors to determine the sale price of the merchandise in their units. The vending equipment has an extra-large coin capacity and an adjustable coin mechanism that can accept up to eight coins.

Protocol distributors do not have to operate on a full-time basis. Many choose to start out slowly, working only a few hours a week. This schedule gives them a chance to build a successful route and learn the vending business thoroughly.

A Protocol distributorship can be operated by one or two persons, depending on the number of vending machines in operation and how often they need to be stocked.

An investment of $15,000 purchases 50 protocol vending units with one-year guarantees, merchandise, and an exclusive territory. Protocol determines each territory individually according to each distributor's goals and financial capabilities.

As part of the investment package, distributors receive training and marketing support. Protocol requires each distributor to attend a one-on-one training seminar at their corporate headquarters in Mendota Heights, Minnesota. During this training, distributors learn to set short- and long-term goals and implement plans of action to attain these goals. Distributors also receive in-depth education in sales promotion and generating leads, and the company provides a step-by-step marketing manual that outlines the various marketing programs that have proved successful for other distributors.

Protocol estimates that entrepreneurs will need an additional $3,000 for business start-up expenses such as marketing and promotion, business insurance, and working capital.

Future Outlook

Protocol has capitalized on the consumer's need for convenient personal-care products. The discreet location of the vending equipment in rest rooms or customer lounges attracts customers who might otherwise be embarrassed to purchase some of the merchandise.

Protocol supplies ample support for its distributors. The company assists them in securing locations as well as in installing and maintaining the equipment if needed. The home office also encourages frequent telephone contact.

The overhead on this type of business is low, and the profit margin can be very high depending on the choice of products sold and their location.

Contact Information
Address: 1370 Mendota Heights Road, Mendota Heights, Minnesota 55120
Telephone: 1-800-227-5336 or 1-612-454-0518
Contact person: Brett McKay, vice president of sales

THE VENDOR$ CHOICE
(D. J. Gills Associates, Inc.)

Initial investment: $2,000 to $50,000
Total investment: $2,000 to $50,000
Ongoing fees: None
Right to use trademark and logo: No

Expansion History
Company operating since: 1981
Offering business opportunities since: 1981
Number of machines sold and number of distributors: Not available

Industry Focus
Vending machines can provide first-time entrepreneurs with an inexpensive entry into business ownership. Entrepreneurs can start with one or two machines and build a route business.

Company Advantages
Vendor$ Choice is a distributor for all leading manufacturers of vending equipment. The company sells more than 100 models of coin-operated vending machines. Company owner Don Gill is a manufacturer's representative for all machines his company sells. He guarantees route operators the lowest prices.

Vending-machine route operators can graduate to distributor status with the company. Don Gill insists distributors maintain active operating routes so they do not lose touch with the daily operations of the vending-machine owner.

Vending machines are a familiar sight in every office, school, and public building. Vendor$ Choice is one reason these coin-operated machines have gained such popularity. Established in 1981, the Thorofare, New Jersey–based Vendor$ Choice sells more than 100 varieties of coin-operated vending machines and snack trays to new and established route operators throughout the United States.

A vending route requires a person to be both a salesperson and customer service manager. Those who choose to enter the industry by purchasing machines from Vendor$ Choice usually begin by placing two or three machines in one location. Route operators do not need experience in vending, and they are not required to locate sites for their machines. Vendor$ Choice assists entrepreneurs in placing their machines. The company allows operators to set their own prices, and it does not disclose average profit margins of its operators.

Route operators need a minimum of $2,000 to break ground in the vending-machine business. This initial investment covers the purchase of one or more machines and their contents. Vendor$ Choice guarantees the lowest sales prices on all products, plus it includes the costs of all training materials, videos, and promotional flyers. The investment also covers the $50 to $200 fee per machine paid to a site placement company.

As route operators gain experience, they can purchase new machines and expand further into their territory. Vendor$ Choice does not offer exclusive territories, but it will not put a second operator in an area that is being developed properly. Route operators can expand their business further by becoming distributors. The company requires that all distributors have at least six months' experience as route operators. Distributors pay a $500 refundable fee for a nonexclusive distributorship, and the company returns it after the first sale. Vendor$ Choice monitors distributors' sales and terminates distributor agreements if they overstep the company's price policy.

Future Outlook

The vending machine industry breeds serious competition. To ensure a profitable return on investment, consumers should investigate all machine prices thoroughly. Vendor$ Choice keeps a watchful eye on both the machines and the placement service companies.

Contact Information

Address: P.O. Box 591, Thorofare, New Jersey 08086-0591
Telephone: 1-609-384-0440
Contact person: Don Gill

WESTROCK VENDING
VEHICLES CORPORATION

Initial investment: $2,000 to $60,000
Total investment: $2,000 to $60,000
Ongoing fees: None
Right to use trademark and logo: Yes

Expansion History
Company operating since: 1971
Offering business opportunities since: 1978
Number of machines sold: 3,000+

Industry Focus
Mobile vending carts allow entrepreneurs to take their food products and consumer goods to the customer. Mobile vendors do not have to wait for the customer to come to them.

A mobile vending operation can be transferred easily to another location. The carts or vehicles need only a small amount of space, and this reduces overhead operating expenses.

Company Advantages
Westrock manufactures the carts and vending vehicles and supplies all needed equipment. The company has a 21-year track record in the industry, and it can accommodate special orders from vendors.

Westrock continues to develop products that address vendors' needs. The company is the designer of a mechanical refrigeration recharge system that eliminates the need for dry ice in ice-cream carts, and it also pioneered a fuel-efficient moped cart.

Business owners are often in the position of waiting for the customer to come to them. Westrock Vending Vehicles Corporation eliminates the wait with its specially designed line of mobile vending carts and vans. Established in 1971, the Bayshore, New York–based company manufactures in its 25,000-square-foot plant manually and motor-operated push carts and trucks as well as refrigeration and kitchen equipment needed for these vehicles.

Westrock customers range from the mom-and-pop operators to large food corporations looking to increase their market share through mobile sales.

For first-time business owners who may not have a great deal of investment capital, Westrock offers vending vehicles for as low as $2,000. These vending vehicles are the typical hot-dog or ice-cream carts that are manually pedaled or pushed. Westrock also accommodates food and beverage vendors looking to expand their busi-

296 • THE BEST NONFRANCHISE BUSINESS OPPORTUNITIES

nesses with a larger vehicle. For these entrepreneurs, Westrock custom-designs vans and trailers. These larger vehicles can cost up to $60,000 or more, depending on the interior and equipment installed.

Food-vending entrepreneurs usually establish their food and beverage posts in well-traveled pedestrian areas such as corporate centers, hospitals, or college campuses. These vendors have an advantage over stationary store owners since they can move their stands depending on the volume of customers.

Vendors usually need permission from property owners or managers to operate their cart or park their vans. Property owners may impose a small monthly rental charge on vendors. It is also the vendors' responsibility to stock the cart. They enter into contracts with well-known food companies, or stock the carts with their own food or merchandise.

In its role as manufacturer and equipment supplier, Westrock does not make any type of earnings claims for vendors, but the company is aware of vendors who earn more than $800 per day in this type of business venture.

Westrock has also successfully experimented with collapsible retail carts for merchants. These portable stores are set up in mall corridors or other shopping arenas on a permanent or temporary basis. Cart owners sell their own crafts, jewelry, or other merchandise. They do pay a rental fee to the mall or shopping center management, but it is far less expensive than a storefront retail location.

Future Outlook

Westrock provides a variety of vehicles to take an entrepreneur from a small cart operation to a larger, full-scale motor-vending business. The company continues to develop new technology for the food-vending vehicles. This trend toward research and development has made this company one of the largest manufacturers of these types of vehicles in the world today.

Contact Information
Address: 1565 Fifth Industrial Court, Bayshore, New York 11706
Telephone: 1-800-831-3166 or 1-516-666-5252
Contact person: Stephen Kronrad

List of Companies
that Appear in Part II

About the Authors

Andrew J. Sherman is Of Counsel with Silver, Freedman, and Taff, a Washington, D.C.–based law firm specializing in corporate securities, franchising, intellectual property, real estate, and emerging growth companies. Considered a national authority on legal issues for small and growing businesses, he writes for major publications including *Dun and Bradstreet Reports* and *Nation's Business*. He is the author of three previous books: *One Step Ahead: Legal Aspects of Business Growth, Franchising and Licensing: Two Ways to Build Your Business* and the recently published *The Franchise Management Handbook*. Prior to practicing law, he worked for The White House Conference on Small Business and the Department of Commerce.

Donna Tozzi Cavanagh is a former newspaper reporter who covered general news for the *Montgomery County Times-Herald*. She is currently a free-lance journalist specializing in business writing. She lives in East Norriton, Pennsylvania.